DAVID LAM
A BIOGRAPHY

REGINALD H. ROY

Douglas & McIntyre
VANCOUVER/TORONTO

Copyright © 1996 by Reginald H. Roy
96 97 98 99 00   5 4 3 2 1

All rights reserved. No part of this book may be reproduced, stored in a retrieval system or transmitted in any form or by any means, without prior written permission of the publisher, or in the case of photocopying or other reprographic copying, a licence from CANCOPY (Canadian Reprography Collective), Toronto, Ontario.

Douglas & McIntyre Ltd.,
1615 Venables Street,
Vancouver, British Columbia V5L 2H1

CANADIAN CATALOGUING IN PUBLICATION DATA

Roy, Reginald H., 1922–
    David Lam: A Biography

    Includes index.
    ISBN 978-1-55365-685-2

    1. Lam, David C., 1923– 2. Lieutenant governors—British Columbia—Biography. 3. Philanthropists—British Columbia—Biography. I. Title.
FC3828.1.L36R69 1996   971.1'04'092   C96-910303-4
F1088.L36R69 1996

All care has been taken to trace ownership of images in this book. Omissions will be corrected in subsequent editions, provided notification is sent to the author.

Editing by Andrew Wilson
Jacket design by Peter Cocking
Front cover photo by Jeff Barber
Back cover photo courtesy of the *Vancouver Sun*
Text design and typesetting by Val Speidel
Printed and bound in Canada by Friesens

The publisher gratefully acknowledges the assistance of the Canada Council and of the British Columbia Ministry of Tourism, Small Business and Culture.

To Franklyn Ann

CONTENTS

	Preface	vi
ONE	Boyhood in Hong Kong	1
TWO	The Wartime Years	19
THREE	Branching Out	42
FOUR	Return to Hong Kong	57
FIVE	Working for the Family	76
SIX	Arrival in Canada	94
SEVEN	Lift-Off	109
EIGHT	In Full Flight	125
NINE	Expanding Horizons	140
TEN	Active Retirement	151
ELEVEN	Caring and Sharing	170
TWELVE	Queen's Representative	191
THIRTEEN	Cultivating the Future	213

PREFACE

A FEW YEARS AGO on a visit to Government House, I happened to meet Michael Roberts, private secretary to the lieutenant-governor. He knew I had written a biography of a previous lieutenant-governor of British Columbia, Major-General G. R. Pearkes. He suggested to me that the current incumbent, David Lam, was an interesting man with a colourful background and that I might be interested in writing a book on him. I did not know David Lam, but I suggested that Michael arrange for me to do a few tape-recorded interviews with him. Once I had talked to him I would be better able to judge.

It took only two or three interviews for me to decide that David Lam was a remarkable man. He was also an exceptionally busy man. We decided that the interviews should continue, and for several years, depending on his schedule, we would try and meet for one or two hours once a week or fortnight to talk about his life. These interviews were all taped and transcribed, and remain in my possession. I also had the opportunity to interview many of his friends and business acquaintances, as well as some members of his family. There have been others who have contributed to this story ranging from academics to civil servants, sometimes by correspondence or by interviews. I have benefited from all of them and wish to express my appreciation to all for being so generous with their time.

Frequently, I have used his own words to describe his thoughts and feelings on a wide variety of topics. Some of these quotations have come from journals or newspapers. More frequently, they have come from our interviews or from speeches he has made over the years. The latter needs a little explanation. David Lam does not like to speak from a prepared text. As lieutenant-governor he had no one to research or write speeches for him, yet there were times he had to give several speeches a day. Fortunately, he has a very retentive memory coupled with an inherent ability to speak well to an audience of anything from twenty to two thousand. Before speaking he would make a few notes outlining what he wanted to say, sometimes on the menu of a dinner where he was to speak. These few notes would be expanded to a 20- or 30-minute speech. Since he was frequently asked for a copy of the speech (which, of course, he did not have), he decided to buy a small tape recorder which fit easily into his shirt pocket. He would switch it on when he started and, once back in Government House, he would give it to his secretary to be typed. These transcriptions were available to me when I was doing my research as were other documents, newspaper clipping books, appointment books and other items at Government House. Other material and correspondence relating primarily to his philanthropic work were made available to me by Regent College and the province's three universities.

There are many people I must thank for their help during the four years I spent doing research and writing this book. The presidents of the University of British Columbia, the University of Victoria and Simon Fraser University provided financial grants and also allowed me access to their files respecting their association with David and Dorothy Lam. On my frequent visits to Government House, the staff was more than courteous and willing to assist me in locating files and correspondence. I owe a particular debt to Michael Roberts, private secretary to the lieutenant-governor, and Brian Rowbottom, the Operations Manager, whose contribution to the last two chapters was most welcome. Dr. David Lai of the University of Victoria read most of the text to make sure I had Chinese place names correctly spelled. Mrs. June Bull did a remarkably fine job both transcribing the taped interviews and typing the chapters of the book. I have not attempted

PREFACE

to impose any particular spelling system on the Chinese names of individuals, preferring to use the spellings as they were given to me or appeared on original documents. A fully footnoted version of the manuscript is on file at University of Victoria library for anyone wishing to do further research.

I am particularly grateful, of course, to David and Dorothy Lam. Without their cooperation it would have been almost impossible to write this book. They never avoided any questions I posed to them nor did they ever suggest a rewording of what I had written except to correct certain facts such as names or dates.

David Lam has made hundreds of friends in his newly adopted country, and readers of this book will soon understand why. Whenever I mentioned that I was writing his biography, the immediate reaction was, "Oh, how lovely. What a nice man. When is the book coming out?" Well, here it is. Meet the Lams. I feel sure you will like them.

R. H. Roy
Victoria, B.C.
May 1996

ONE

Boyhood in Hong Kong

DECEMBER 8, 1941, was turning out to be a bright, clear Monday morning. David Lam got up from an early breakfast and made his way to the third floor of his father's house to do some gymnastics. A large house set in spacious grounds, by almost any standards it could be called a mansion. It had been built only four years earlier in Kowloon, just across the harbour from the main island of Hong Kong.

The house was large but every room was occupied. Aside from his parents and several grandparents, there were nine children in the Lam household. The oldest boy, Daniel, was not at home. He had left several months earlier for Manila where he was attending the University of the Philippines. That left David as the senior among his five brothers and two sisters still at home. The absence of one of the brothers had little impact on the level of activity in the house. There were numerous servants bustling about—indeed, there were more servants than children. The cook and his helper were busy in the kitchen, the chauffeur had brought the car around to take David's father to his office, the maids were helping his mother get the children ready for school, and others were preparing to undertake the numerous tasks his mother had laid out for them.

His father, David knew, would be leaving shortly for his office on the island, only a short drive and ferry ride away. Lam Chi Fung (Lam is the family name and Chi Fung the given name) was an active, middle-aged man who believed in lots of physical exercise both for himself and his children. His business as a coal importer and distributor had flourished over the previous decade and he had become modestly wealthy. This had allowed him not only to provide well for his family, but to devote extra time to the numerous charitable activities in which he was involved.

As David mounted the steps to his bedroom, he thought about how he would spend his day. He was eighteen years old. He had been accepted a few months earlier as a second-year student at Lingnan University and, with Christmas examinations looming, he knew he would have to devote some time to his studies after he had finished his exercises.

The fact that he was attending Lingnan University was a disturbing reminder of the continuing warfare in China, whose borders were only a short drive from his home in Kowloon. The university had started in 1888 as Christian College. Renamed Lingnan College in 1912, it achieved university status in 1927. It had occupied a pleasant campus in the city of Canton (Guangdong), about eighty miles up the Pearl River from Hong Kong. The steady and brutal encroachment of the Japanese army into mainland China had forced the university to move to Hong Kong where, everyone hoped, it could continue to operate in temporary quarters safe from Japanese domination.

Although Hong Kong offered refuge to the university's professors and scholars, the colony was in a precarious position. A hundred years earlier, the British flag was run up over Hong Kong as a result of a trade dispute between Great Britain and China. Shortly afterwards, following the First Opium War, the colony became part of the British Empire in 1843. Captain Charles Elliott, the Royal Navy captain who took the island for the empire, was later reprimanded for his action by the British Foreign Secretary Lord Palmerston. The foreign secretary's position was understandable enough: Why should anyone in London, about eight thousand miles away, be impressed with the addition of twenty-nine square miles of irregularly shaped rock, roughly ten miles in length and varying from two to five miles in width? There were less than six thousand inhabitants on the island at the time and little agricultural land available. It lacked sufficient drinking water to support more than a small town, and there were few level areas on which to erect dwellings.

In spite of Lord Palmerston's reservations, the colony slowly began to thrive. In 1860 the Kowloon peninsula, where the Lam family now lived, was ceded to Great Britain and at the end of the century it acquired the New Territories on a 99-year lease. This brought the colony an additional 355 square miles that formerly had belonged to the Chinese province of Canton.

In the following years, the population had increased at a tremendous rate. British rule brought with it a measure of law, order and stability which contrasted with the insecurity and turmoil in China. With its fine harbour and strategic location, Hong Kong's trade grew steadily, and its merchants and shipping firms flourished. As the flames of civil strife and, later, the invasion by Japan brought more refugees from China, the colony's population continued to expand. In young David's brief life, for example, the number of residents had more than doubled to 1.6 million. During the same period, however, the colony's exports to China fell by more than 75 per cent as Japan gained greater and greater dominance over the mainland and its economy.

The beginning of the Second World War did little to change the pattern of life in Hong Kong, despite increased tension between Japan and Great Britain. In 1940 and 1941, as the German armies swept over Europe and then plunged into Russia, Japan became more arrogant in its demands. In July of 1941, Japan, knowing the weakness of the Vichy government in France, sent several warships to occupy bases in Indochina. This show of force, together with other belligerent moves, caused further deterioration in the diplomatic and trade relationships between Japan and the United States. With German forces on the outskirts of Moscow and the British hard pressed to keep a foothold in North Africa, Japan was able to push its expansionist policy to the limit.

All of this had its impact on Hong Kong. The demands of the war in Europe and the submarine threat in the Atlantic had resulted in a weakening of the garrisons in most of Britain's imperial outposts.

Despite the fact that the colony bordered on Japanese-occupied territory, the British garrison consisted of only two British and two Indian battalions. The British government had asked Canada for reinforcements in September 1941, and in mid-November two Canadian battalions arrived and were stationed in Kowloon.

David Lam's father had more than a passing interest in these events. Lam Chi Fung imported coal not only to Hong Kong but to other distribution points up and down the China Coast. One of his coal depots was located in the Portuguese colony of Macao, a small island about a three-hour ferry ride across the Pearl River Delta from Hong Kong. Several years earlier, apprehensive about a possible Japanese takeover of Hong Kong, he had rented a house there in case he had to move his family out of danger. When the Japanese had made no move, he gave up the lease and, like many other merchants, hoped that the Japanese would not attack. As David recalls the situation, "The Japanese were extending themselves very thinly in China. They were able to occupy only the cities and patrol the railway lines. There was no massive land occupation like France or the Lowlands being occupied by the Germans. We figured that the Japanese were trapped in the morass of the vast territory of China. Why would they want to do something so drastic as attacking British or American territories?"

Nevertheless, the people of Hong Kong were pleased with the arrival of the two Canadian infantry battalions in mid-November 1941. At that time, David's father was president of the YMCA. Once the troops were settled in, he invited the two commanding officers for dinner. David remembers talking with them: "They were very concerned about the possibility of a Pacific war and about the Japanese. But we didn't seem to be too concerned." During their visit, the colonel told David's father that the soldiers were very homesick. There wasn't much recreational activity for them. "My father turned to me and said, 'Go and do something,'" recalls David.

The Canadians, the first David had ever met, had been to dinner only a week previously, but he had already arranged a basketball game for them and was planning a tea-dance in the coming week. Meanwhile, there was a lot to do and the first thing on his schedule that Monday morning was his exercises.

David kept a punch-ball in his bedroom on the top floor, and he began to hit it like a boxer in training. Suddenly, air raid sirens began to sound. The Lam residence was not far from the Kai Tak airport and at first David thought there was another exercise in progress. He looked out the window and saw an airplane making a slow turn down Happy Valley. As it swooped closer, he could make out two red circles under each wing and eventually he could even see the pilot. Almost immediately there came the sound of exploding bombs. One of them landed only a few blocks away, demolishing a building and killing a friend of his father, the secretary general of the YMCA.

What David and his family thought might never happen had occurred like a bolt from the blue. Twenty miles away, Japanese troops began to pour across the border into the New Territories. For the Lam family, and for the other residents of Hong Kong, life would never be the same.

At the time Japanese bombs began to fall on Kowloon, three generations of the Lam family were living in the same house. The oldest was Lam Siu-Fun, David's grandfather.

Lam Siu-Fun grew up in a small village called Gum Hong ("Golden Valley"), not far from Swatow, a coastal port about two hundred miles northeast of Hong Kong. He became a school teacher in Kit-yang, a poor village where, because he had some education, he was regarded as a scholar. During this period, the village was visited by some Baptist missionaries. Although the villagers had no concept of Christianity, they felt that the foreign missionaries were well-to-do and came from a wealthy country. The village elders held a meeting and concluded that if they could attract the foreigners to the village, they might benefit from some of the wealth or protection they might bring with them. The best way to do that was to offer a convert. As David tells the story, "The village elders decided that my grandfather should be the designated Christian. When the missionaries held their meeting, he was to stand up and say he wanted to be a Christian. Grandfather said 'Why me?' They said, 'Because you are the scholar.' So at the meeting he stood up, and hallelujah, he was saved. I even met those missionaries myself when I was very young. They came to Hong Kong and stayed in my father's home and said, 'We were the ones who saved your grandfather.' "

As it turned out, Lam Siu-Fun's "conversion" brought no wealth to the villagers. Siu-Fun was, at best, a reluctant convert bowing to the persuasion of the elders. Nevertheless, either out of curiosity or due to the request of the elders, he agreed to go to Swatow and study at the Ling Tung Baptist Mission. It was there that he became a true and strong convert to the Christian faith.

In due course Lam Siu-Fun returned to his village and began work as a missionary himself. He established a chapel in his old schoolhouse and, with more successful conversions, he became the pastor of the Gum Hong Baptist Church. He married a woman who, like himself, was a devout Christian and they became the parents of a fairly large family. Their first son, Chi Fung, was born on November 6, 1892. He was David's father.

Although Pastor Lam was now considered well educated and had thus become a respected man in the village, he still had very little money. Anxious that his children obtain a proper education, he exerted great efforts to provide it, going so far as to sell the remaining meagre portion of farm land left to him by his father. This allowed his eldest son, Chi Fung, to be sent to the Tung Man College in Amoy, a city about a hundred miles further up the coast from Swatow.

After Chi Fung graduated from Tung Man College, his father urged him to try to become a medical doctor. If successful, his income would help support the family. Pastor Lam again made sacrifices to send his son to the Peking Union Medical College. Saving what he could, he put aside some money, borrowed from the bank and then approached friends to lend him money. Eventually enough cash was raised to send Chi Fung to the medical college.

The young man left Swatow by boat, going north to Shanghai and then on to Peking (Beijing). He was a deck passenger, the least expensive way he could travel. He ate and slept on the deck, which was crowded with others passengers, all exposed to the elements. It was the first major trip he had ever made, and perhaps he was unaware of some of the dangers he might encounter. During the voyage someone cut into a corner of his suitcase and stole about half the money he was carrying. This was a tragedy for the young man, but he continued on and duly enrolled in the medical school.

Chi Fung never became a doctor, however. The lack of funds was a major obstacle but a second appeared when he attended the first operation he had ever witnessed. According to his eldest son Daniel, "It was an operation on an appendix. When the surgeon took out the patient's appendix and held it up to the students, my father took one look at the bloody object and fainted."

It was obvious that fate did not intend Chi Fung should enter the medical profession. Nevertheless he had to earn a living. Peking, the capital of China, apparently had little appeal to him. The country before the First World War was in a chaotic state as the Manchu dynasty was losing its ancient control and new leaders like Sun Yat-sen were attempting to reform the crumbling government. The Great Powers of Europe, taking advantage of China's weakness, were increasing their demands for economic concessions, and Japan was exerting great pressure for geographical annexation of Chinese territory.

There was one place, however, which offered a measure of stability and possible opportunity—Hong Kong. Chi Fung had learned English while a student and it was to this British colony that he made his way shortly after the war broke out in 1914. It was no use returning to Swatow. It was a poor district when he left and little had changed in the years he had been away. He had to make a fresh start and, with his education, he felt confident he would succeed.

Arriving in Hong Kong, Chi Fung met a friend who recommended him to the proprietor of Messrs. Kwong Yuen Shing, a large importing firm. There he started work as an English language clerk. He found business an interesting occupation, worked hard and eventually was promoted to manager of the firm.

Once he was employed and earning enough money to support a wife, Chi Fung decided to get married. He returned to his native village where a schoolmate named Tan had a sister whom Chi Fung liked very much. En route to the village, however, he stopped off at Swatow and visited his old high school. There he met a girl he liked even better, Chan Chik-Ting, and ended up marrying her. (As things turned out, the Tan family moved later to Hong Kong and prospered. One of Chi Fung's sons, David, would later marry the daughter of his old school chum.)

Chi Fung was married shortly after the end of the Great War and the first of their nine children, Daniel, was born in 1922. Theirs was a religious household. Many years later, in a booklet celebrating the 1962 opening of one of his factories, Chi Fung would write: "From the beginning, my wife and I have resolved that we would raise our family with Jesus Christ at its centre. In doing so, we have preached to every member of the family to accept God as their saviour. We held family prayer meetings regularly as both my wife and I believe the teaching of the Bible to be more important than any worldly knowledge."

Chi Fung was the type of man who practised what he preached throughout his life. For example, in 1922 his former village was struck by a typhoon. He made a visit to the area and saw that most of the rice fields had no irrigation system. Flooding and drought occurred constantly. Chi Fung offered all his personal savings for the building of an irrigation system some twelve miles in length. In the booklet mentioned above, he commented: "Under the guidance of our Lord and the assistance of good friends of my village, all obstacles were resolved resulting in the canal being dug."

Considering that Chi Fung had just been married and had a new baby on the way, this was a remarkable gesture of Christian generosity. He was to be generous with his time and money throughout his life and he strove to impress on his sons and daughters the Christian values which he had inherited from his own father. His gift towards the irrigation system in his village, together with the assistance he was to give to immigrants from the Swatow area to Hong Kong, gave him great respect, and made his name known well beyond the borders of the British colony.

During the 1920s, the company for which he worked prospered, but with the onset of the worldwide economic depression in 1930, business slowed to the point where it had to declare bankruptcy. As its manager, Chi Fung had acquired a great deal of knowledge about the import business and he decided, with a couple of friends, to form his own company. The Sze Wai Company dealt with the importation and distribution of anthracite coal from Haiphong in French Indochina. This hard, smokeless coal was in great demand not only by industries but by domestic consumers as well. The firm flourished and as the economic situation began to improve, he established branches along the coast of China and expanded into shipping and the rice trade.

Chi Fung's business success did not change or weaken the solid Christian foundation of his beliefs. He was a firm supporter of the Baptist church in Hong Kong, and was elected chairman of the Hong Kong YMCA. He also supported new arrivals from the Swatow area, doing what he could to provide them with medical care and better education. By the end of the 1930s, he probably spent as much time on activities normally connected with Baptist missionaries as he did on business affairs. He was not the sort of man to pile up money merely for the sake of becoming more and more wealthy. It was to be used for good works, helping the poor, educating the illiterate and spreading the word of God. There was much to do, but he made sure that first of all, his own children should learn the Christian message which his own father had imbued in him.

Chi Fung's second son, David See Chai, was born on July 25, 1923. His Chinese name came from a Confucian epigram which means "aspire to equal the nobility found in others." David's father told his secretary to go to the proper authorities and register the birth. The secretary went out and celebrated the event but forgot to go to the registry. When he remembered about six weeks later, the officer in charge of the registry refused to backdate the birth. Anxious to get the certificate for his employer, the secretary suggested that the present date, September 2, be inscribed. As David related the story later, "The secretary put the certificate, nicely folded up, in an envelope and gave it to my father. Father didn't look at it and gave it to mother, who locked it in a safe. Years later, when I had to get a passport I looked at it and said to my mother, 'You always celebrate my birthday in July. How come the certificate says September?' Mother said, 'I know the date, the exact date.' Then we went to Father. He was surprised and tried to explain without success. He then went after his secretary, who finally confessed what had happened. So I had a real birthday and an official birthday, almost like royalty."

The other children arrived during the twenties and thirties—Alex, Julia, John, Joseph, Samuel, Alice and Timothy. Timothy was the seventh boy and last child in the Lam family. He was born at about the same time Chi Fung decided to buy land and build a house over in Kowloon. Up to this time, the family was living part way up the hilly area of Victoria. As the city expanded, conditions were becoming more crowded and Chi Fung wanted more room where his growing children could play. Moreover, because of its location, his home was in the shade about mid-afternoon.

Across the harbour, the colonial government was opening up a new area just north of Kowloon. They had recently built Grampian Road, adjacent to which was some residential property. Chi Fung purchased a large section, about the equivalent of a city block. On this land, he decided to build his dream house, one that was large enough to allow space for everyone as well as quarters for some of the servants. Under his direction, the architect designed a house with curved balconies and other features different from the rectangular houses common in their former neighbourhood. The finished house was a showpiece. Next to the house, he built a tennis court. The remaining third of the property was left undeveloped. It was fenced off and, as undeveloped land, it was not subject to residential property tax.

Chi Fung had definite ideas about how his children should be raised. First, they should be Christians in mind and in deed. Second, they should receive a good education in their chosen field. Third, they should keep healthy through exercises. Finally, they should receive instruction in the philosophy of Confucius and remain proud of their Chinese origins.

Education in Hong Kong was not a right that families could expect the government to provide for their children. Parents had to pay to put their sons and daughters through school. This was a hardship for most families, but many were willing to sacrifice the money if they possibly could. An education was an immediate advantage when it came to looking for a job and increasing one's chances for advancing up the economic ladder. For a family of limited means, it was important that the elder children should receive the benefits of schooling even if the younger members had to do without. It was also expected that if the elder children derived the economic benefits of their families' sacrifices, the families in turn should expect to share in the economic success of the educated children. One result of this system was an emphasis on hard work and continual study for school children. They were made aware of their privileged position and their obligation to succeed. Another result was that from the earliest grade, the children stayed in school longer and started their academic learning from the day they arrived. Since school fees were paid monthly and a family might not be able to pay if there was an economic downturn, teachers were under pressure to provide as much education as they could in the shortest possible time. The system laid a great deal of stress on the child, and classroom discipline was such that every minute in school was aimed at educating rather than entertaining.

David started his education in the YMCA primary school and soon found himself involved in some of his father's Christian endeavours. When he was about seven, the teacher told his class that they had to go out and try to raise money for the YMCA campaign. "I didn't know why," David remembers, "but everyone got a little book to get people to sign up and pay money. I didn't know where to go and I asked my father, 'Who can help me?' He said, 'Why don't you come to the office?' I went there and one of the fellows took me to some of my father's business associates. I would go to them and say 'I want money.' The fellow would say, 'Why?' I would say it was for the YMCA. 'What is the YMCA?' I didn't know, but they would pinch my cheek and ask, 'How much money do you want?' I said I wanted ten dollars. They would say, 'How about I give you five?' I would say, 'Thank you.'"

He got more one-, two- and five-dollar bills than he did tens, but when the campaign was over David had raised over $500, more than any other child in the school. In appreciation, he was given a small silver cup with his name inscribed on it. This was his first effort at raising money for an educational institution. Many years later, he would still be at it, but instead of asking for ten dollars, he would be asking for millions.

In Hong Kong, there were two streams of thought about a child's education. Should the child be educated as he would be in China, with instruction in Chinese on Chinese history, literature and so on? Or should he accept the fact that he was living in a British colony and therefore go to a school where he would be instructed in English, with a minimum of time spent on Chinese topics? David's father believed his children should be Chinese in thought, language and everything else. David, therefore, was sent to primary school under the Chinese system.

After completing his junior years, David and his older brother were sent as boarders to a Pui-Ching school in Canton. The new school was something of a shock to both boys. Instead of the comfort of their own beds in their own home, they now slept in a large room with twenty-eight other boys. There was no privacy, but, on the other hand, there was much camaraderie and lots of time for sports.

Some time later, the boys' parents visited the school and were distressed at the rather spartan life the school offered. They decided to move them to Lingnan High School, an institution which prepared students for entrance to Lingnan University. Once again, it was a dramatic change. As David remembers, "We were moved from a low, grassroots type of existence to a luxurious American high school environment, with only four boys to a room. Everyone had a bicycle—that's almost equivalent to having a private car. We had pocket money to spend, better food, American-style Boy Scouts, a uniformed band and cheerleaders. It was like an American institution with nice buildings, lawns, trees, ice cream parlours, everything luxurious. But I found we were not really liked by the Cantonese people who jeered at our uniforms and our band and cheerleaders. So we were torn again. It was a Chinese education with a very heavy missionary influence."

The new school may have provided better living conditions but neither the boys nor their father felt they were in the right place. David spoke to his father about it and recalls being told, "Look, you boys are not having very good grades because you are living it up when you are only in grade eight. You have bicycles. You have ice cream every day and good food. You're spending money. You are going to come back to Hong Kong so I can keep a closer rein on you two." David adds, "When he said so, it was like Chairman Mao—end of discussion."

David started grade nine in Hong Kong, where his father was on the board of directors of Munsang College. This was a bilingual school where instruction was given in both Chinese and English. It was the beginning of four years of very hard work. David knew very little English and when he went to a class where the teacher instructed in that language, at first he didn't know what was being said or written. He was faced with the problem of both learning the English language and at the same time trying to absorb the lessons. It was very difficult, but he kept at it with great determination.

"I can never forget it," he says now. "I would go home and do a quick exercise and take a walk around my garden. Then I would prepare myself to study. When I became sleepy, I would pinch my leg to wake myself up. I got black and blue on both my legs, pinching myself to give me pain to keep awake. For relaxation, I would take a break and play some classical music on an old, wind-up Victrola gramophone, and then back to my studies."

About the classes themselves, he remembers, "It was a torture to study English and to study a lot of things which, to my young mind, I considered totally irrelevant. We learned about Glasgow, Edinburgh and the Midlands—what the heck for? We learned about the Clyde, shipbuilding, London, the Thames. I kept asking myself, what for? We studied English and European history but never touched Asian history or geography. We studied like crazy and every day I asked—what for? It was really hard work, just transforming a person from a totally Chinese educational and cultural background into an English-style one."

The Munsang College offered a high school curriculum designed to bring its students to an educational level where they could take a Cambridge matriculation examination which would allow the student to enter Hong Kong University. It was a stiff and demanding exam, so in his final year David studied harder than ever. Of the thirty-two students in his class, two passed. David was one of them and he received an "A" grade, a remarkable achievement considering he could not read, write or speak English when he entered grade nine.

With his matriculation certificate, David went to the registrar's office at Hong Kong University to enroll as a student for the next session. It was his first visit, so he decided to see some of the buildings. Dropping into Lugard Hall, one of the dormitories, he was amazed to hear the students talking half English and half Chinese, all in the same sentence. He felt this insulting to both languages. Moreover, he talked to people and found there was no particular depth in their conversation. It was only a first impression, but he felt that perhaps he might try to enter another university.

After his exhausting four years at Munsang College, his father allowed him a short vacation in Shanghai. He was shown around the city by a young friend who took him to visit St. John's University. David found that it placed a great deal of emphasis on Chinese studies. Since he liked the city and wanted to focus on Chinese and Asian topics, he wrote his father asking for permission to attend St. John's. Chi Fung had other ideas. Big cities like Shanghai, he pointed out, were filled with sinful activities like gambling and prostitution. He had no intention that David should be exposed to such contamination. He appreciated his son's desire to pursue Chinese studies but told him he could now do so in Hong Kong.

Owing to Japanese advances in mainland China, Lingnan University had been forced to evacuate its campus and move to Hong Kong. Arrangements were made for the faculty and students to share the facilities at Hong Kong University. Each institution kept its own identity, and by sharing classroom schedules, the library, laboratory space and so forth, the two were able to function on the congested campus. It was awkward, but at least they could pursue their work free of Japanese domination and control. David agreed with his father's choice and became a freshman student at Lingnan in 1940. He could easily commute from his home in Kowloon to the campus on Hong Kong island, and the house was large enough for him to find a quiet place for study in the evening.

Both as a boy and a teenager, David enjoyed a security which came partly from his father's financial status and partly from his solid Christian upbringing. As a strong Baptist, Chi Fung made every effort to ensure the children were raised as Christians in the most complete sense of the word. On Sunday mornings, the family attended church and the younger children attended Sunday school. Each child was given an allowance, but it was made clear to them that a portion of their allowance was for the Sunday school collection plate. This was early training not only to support the church but, indirectly, the poor as well. Many years later, when David began to earn a salary, he would voluntarily put aside 10 per cent of his wages for charitable giving, a practice he continued no matter how small or large his income might be.

Aside from church services, Chi Fung had the entire family attend a Saturday afternoon prayer service at home, sometimes with the local Baptist pastor in attendance. If there was a Baptist evangelical meeting in the city, the Lam family would probably be there. During summer vacations, the children might go to a Baptist church camp. It was while attending these church events that David gained his first experience as a public speaker. At Sunday school, he and the other children were expected to stand up and recite verses from the Bible from memory. Later, when he had learned to play the guitar, he would be asked to sing songs to entertain the school. For a while, he taught Sunday school lessons to the junior classes. According to his younger sister, David had a knack for telling stories and, even as a young man "could charm the birds from the trees." Like his father, he grew up with strong religious convictions, secure in his faith in God and sure of His guiding hand in his life.

During the pre-war years, there were many activities for the Lam children. David's father was a great believer in physical exercise. He liked walking and when he went, the entire family came too. It wasn't a matter of walking for a mile or so; rather, it was more like a small route march which would go on for several hours. A favourite outing was to go to the beach for a picnic and a swim. Chi Fung was a good swimmer and insisted that all the children should learn how to swim. Again, this did not mean dashing into the water for a quick dip and then out again. It meant completing certain distances non-stop, the distance depending on the ages of the children. David became a good swimmer, fortunately, and continued to enjoy it for many years. Tennis was another sport most of the family enjoyed.

For David, however, there was more to life than studying and sports. He enjoyed playing with other children, bicycle riding, reading and music, and was a movie fan from an early age. As with others of his age, it was a treat to go to the theatre and see serial films such as *Rin Tin Tin* or *Anne of Green Gables*. One serial film he remembers was *The Burning of the Temple of the Red Lotus*. It went on for twenty-eight weeks and even then, he recalls, "It still didn't burn down." His musical tastes were mainly Western rather than Chinese. Daniel, his older brother, recalls that the family had a small band: "David played the Hawaiian guitar. I played the Spanish guitar accompaniment and our number three brother, Alex, played the ukulele. We were so popular in those days, 1938–39, that at Christmas time we received many invitations to play at boys' and girls' schools. There was a lot of fun in those days."

Part of the reason for liking Western songs was the influence of British and, particularly, American tunes David heard at the theatre or on the radio. Equally important in forming his tastes was the music he heard at home. "The music I was brought up on," he says now, "was mostly church music. Also, my uncle and my aunt liked to sing. They had one book called *The 101 Best Songs*. It had tunes like "Darling, I Am Growing Old," "Old Black Joe" and "My Old Kentucky Home." So, as a kid, I just kept hearing all those tunes. I couldn't sing the words, of course, but I got to know the tunes."

There was one activity which he pursued on his own, starting when he was fourteen years old. Gardening was his first money-making venture, yet probably gave him as much pleasure as anything else he did at home. It began when he was in grade school and ran across a seed catalogue from Sutton Seeds. With all the photographs of beautiful flowers, David could not put it down. He recalls, "I took it to my school and during the class I looked at it. The teacher came by and grabbed it. He could not believe his eyes, that I was secretly reading the seed catalogue."

David's interest in gardening was primarily as a spectator until the Lam family moved to Kowloon. Since his father had purchased the equivalent of a city block of property and about one-third was unused, David asked his parents' permission to turn it into a productive garden. One of the first things he did was to get some letterhead stationery printed, with "David Lam Farm, 7-11 Grampian Rd.,

Kowloon" on the top of each page. With such a letterhead he felt, quite correctly as it turned out, he could write to the seed companies and purchase their seeds and bulbs at wholesale prices. He also could ask for the free samples they always seemed anxious to send.

The next step was to prepare the ground. That took a lot of hard work. He was helped at times by a refugee who was staying with the Lams until he could find a full-time job. Someone suggested David should get some horse manure to mix with the soil. That sounded like a good idea so David telephoned the Hong Kong Jockey Club and they sent him a whole pile of it. Fortunately, the garden was far enough from the neighbours that there were no complaints. Someone else suggested he should get the discarded "cakes" from a plant which pressed peanuts for oil. They were good for fertilizer. He contacted the firm and got a load. When they arrived, he found they were as hard as a board; apparently they had to be soaked in water. "So I got urns," he says, "and put the cakes in. After a while they all became soft and started fermenting. It stunk sky-high. You couldn't walk near it, and flies started to come."

David was learning about gardening the hard way. An early experiment was to write the Burpee seed firm in Philadelphia to order three different kinds of corn seed. He planted each package of corn seed in a different row to see which would grow best in the Hong Kong climate. While engaged in these experiments, he recalls, "A fellow came by and said, 'You should plant gladiolus.' I said, 'What's that?' and he replied 'It's like a corn. Put it in the soil and sixty days later they start to have flowers. You harvest them and get lots of colour. They are easy to grow.' The man talked me into buying a thousand bulbs from him, wholesale. I didn't have the money so I borrowed it from my father. I got the bulbs, planted them, and lo and behold, they grew. I started sending the gladiolus flowers, my lettuce, beans, corn and so forth to various friends of the family and to the church."

As his garden increased in size, David grew more flowers and decided to sell some at the open flower market which he passed on the way to school. He sold them slightly below market price so usually he could dispose of them. If he was left with a bundle of flowers before he had to go to his first class, a flower broker called Fat Tim would take the remainder from him at a reduced price. It was a nice venture into business, one he continued through high school and into his early years at Lingnan University. It meant he always had money to spend.

By the time he was in his late teens, anyone who knew him would consider David to be a well-rounded young man. He was athletic, well educated, a good conversationalist and becoming more acquainted with the English language. Although his native dialect was Cantonese, his father brought a Confucian scholar to the house twice a week to teach the older children both Confucianism and how to speak Mandarin. Chi Fung thought that every Chinese should be able to speak the standard or "official" Chinese dialect. Although the writing is identical, the pronunciation of the two dialects is very different. David found Mandarin very difficult to understand. Nevertheless, he plugged away at it and in time he won first prize in his school for public speaking in Mandarin.

Until that fateful December day in 1941, David lived a pleasant and largely uneventful life. If it wasn't exactly exciting, it was too active to be dull. He had security, a strong Christian faith and the foundation of a Confucian philosophy that he was to find invaluable in time of trouble. That time was about to begin. As the Japanese planes swept in to bomb Kowloon and Hong Kong, David Lam knew his peaceful life was coming to a shattering end.

TWO

The Wartime Years

The Japanese bomber that swooped over David Lam's house early on December 8 was one of forty-eight aircraft involved in the attack on Hong Kong. Dropping bombs and spraying machine-gun fire, the aircraft concentrated on military targets or buildings which might contain government offices. Within minutes of the first air strike, all the aircraft—both military and civilian—at the Kai Tak airport had been destroyed or damaged. Two blocks from the Lam house, an apartment building with a Chinese flag flying from its flagpole was bombed. David could see the flames billowing from its windows. The howl of air raid sirens, the thump of bombs falling and the noise of fire engines and ambulances dashing to emergencies caused both confusion and apprehension, bordering on panic.

At the same time as the bombers struck, Japanese troops crossed the border between China and the New Territories. The border was over fifteen miles from Kowloon, and between it and the city lay a rough territory of hills, winding roads and deep gullies. North of Kowloon was a defensive belt of field fortifications called the "Gin Drinkers Line."

It was to take the Japanese several days before they reached the city. Meanwhile there was a rush of people in Kowloon trying to get across the harbour to Hong Kong, fearing that Kowloon's proximity to the airport would bring more bombers. On the island of Hong Kong, a similar stream of people scrambled to get on the ferry—or indeed any boat—to take them to Kowloon. They reasoned that since Kowloon had been badly hit, Japanese bombers would soon turn their fury on Hong Kong. With turmoil and confusion in the streets and the sound of mortar and artillery fire coming closer each day, David's father decided to stay where he was. Hong Kong, he felt, could not hold out for long, so why go through the motions?

As the fighting drew closer, the family decided to make the house safer. There were no air raid shelters nearby, so the next best thing was to collect as many bags as possible, fill them with earth and place them on the ground floor of the house by the windows. With everyone working feverishly, this was accomplished in good time. Shortly after, the family noticed a crowd lining up outside their gate. Food supplies had been disrupted, and to people looking at the Lam house from the outside it seemed that Lam Chi Fung was storing up bags of rice. The crowd began to get a little ugly. People with empty stomachs are not particularly receptive to reason and they would not believe the sacks behind the windows were not filled with rice. David's father finally persuaded them to elect three representatives who came into the house, poked into the bags and assured themselves the bags were filled with earth. That done, the crowd at the gate melted away to seek food elsewhere.

After constructing some protection for the ground floor, the Lam family decided to become as self-sufficient as possible. The garden, including David's flower garden, could be dug up and planted with vegetables. Since the water supply might be cut off at any moment, they resolved to dig a well. David, some of his brothers and others in the house set to work at once with pick and shovel. The well was about four feet in diameter and as they laboured away, it became became deeper and deeper. None of them had ever dug a well before, and nobody realized its walls needed constant reinforcement. When they had dug to about fifteen or twenty feet, water began to seep in. It was the end of the day so the young men left, happy their hard labour had paid off. Sometime during the night, the side of the well gave way and the lower half was filled with earth from the cave-in. It was pure luck it hadn't happened earlier.

Within four days of their initial attack, the Japanese had seized all of the New Territories and the Kowloon peninsula. Across the water lay the city of Victoria on the island of Hong Kong. Already, some of the colony's key personnel were being evacuated by fast naval speedboats to Chinese ports still unoccupied by the Japanese. On the island itself, a few British, Indian and Canadian battalions were preparing to battle to the end. The short but vicious campaign started on December 18 and ended with the surrender of the island on Christmas Day.

Once the fighting had stopped, the Japanese began to look around for quarters for their officers and men. What they wanted they commandeered. An officer would come to a house, bang on the door, warn the occupants they had three hours to clear out, and put up a notice saying the building was under Japanese control. The Lam house, which was undamaged and contained about 30,000 square feet of living area, looked very attractive.

There was a period after the invasion when the police force was not functioning. Taking advantage of the situation, small groups of criminals began to prey on citizens, demanding money or goods, and threatening bodily harm unless they got what they wanted. Some of these gangs began to visit the Lam house, forcing their way in and returning repeatedly with the same threat—money or else. Chi Fung bought them off to the extent he could, but he did not keep a great deal of money in the house. On one of these repeat visits, he could offer them nothing. The intruders drew their knives.

At that very moment, there came a hammering on the front door. It was a Japanese officer accompanied by a few soldiers, who had come to confiscate the house for the army. He quickly saw what was going on and had his men seize the extortionists and hustled them outside. The leader of the thugs pleaded with Chi Fung to tell the officers he was a member of the family and not a criminal. Chi Fung said nothing. His primary concern now was that a notice had been pinned to the door, ordering everyone to leave.

Luckily, help was nearby in the form of a family connection. Chi Fung's younger sister had married Dr. C. K. Chan, a medical doctor who had graduated from the University of Nagasaki. He spoke fluent Japanese and had actually practised medicine in Japan. They lived just next door. As David tells the story, "When we saw we were being commandeered, we ran over to his house and got him and he came over. He looked and behaved like a Japanese because he had been there since his teens. The way he wore his hat, his little Hitler moustache—he looked more Japanese than the Japanese."

When the Japanese colonel came, Dr. Chan spoke to him in his own language, emphasizing that this was his brother-in-law's house, that he had a large family, and was a good citizen. It must have been a convincing argument, for the colonel gave way and ordered the official notice to be taken down. That was a relief, but the doctor pointed out that some other official might come by and put another claim on the house. The colonel pondered that remark and asked for a piece of paper. He wrote on it and said, "Put this up. Nobody will dare tear it down. This house is excluded from confiscation." From that time on, there was no further attempt to take over the house.

During the next several months, the Lam family had to cope with numerous hardships common to all the people in the colony. Japanese soldiers were ruthless when enforcing their regulations and they demanded respect for their armed forces. If a Hong Kong citizen walked in front of a Japanese sentry, he was expected to bow and remove his hat. If a citizen accidently wandered into an area declared by the Japanese to be out of bounds, he would be shot immediately. Sentries were posted throughout the city, and David found it best to avoid meeting them even if it meant travelling a zigzag route through the streets. There was an almost total lack of communication between the Japanese troops and the citizens but, with the thousands of refugees in the colony from mainland China as witnesses, everyone knew that their conquerors were domineering, ruthless and frequently pitiless in their attitude toward a subject civilian population.

Japanese occupation was not made any easier by the series of victories they achieved during the first half of 1942. British and Dutch territories bordering the Pacific were invaded and overrun. Australia was threatened. The Philippines were seized and in Manila, David's older brother Daniel was put in a concentration camp. The British naval presence in the Pacific was almost eliminated, the United States Navy had been hard hit at Pearl Harbor, and French Indochina was under Japanese domination. Having captured Malaya and advanced through Burma to the gates of India, the Japanese armies seemed to be invincible. Their victories, broadcast over the Hong Kong radio stations month after month, had a depressing effect on the people of the former British colony. But life had to go on. Finding enough food to feed the family was becoming increasingly difficult even for the well-to-do Lam family, and the strain of living under Japanese domination added to Chi Fung's difficulties.

The Japanese attack had come almost in the middle of David's second term at Lingnan University. Classes ceased immediately with the onset of war and, for a while, all the schools in Hong Kong closed until Japanese control was established. Left with nothing to do, David began to teach his brothers and sisters at home. Then an opportunity presented itself for him to broaden his own education.

"There were a lot of Japanese language schools springing up like mushrooms," he remembers. "Everybody was trying to capitalize on teaching Japanese over Chinese so the people could make a living or work for the Japanese. A friend of ours happened to open a Japanese language school only two blocks from where we lived, so I went there every morning and studied. I did quite well. I was able to converse and suddenly I could read with no problems." Some time later, David was to find his basic knowledge of Japanese very valuable.

With life in Hong Kong getting more difficult every week, David's father decided it would be best to move the family over to Macao, the small Portuguese island colony a three-hour ferry ride from Hong Kong. Portugal was a neutral country so its tiny colony enjoyed a freedom from Japanese control which was a rarity along the Chinese coast at the time. There, the Lam children would be able to continue their studies without interference and avoid the omnipresence of Japanese control in Hong Kong. As for himself, Chi Fung felt he had to remain in Hong Kong and try to reorganize his coal import business. The Japanese had seized his coal depot and somehow he had to renew his connection with Charbonnages du Tonkin, the French coal mining company in northern Indochina. While Chi Fung dealt with his business interests, David would have to assume the burden of establishing the family in Macao.

This was a tremendous responsibility for an eighteen year old but it couldn't be helped. "I don't have an ox. I have to use a horse," Chi Fung said when they discussed the matter. David asked him what he meant.

"In farming in China," his father explained, "you use an ox to plough the field. Farmers never use a horse. If you don't have an ox, then you are forced to take the second best." David was a bit miffed at first, thinking perhaps his father wished his elder brother was available rather than himself. But his father made it clear that there simply was no other choice. "Look after your brothers and sisters," he instructed. "Here is some money. Go and get established in Macao. Put them in school. Get them settled in."

Fortunately, by the spring of 1942 the Japanese authorities were encouraging the Chinese residents of Hong Kong to leave the colony and return to China, where many of them lived before emigrating. Tens of thousands left, urged on by the Japanese who had no desire to provide the food which had to be imported. There was no problem leaving so at least David did not have to obtain permission from the authorities.

It was David's first visit to the Portuguese colony. As a neutral haven in a war zone, it was to remind David in later years of the film *Casablanca*: a hotbed of intrigue, a home for intelligence agents and a transfer point for many people on mysterious business. All that was missing was a Humphrey Bogart or a Peter Lorre.

While lining up on the dock in Hong Kong to catch the ferry to Macao, David and his young brothers and sisters ran into trouble with the Japanese soldiers who were examining the baggage. When David came along with a pile of suitcases, they thought he was engaged in smuggling. Their first reaction was to aim a blow at him, but before they did David used his basic Japanese to explain that the suitcases belonged to the family members behind him in the line. That seemed to satisfy them and all got on the ferry safely.

David's father had a coal depot in Macao so when they arrived there, David and his party went directly to the manager's office. There the group settled in while David and the manager tried to find a house to rent. Macao was crowded with refugees and space was at a premium, but in time they found one. As he recalls, "I considered myself extremely lucky to have got hold of a small house, but it was wedged in between two big buildings. It was a small, old-style Chinese kind of house. On both sides were three-storey-high apartment buildings. It was not the best because there was only one way of cross-ventilation, from one end of the house to the other. There were no side windows because of the closeness of the side buildings. We moved in and boy, it was hot when the wind was not blowing in the right direction. But what I didn't know is that I had rented one of the most notorious haunted houses in Macao."

It was the reputation of the house that made others avoid it. Whether the local manager knew about it is unknown. If he did, he may have balanced that against having ten members of the Lam family temporarily occupying his office. Without a doubt, he would have been happy to see them move into their house and so regain his lost office space.

In David's memory, only the servant and an aunt who accompanied them to Macao ever saw ghosts or spirits in the house. However, his youngest brother Timothy, who was four years old at the time, says he saw some inexplicable things in the house at night, rather like the cartoon character "Caspar the Friendly Ghost." Whatever its reputation, at least the house provided a shelter for the family, and several weeks later David was able to return to Hong Kong and report to his father.

Once home, David tried to persuade his parents to move to Macao. Why should his father face the daily humiliation of having to bow when passing a Japanese sentry on duty? Why should he run the risk of being slapped or kicked if the sentry thought he did not bow low enough? Moreover, an entire shipload of coal had arrived at the depot at Macao just before the Japanese attacked. Since it was in neutral territory the coal remained his property. In fact, this coal deposit was to be the source of the Lam's income throughout the remainder of the war. Chi Fung, his wife and the older members of the family did eventually move to Macao in the autumn of 1942, leaving their house in Kowloon occupied by his mother's relatives.

David now had to consider his own situation. His father suggested he had two options. One was to continue his studies. There was no university in Macao, but by making his way through territory partly controlled by the Japanese, he would be able to attend a Chinese university on the mainland still free from Japanese domination. The other option was to help his father by going to the Vietnamese port and making contact with Charbonnages du Tonkin, the French mining company which supplied the anthracite coal distributed by Chi Fung's company.

David was just turning nineteen when his father put these options to him, but he did not hesitate for a moment. It was time to put his studies aside. His father needed help and David was eager to do what he could.

Aside from selling his flowers at the flower market, David had absolutely no business experience. However, he was to represent his father and carried his father's instructions with him. This endowed him with some authority, and since his father was held in great respect, what young David had to say would be heard.

During the remainder of 1942, David worked with his father. Despite the war, a maritime trade continued to exist along the coast of China. The necessities of life still had to be provided, but with Japan now regulating all sea commerce, merchants had to revise many of their previous business arrangements. French Indochina, under the rule of the Vichy-French government since the defeat of France, was neutral but Japan dominated its government, imports and exports. All of this further complicated the business of Chi Fung.

David's primary task was to keep in personal contact with the various coal distribution bases his father had established. To do so, he took numerous trips by freighter down the coast of China as far south as Fort Bayard, a small port which had come under French administrative rule in 1898. Owing to the irregularity of shipping, David occasionally spent time in Fort Bayard waiting for the next ship to go north to Macao. On one of these trips he met the local governor, a pleasant man who took an instant liking to David and sometimes invited him to his residence on social occasions.

In his first conversation with the governor, David spoke in English, which the French official understood. In passing, David mentioned that he was studying French in Macao. The idea of a Chinese youth studying French in a Portuguese colony intrigued the governor and he asked David to explain. "Well," David said, "there was a fellow who came to the house we rented in Macao to take the electric meter reading. I talked to him but he didn't speak Chinese too well. I said 'What is your language?' He said, 'I speak French.' I said, 'Why?' He said, 'I'm from Vietnam. I got stranded in Hong Kong and came to Macao. I couldn't get back to Vietnam.' So I said, 'What were you?' He said, 'I'm a teacher just travelling and got stranded. I've got to make a living.' So he got a job reading the meters for the electric company. I said, 'What else do you do?' He said, 'Nothing.' 'Are you good in French?' I asked. He said, 'Yes. Why don't I give you lessons when I'm not working?' I said, 'Yes, that makes sense. One-on-one tutor.' So he has been teaching me French."

The governor was amused with the story. He told David to return later when he would introduce him to a resident priest who would help him continue his studies in the language. David met with the priest who, in turn, introduced him to some Roman Catholic nuns who were running an orphanage. With time on his hands, David visited the orphanage and noted the poor condition of many of the youngsters. He suggested to the priest and the sisters that with their help, he could go to Vietnam, buy some scarce government-controlled goods and ship them to Fort Bayard. There he would sell them and make a profit, a good part of which would go to the orphanage. They warmly embraced the idea.

David continued on to Haiphong shortly after and while there he took the opportunity to look around for a suitable commodity. There was much to choose from—rice, beans and spices being possibilities—but he felt the best item to buy was crepe rubber.

Returning to Fort Bayard, David had a meeting with the sisters of the orphanage about his plan to import rubber. He could not do it by himself as a non-resident; it would have to be done by the orphanage. The nuns agreed, the necessary documents were completed and as David now sums it up, "I applied and they signed for eight tons of crepe rubber. We imported that and made lots of money." It was a one-time venture, but it helped the orphans and David was more than pleased that his entrepreneurial skill had paid off.

While at Fort Bayard, David found another way to help his father. By this time, Chi Fung was living in Macao where he had volunteered part of his time as principal of a Baptist High School. Many of the graduates wanted to go on to a Chinese university in an area still free from Japanese domination. One route open was to go to Fort Bayard, and from there to walk across the border to Chan-chiang and into unoccupied Chinese territory. David received these students when they arrived in the French colony and did what he could to assist them on their voyage into the interior of the mainland.

David's long stay-overs at Fort Bayard were due to the fact that his father's company had stored several thousand tons of coal there, which represented a great deal of money. His coal in Hong Kong had been confiscated, but he still had the large depot in Macao. There the Portuguese colonial authorities had imposed rationing and price controls on his coal, but at least it was his and he gave thanks to the Almighty for his good fortune.

In Fort Bayard, time passed rather slowly. David lived above the branch office of his father's firm, and the quarters he had were not particularly comfortable. There was no running water in the building but a "dry toilet" was available. All water had to be drawn from a well, and even that was muddy until one added crystals which caused the sediment to sink to the bottom. Drinking water had to be boiled. There was no bathtub, so taking a bath was a matter of sponging from a basin. Looking back on that period, David says, "It was hard, but when there is no other way to handle it, you just let it go. When everyone is suffering the same, it's okay."

The French colony was slightly larger than Hong Kong in area, and Fort Bayard, its main port, had a distinct French flavour to it. The town had wide boulevards lined with poinciana and jacaranda trees, and David loved to take long walks all over the port, enjoying the exercise as well as the opportunity to meet people. In the evenings, he sometimes attended a Chinese opera. Many famous Chinese opera stars had fled to the freedom offered by the French colony, and some of their operatic productions were highly professional. "I would just go and sit through it," he remembers, "and before you know, it started to sink in. I was beginning to enjoy opera. At least I could follow the rhythm and get the gist of it." Better still, he liked to go to the movies. One in particular he watched time and again was *Sun Valley Serenade* which had been distributed just before the war and had many catchy new tunes in it. It was pure escapism, but it was relaxing and available in local theatres.

Sometimes in his walks around Fort Bayard, David would come across amateur basketball teams playing in a park. The teams were composed of young men who were not professionals but who played and competed for the fun of it. David enjoyed the game, became friendly with some of the players and was asked to become the "owner" of a team called the Jumping Beetles. He agreed after finding out that his main duties would be to supply the team with uniforms, basketballs and a trophy, and to treat the team to an occasional Chinese dinner when it won. It was good fun and helped David while away the time. Personally, he liked to play the game but was not good at it. This was quickly apparent to the other players who liked their "boss" but preferred him cheering from the sidelines when there was an important game coming up. Looking back on it, he says, "When we were winning, then I would go in to play. They wouldn't dare let me play when they were losing. When we were winning a lot, then they didn't mind asking the boss to play because I never could shoot the basket. I tried, but never once in my history of owning the team and playing in competition have I scored."

During the long periods he spent in Fort Bayard, David made periodic trips home to Macao. The first sea voyages along the China coast were not particularly dangerous, but by the summer of 1942, Japanese naval and military forces had reached the limit of their expansion. In May of that year, the Japanese navy was dealt a hard blow in the Battle of the Coral Sea. In June, another Japanese naval force was dispersed with heavy losses when it attacked Midway Island. In November, a three-day naval battle in the Solomon Islands again saw the Japanese naval force turned back with heavy losses. Aircraft from land bases and American aircraft carriers began to make the waters of the South Pacific more dangerous. With its growing strength, the United States and its allies began to reconquer some of the territories and bases lost to Japan in its triumphal sweep of 1941–42. The tide of war was beginning to turn and, as it did, the danger in the Chinese coastal trade increased.

Early in 1943, David was in Macao when his father asked him to go to Haiphong again on business. Arrangements were made for him to travel on a ship called *Wing Wah* which was due to leave shortly. There were a large number of passengers on board, but David shared a cabin with the son of the ship's owner so he was fairly comfortable. En route the ship put into Fort Bayard briefly before proceeding to Haiphong. While loading cargo in the French colony, David was contacted by his father's representative there. He had run into problems with the French authorities and begged David to help him since he knew of David's friendship with the governor. David protested. He had to get to Haiphong, the *Wing Wah* was going there and it might be weeks before another ship could take him. He was assured that a ship, the *Dennies Frères*, was due in a few days' time and he could board that one for the same destination. David agreed and managed to take his suitcase from the *Wing Wah* minutes before it left the dock. He waved goodbye to his friends and then arranged an appointment with the governor.

A few days later, David boarded the *Dennies Frères* and again set sail. The ship kept close to the coast of Hainan Island, slipping into its bays and harbours because there were American submarines in the area. After five days, the captain decided it was too dangerous to go on, and cautiously returned to Fort Bayard. There, David was informed that the *Wing Wah* had been torpedoed on approaching Haiphong. Very few of the crew or passengers had been saved.

Back in Macao, David's father heard about the *Wing Wah* sinking, and thought his second son had been lost. Later, when he learned David was alive, Chi Fung made a quick decision: David would no longer be used to maintain contact with the coal depots along the coast. He was to return to Macao. From there he would make his way to Shaoguan in mainland China, where Lingnan University had re-established itself the previous year. It was time to resume his university studies.

Lingnan had already moved once from Canton to avoid the Japanese, and it determined to do the same when Hong Kong fell. It was a difficult task, to put it mildly. The essence of a university is its professors and scholars. Classrooms, student housing, libraries and laboratories can be built later. With this philosophy in mind, the first priority was to move the faculty and staff to an area about a hundred miles inland from Hong Kong, an area which could provide food for the students, construction material for buildings and—most important—academic freedom.

Travelling from Macao to the northern part of Canton province where the university was located involved a lot of planning. Small boats travelled between Macao and the mainland, which was only a short distance away. The Japanese did not have the manpower to patrol every mile of the coastline and even though their army occupied the coastal strip, their presence was concentrated in the larger towns and along the main transportation routes. For a price, "agents" were willing to guide people through the Japanese-held territory, across a no man's land where law and order was at a minimum, and on to "free" China controlled by the Nationalist government of Chiang Kai-shek. This underground railway had been developed in 1942 and was utilized by students and faculty from both Hong Kong University and Lingnan University.

David retains vivid memories of the journey: "We had a little group of students all wanting to go to Lingnan. We took off carrying a minimum of baggage. There was always one fellow who knew the way . . . but we didn't. We just kept walking from early in the morning until nighttime and then we stopped. The thing that bothered me most were the mosquitoes—they would just chew me up. We would sleep anywhere, sometimes in a restaurant. We would ask the owner to allow us to put the tables together and we would sleep on top of them. The next morning we would put the tables back. The next night we might sleep at a place where there were peasants. We would give them a few cents so that we could sleep on their bed and they would go somewhere else. It was just one thing after another."

One very strange incident occurred on a night when the group stayed in a small hut: "It was just several rooms inside with partitions. The beds were hardboard planks with a piece of wood as a pillow. I was tired and I went to bed. It was a full moon and my three student companions went out to enjoy the moonlight. I heard them calling me to join them because the moon was beautiful. I was praying so I didn't answer them. They came to my door but quickly left. The three of them all stayed in one room that night so I was alone. I never thought about it further.

"On the last leg of our journey, we were in a small boat pulled by a boatman, walking along the bank, pulling it against the current. I heard my companions at the bow of the boat talking. I heard my name mentioned and I went up to them and said: 'What are you fellows talking about?' Then they told me that the previous evening, when they went to the door to call me, they saw a woman sitting on my bed. She had long hair, was dressed in white and was kind looking. When they called my name, she looked up at them and looked back down on me. It scared the daylight out of them and they rushed out. They never did come back into my room again. They didn't intend to tell me."

David told them, "It must have been an angel because I was praying." He had seen nothing of this. His eyes had been closed in concentrated prayer, and he had immediately gone to sleep, peaceful in mind and spirit.

When the group reached the new campus of Lingnan University, David was astonished at what he saw. Seemingly in the middle of nowhere, there were buildings, classrooms, dormitories, gardens and auditoriums. These had been built largely by the students and faculty members themselves. Most of them had been constructed by splitting bamboo trees, weaving them together, covering the walls with mud and then whitewashing the walls when the mud dried. There was no running water available so it had to be brought in pails from wells and nearby streams. There was no electricity either, so oil was used for heating meals. This was expensive and the university decided to make use of a huge grove of nearby camphor trees, pressing the seeds into oil. "We used camphor seed oil for our lamps," David recalls. "It's fantastic if you can stand the smell because it's so strong. After a while you get used to it and it repelled the mosquitoes."

Life at this rural campus was primitive. Everyone pitched in so that it operated almost like a commune. Everything was lacking except enthusiasm and innovation. For example, paper was very scarce so rice straw was collected, ground up fine and a rough paper made. In its primary stage, it looked like toilet paper and blotted any writing in ink. Eventually someone devised a type of diluted paste which, when brushed on the paper and allowed to dry, gave it a coating which took pencil or pen quite easily.

For relaxation, there were sports like basketball and softball, and sometimes the students arranged a music appreciation night. The university had managed to obtain a hand-cranked, floor model RCA gramophone and some records of classical music. Although some of the sets of records were incomplete, they nevertheless included the best of such composers as Tchaikovsky, Mozart and Beethoven. The concerts were held in the evening just before sunset. A student would describe the life of the composer or the importance of the particular piece about to be heard. There was no public address system but the four or five hundred students sitting on the grass would be perfectly quiet so when the record was played everyone could hear it. For David, with his love for music, it was a particularly moving experience to attend such a concert. Amateur theatricals were also put on in the evenings but music was his special delight.

Lingnan University was not concentrated on one campus. David was on the College of Arts campus. Other locations some distance away were occupied by the Faculty of Agriculture and the Faculty of Medicine, for example. One of David's young uncles, Shu-Kee, was a medical student at Lingnan, and the two of them managed to visit each other frequently. David also ran into a friend from the Lingnan campus in Hong Kong, K.T. Yue, who was also studying medicine. Yue was helping to run the medical clinic. With only a minimal supply of drugs and medicines at the clinic, he hoped fervently that none of the students would get sick.

Communication with the outside world was difficult. Trips by agents such as the one who guided David and his friends from Macao were infrequent and beset with danger, but an occasional message could be sent so David could inform his parents about his own situation. Fortunately, his health was good and his natural optimism and cheerfulness more than balanced the austerity of his surroundings. He made friends and found a tremendous camaraderie in sharing the hardships of campus life. Years later the alumni from this period would continue this bond of friendship.

David was at the university for about a year and a half. Periodically there were Japanese air raids near the campus, but for a long time there was no danger to the university itself. During 1943, radio reports confirmed that the tide of the war was changing. In North Africa, the Germans had been defeated and Allied forces invaded Italy in July. On the eastern front, the Russian armies were steadily grinding down the Germans. In the Pacific, Japanese naval forces were being hit hard and American troops were seizing one island after another as they thrust towards Japan.

By 1944, the pace quickened. In June the Allies landed in Normandy. Meanwhile in the Pacific, after seizing the Marshall Islands and Guam, American forces prepared to launch an attack on the Philippines.

In the interior of China, however, the Japanese were holding their own, and in some areas were making inroads into previously held Nationalist territory. Late in 1944, Japanese troops fought their way closer to the Lingnan campus. The university authorities were aware of the menace but only at the last moment gave the order for everyone to leave. David had talked to his uncle about such a possibility and they had agreed that, come what may, they would travel together. When the sudden announcement came to evacuate, the problem was how and in what direction. No longer could an agent guide a few students through the Japanese lines, walking through fields and sideroads. The Japanese front was advancing from the north and the south. The previous route led straight to the battlefield.

David considered his options very carefully. He had little money in the money belt he carried around his waist, and his uncle was in a similar position. If they went northwest and travelled inland they might reach Chungking. There David would be able to study but he had no funds to maintain himself. Another possibility was to go east and then south to his father's village. Here he would probably find a place to live and food to eat. Again it would involve slipping through Japanese lines, and once there, he would not be able to study. A third alternative was to take a very circuitous route to Fort Bayard, and from there try to return to Macao. He had many friends in the French colony, and once there, he could count on a measure of safety and support. This was the route he decided on.

When the word came to go, there was almost a panic. No orderly evacuation could be organized and there was turmoil as students collected only what they could carry and set out, singly and in groups, to flee the Japanese. David and his uncle walked to the nearest railway station hoping to get to Kwei-lin. As David recalls the scene, "It was a madhouse. When the train arrived, people climbed in the windows and doors. We managed to get a seat. The train journey took about two days. By the time everyone got on the train, it was hot and noisy. People were sitting on the floor. We gave up our seats to a mother with a crying baby. . .

"The train was going very slow because every time a Japanese warplane would come, everyone would evacuate the train until the danger was over. Then everyone got on and the train would slowly chug forward. My uncle and I ended up on the roof of the car. That was good. It was cool up there except when going through a tunnel. It made your heart skip a beat because you didn't know whether you would get knocked off or something, but by sitting down or stooping low, there was no problem. The only worry was in the tunnel, we didn't know if there were any crosswires."

The pair reached Kwei-lin safely, only to find that the city was also evacuating in considerable disorder. He remembers it as being like the scene of the burning of Atlanta in *Gone with the Wind*.

Fort Bayard lay about 250 miles due south of Kwei-lin. After about a week of rough and hazardous travel by bus and by foot, David and his uncle reached a town a short distance from the French colony. Since the latter had been subjected to occasional bombing, and since some of his friends had moved to the town from Fort Bayard, they decided to wait for a few days. The father of one of David's friends owned a hotel so they had no trouble getting a room, and for the first time in a fortnight they enjoyed a comfortable bed and the luxury of a bath.

Shortly after, David met a gentleman named Mr. Fok who claimed he had met David and his father on a previous occasion. David could not remember meeting him. Mr. Fok managed a small business and seemed a very bright young man. As David tells the story, "He asked me to go to his office. So I went there. He said, 'Why don't you have your meals here. It costs money outside.' I said to him, 'But I don't know how long it will take me to get a passage on a boat.' He said, 'Don't worry about it. You eat here. Two meals a day.' I will never forget him." (And he didn't. Forty-four years later, David was able to invite Mr. Fok and some of his family to lunch at Government House. It was an emotional reunion.)

David and his uncle remained there for some weeks trying to make arrangements for a trip north from Fort Bayard. It gave him time to renew old friendships, meet new people and observe how business was conducted in the colony. Eventually he made contact with the captain of a forty-five-foot motor vessel going to Macao. The captain had room for two more passengers which, with the crew, made a total of thirteen on the boat. The trip, the captain said, would take about a day and a half. David paid the fare and then asked where their accommodation would be. The captain replied, "There is none. You go to the bow of the boat where we store the anchor chain. You spread the chain a little bit level and put some blankets on it and also your suitcase. You make do there." The captain added that he would sail at the crack of dawn, and that they could come aboard at any time that night.

"So that evening we had a farewell party with our friends," David remembers, "and then moved on to the boat. It was called the *Sin Gin Maru*. Sin, in Chinese, means smoothly. Gin is to go forward. So the ship's name meant to go forward smoothly. It's a good omen so we slept on board.

"After two or three hours we were awakened by air raid sirens. I saw an airplane—it was first light—coming right at us. Before we knew it, four rockets were fired at our boat and they landed on the left and right of us. The boat went up and down and there was some leaking. The skipper said, 'Wait and see if the planes come back.' By that time, my uncle and I had already climbed to the deck and run away from the dock. Then we looked back. There were no more air raids. The boat was still there. So the captain said, 'We've got to sail. We'll get away from the dockside.' So we got back on the boat."

It was not a propitious beginning, but things were going to get worse. As the boat eased its way out of the harbour, the captain felt there must be seepage in the hull because the bilge pump was working constantly. He went down the channel and started along the coast until he neared a fishing village. There he decided to beach the boat, and at low tide, the crew set to work repairing the leaks. That took an entire day. When the tide came in, the boat was refloated and made its way out to sea. By this time, however, the winds had come up and waves crashed over the bow. It was heavy going as the boat struggled to keep on course.

After a few hours at sea, David saw first one and then another boat approaching. The crew became very excited and when David enquired about the commotion, the captain explained that they were pirate boats. Their method was to approach their prey, and wait to see if it would fire a machine gun at them; if unopposed, they would approach and overcome their victim. If, on the other hand, they were met by fire, the pirate boat would come close, draw fire, move away and then repeat the manoeuvre. Their objective was to have their quarry use up all its ammunition—at which point the pirates would move in for the kill.

The captain of the *Sin Gin Maru* had rifles and a machine gun on board. The first pirate boat was kept off and fell behind. Shortly after, another one came at them using the same tactics. As David describes it, "I recall our engine conked out owing to the water coming in. The engineer was on the deck firing at the pirate. The skipper told him, 'Your job is down there in the engine room to make sure we can get away. We don't need you up here firing.' So he went down. I really prayed that he would be able to fix the engine. The engineer did get the engine going and the *Sin Gin Maru* moved away."

Once out of sight of the pirates, the captain decided to seek shelter from the high winds and rough seas. He put the ship into a cove near Yangjiang, close to an island which gave some protection. Neither the crew nor passengers had eaten all day. The captain ordered the anchor to be dropped and the cook to prepare some food. Soon, everyone was below deck eating. With the ship still heaving, nobody noticed the anchor chain had broken until, with a sickening thud, the ship crashed between two huge rocks about five hundred yards from the beach. It was dark by this time. Before going aground, the ship had drifted away from the sheltered area, and the waves began to pound it relentlessly. It was terrifying when the pounding of the surf broke the ship in two. David recalls the incident vividly: "Everybody came to the bow area that had caught in the rocks. By that time, nothing was level. Everyone was clinging on. There was an elderly crew member who told me 'I'm cold, I'm cold.' I held him in my arms for hours but he never had any motion. I asked the skipper, 'How come?' He took a look, opened his eyelids and he was dead.

"At that time—it had to be about two or three in the morning—I told my uncle, 'I'm feeling sleepy.' He said, 'That's bad.' I said, 'I would rather swim for the island than stay here in the cold.' "

The miserable situation was made worse by the action of the crew. There were not enough life jackets to go around so crew members with guns grabbed those that were available. There were no life rafts or lifeboats; indeed, only half of the *Sin Gin Maru* itself remained, wedged between two rocks. The decision by David and his uncle to try to swim to shore through the heavy surf was probably a good one. Taking off their shoes, they dived in. The surface of the water was covered with diesel fuel from the wreck and both men were soaked with it after they pulled themselves on shore. Ahead of them was a steep cliff, but in the dark David could see a light. They made toward it, their feet being badly cut as they made their way over the beach.

The light came from a small fishing boat on the beach. The fisherman's son was sick and he and his wife had just prepared some hot water with ginger in it. When David and his uncle appeared at the cabin doorway, the fisherman took one look at them—cold, wet, covered with oil, their feet bleeding—and insisted the two survivors have the hot ginger first. David, grateful for this bit of warmth, enquired about the place. They were on Nanpang Island. The date was December 7, almost exactly the third anniversary of the bombing of Hong Kong. On the island, further up the hill, the Japanese maintained a weather station. There were some small warehouses nearby so David and his uncle headed there. It provided shelter, if nothing else, and it was no more uncomfortable than sleeping in the anchor chain locker on the *Sin Gin Maru*.

When they woke up in the morning, the wind had died down. The small cove now held over half a dozen fishing vessels which had run in for shelter. They had rescued the crew and passengers from the wreck and soon they too came to the warehouse. Some of the ship's cargo was off-loaded and brought to the warehouse as well—cowhides, lard, preserved pork and other goods. The survivors were able to purchase some rice and used that and the preserved pork for food. However, the food attracted rats. "We would be smelling of food," David remembers, "and when we went to sleep, the rats would climb over us and that would wake me up. It was like a horror movie to be awakened by a rat looking at you, perhaps trying to see if they could take a nibble from my face."

After about a week, a small Japanese naval trawler arrived. Straining to remember as much Japanese as he could from his studies in Hong Kong, David managed to inform the captain about their shipwreck and asked for a passage home. It turned out the ship was headed south, but the captain said another vessel, a naval supply ship, would be coming by heading north. Three days later it arrived. David again used his Japanese to plead for assistance. One of its crew members spoke both the Taiwanese dialect and Mandarin, so David was able to elaborate on their plight. The captain was sympathetic and his cargo was light, so the group was given permission to board his vessel for Hong Kong.

Once aboard, they were put into the ship's cargo hold and the hatch was closed. They were not allowed on deck during the trip to Hong Kong and the only light they had was from a single porthole. Twice a day, the hatch was opened and a basket lowered to the dozen men below. The basket contained rice balls and salted, dried plums, enough to give each one a rice ball and two plums each. "Everyone tried to make themselves as comfortable as they could," David recalls. "There were a lot of oil barrels in the hold and it's very hard to make a bed on a stack of barrels, lying sideways. I had a bag and was using it as a pillow. It got loose and opened up. It turned out to contain the locks of hair, nail clippings, purse, belt and other items of the fellow who died in the shipwreck."

After a most uncomfortable two days' journey, the ship arrived at a dock on the Kowloon side of Hong Kong. Here the survivors of the *Sin Gin Maru* disembarked and were subjected to an interrogation by Japanese military police while still on the dock. To keep his long hair out of his face, David had tied a handkerchief around his head and pushed his hair underneath it. The policeman who interrogated him seemed first to want to hit him. Apparently, he took the handkerchief to be a hat and the Chinese were supposed to take off their hats when speaking to a Japanese official. The policeman grabbed the handkerchief and threw it to the ground. It was not the beginning of a pleasant interrogation.

Just as the questioning was underway, however, the air raid sirens sounded. Allied bombers were near and the docks were a likely target. There was a tremendous scramble to find safety as people ran in various directions. David and his uncle took advantage of the confusion and ran away from the dock. There was no baggage to carry: all they had were the clothes they wore and a few coins in their pockets. Once beyond the dock area, David went to a public telephone and called his uncle, Dr. C. K. Chan, the same person who had prevented the Japanese from taking over the Lam house three years earlier. Dr. Chan was at home. Astonished and pleased to hear David's voice, he told David to come at once. David asked him to contact his father to tell him he was safe.

David and his uncle then hired a tricycle cab, promising to pay the driver once they arrived at their destination. That was agreed upon and off they went. En route, they passed a shop called the Mayfair Studio. David knew the owner who used to take his high school's graduation photographs. On the spur of the moment, he told the cabbie to stop and went with his uncle to have their photo taken. Then they went on to Dr. Chan's house for a joyful reunion, a bath, a good meal and a change of clothes. It was a glorious feeling, he remembers.

Anxious to return to his parents in Macao, David asked his uncle if he could secure tickets for them on the ferry that crossed over to Macao. His uncle promised he would, but despite all his efforts,

Dr. Chan could only get one ticket. They were in very great demand. It was a great temptation but David declined to take the single ticket. He and his young uncle had been through so much since they left Lingnan University several months earlier that he was determined they would stick together to the end. The ferry ticket was given to a cousin, anxious to go to Macao to study. David and his uncle looked for another way to reach there and eventually found a small sailboat carrying a cargo for the island. A deal was struck and the pair got on the boat for their slow journey across the river delta. The regular ferry, called the *Lingnan Maru*, was still in the harbour when they left, but they knew it would easily overtake their slow sailboat.

There must have been a guardian angel looking after David. The ferry to Macao did indeed leave the harbour and easily passed them. Half an hour after it left, just off Castle Peak, the ferry was attacked by an American warplane and sunk. Hundreds of passengers lost their lives, including David's cousin. In Macao, thinking he was on board, David's parents were grief-stricken. Unaware of what had happened, David and his uncle sailed slowly across the wide delta on the last leg of a journey neither of them would ever forget.

THREE

Branching Out

There was no one to greet David and his uncle at the jetty in Macao, nor did they expect anyone. They had no idea that the ferry they were to take had been sunk. The last thing his parents had heard from Dr. Chan in Hong Kong, however, was that David was on the ferry. Word about the disaster had spread quickly in Macao and for the third time his parents thought David had been killed. When once again he turned up on their doorstep, they were overwhelmed. Surely the Lord must be looking after their son and their prayers had been answered. After being bombed, machine-gunned by pirates, shipwrecked, and almost embarking on a doomed ferry, he was back home.

A thanksgiving service was held in their church. It was packed with family and friends, all anxious to hear his stories and welcome him back. He was home in time for Christmas and what better present could he have than that?

David remained in Macao for the next nine months. During that time Germany and Italy were defeated by the Allies, whose forces were now able to turn their full military strength towards the defeat of Japan. In Southeast Asia, the British, supported by the Chinese and Americans, drove into Burma and south towards Singapore. In the Pacific, American forces continued to leap from one island to another towards Japan, all the while subjecting Japanese cities to hammer blows from air bombing. Early in 1945, American forces invaded the main Philippine island of Luzon, and within a few months they had captured Manila.

With the seizure of Manila, the Lam family hoped they would soon hear from the eldest son, Daniel, who had left in the autumn of 1941 to attend the University of the Philippines and had been caught up in the war. As a British subject, he had been confined to a concentration camp until mid-1942, when he and other students were released as harmless. Daniel had been able to get only one message to his family during the rest of the war so they had no idea of how he was faring until the Japanese surrendered. Unknown to them, Daniel had managed to survive by working for meagre pay as a bus driver in Manila, and was even able to continue his university studies in engineering. It had been tough going for him during those three years and his relief when the Japanese had been driven from the city can only be imagined.

In Macao meanwhile, David was recovering from his journey and settling into the routine of living again with his family. His parents had left the original haunted house David had rented and were now living in more comfortable quarters. Lam Chi Fung's coal supplies continued to provide enough money to maintain the family, although without the comforts formerly enjoyed in Hong Kong. Nevertheless, by the summer of 1945 it seemed clear that the era of Japanese domination was coming to an end. Everyone looked forward to returning to their home on Grampian Road, and it seemed that the long months of exile would soon be over.

While David enjoyed getting reacquainted with his younger brothers and sisters, and helped his father to the extent he could, he spent the early part of 1945 anxiously awaiting the outcome of a private venture in which he became involved. When he left Lingnan University to go to Fort Bayard, he stayed for a short time at a town a little distance inland from the port. Friends of his from Fort Bayard had moved there because the port was sometimes subjected to air raids. While there, David had time to visit his friends, who after listening to his experiences, were most impressed with his good luck in avoiding danger over the past years. One of these friends was a former Lingnan classmate whose family was fairly wealthy. He and a few others felt that some of David's good luck would rub off on them. They proposed that they would arrange to send a shipload of raw salt to Macao where it would probably get a good price. David would be there by the time it arrived. They wanted David to be part of the venture and suggested he should have one-third of the shares. Since he had no money, they loaned him enough to buy his share and the bargain was struck.

The arrangement to load a junk with salt and send it to Macao was made before David left Fort Bayard. His own journey home, as we have seen, was a perilous affair that took two weeks to complete rather than two days. A sailing junk would take longer, but once home he expected it to arrive almost day by day. One week passed, then another and still another. David began to despair that it would ever arrive. Perhaps it had gone down in one of the numerous storms that hit the Chinese coast in the wintertime. Perhaps it had been commandeered or hijacked. There was no radio communication with the vessel, and as David thought about his partners, he worried that his integrity might be brought into question.

He was sitting in his father's office in Macao when a man came in and told him the junk had arrived. It had been damaged in a storm and had taken a long time to be repaired. The long delay, although wearing on his nerves, did have an unexpected benefit. When the original deal was made, salt in Macao was selling at about twenty-five dollars for a 133-pound sack. Because of a shortage and the delay in delivery, the price had gone up to about ninety dollars. As a result, David not only made a profit but a windfall. This was not pocket money made by selling a few flowers from his garden; he had made thousands of dollars.

His friends were delighted and invited him to come in with them on another deal. This time he said no. After repaying his loan he had made a profit of about HK$34,000. It had been a gamble for a young man who was only twenty-two, and he realized that had things gone the other way, he would have been deeply in debt.

The question now was which currency he should hold. At this time, there were two types of Hong Kong dollars in circulation: the old notes that had been in circulation before the war began and the new notes that the Japanese had printed. Although the latter were issued under the authority of the Hong Kong and Shanghai Bank, it was known that the Japanese had forced the bank to do so. As the power of Japan waned, the public began to worry that the returning British would not recognize the currency issued under Japanese rule. As a result, people began to hold on to the old notes and the new notes began to lose their value, falling to almost a quarter of their face value.

David decided on a long shot. He felt the British would recognize the new notes at their full face value. If he bought them at a very low price and the British accepted them at face value, the profit from the salt would be trebled again. He was young and he had no debts; he knew it was a gamble, but if he was wrong he could easily live with the error and make up his profit in later years. His mind made up, David purchased as many new Hong Kong dollars as he could. The dollars were easy to come by in Macao, partly because of the trade between the two areas and partly due to smuggling. When he had purchased all he could, he put them in his father's safe and waited to see what would happen.

The rumour mills were working overtime and there was a great deal of speculation about the future of the new dollars, with opinion swinging one way and then the other. David's father was very concerned that his son had bet everything on the "Japanese" dollar. At one point, while David was away on a trip to Hong Kong, Chi Fung decided to take his son's savings from his safe and convert them into the old Hong Kong dollars. David was very annoyed when he found out and protested so strongly that his father reversed his decision and bought back the new dollars. In fact, Chi Fung was so impressed with his son's feelings that he decided to convert his own ready cash into the new notes. He bought somewhere between 100,000 and 200,000 "new" dollars, put them in the safe with David's money, and hoped for the best.

With the defeat of Germany in the spring of 1945, the fall of Japan was just a matter of time. Nevertheless, the Japanese continued to fight furiously all during the summer, defending every island at a tremendous cost in blood. On August 6, an American bomber dropped an atomic bomb on Hiroshima, wiping out over half the city.

A few days later, Japan made an offer to surrender and accepted the severe terms of capitulation on August 16. At long last the war was over and once again the British were in control of Hong Kong. The colony had not suffered a great deal of physical damage from the war but Japanese policies had reduced its population to about 600,000 people. Its trade had been devastated and there was a tremendous amount of work to be done to get the colony on its feet again. In order to restore business confidence and commercial stability, the British government decided that both the old and new Hong Kong dollars would be accepted at face value. David's gamble had paid off. He now had a measure of financial independence which was most unusual for a young man in his circumstances, and he was determined to use his money carefully.

The end of the war brought with it a great many changes. For the Lam family, the first thought was to return to Hong Kong and reclaim their house in Kowloon. It had not been damaged, fortunately, but it took time to move the family from Macao. Thousands had gone to the Portuguese colony to escape Japanese rule, and all wanted to return. At the same time, tens of thousands who had gone to mainland China were slowly making their way back to Hong Kong. Within a relatively short period, the colony's population reached its prewar level.

One of those who came back late in 1945 was Daniel Lam. With shipping in short supply, he took advantage of an offer to travel home from Manila on a Royal Navy aircraft carrier, along with many others who had been stranded in the Philippines. It was a joyful reunion after four long years of separation, but much had changed since 1941. David was only eighteen years old when Daniel had last seen him. He was now twenty-two, with many adventurous tales to relate and with money in the bank. The two brothers had lived quite different lives and readjusting to the new circumstances was not always easy.

Once back in Kowloon, their father began to reestablish his coal importing and distribution business with a good measure of initial success. He also continued to spend a great deal of time on church work. In Macao, he had served as the volunteer principal of the Pui-Ching Middle School, a Baptist high school which he had supported since he had moved there. In Hong Kong, he was asked to assume the same task. Chi Fung not only accepted the job, but in the years following worked steadily to establish a Baptist college in the colony. Meanwhile, as principal of the Baptist high school, he made that institution one of the best in Hong Kong.

Certainly the colony was in need of all the help it could muster, as problems mounted up during the postwar years. Although the war with Japan was over in mainland China there was no reconciliation of the differences between the Nationalist government led by Chiang Kai-shek and the Communist Party led by Mao Tse-tung. Armed conflict broke out between the two rival groups within months of the Japanese surrender. The conflict soon widened into civil war, and between 1946 and 1949 China was again in turmoil. This brought a tremendous influx of people to Hong Kong and drove up the demand for housing, refugee settlement, hospitals and schools.

Chi Fung worked hard to help educate his teenage students while also doing all he could to strengthen the Baptist churches and chapels in the colony. Eventually, he became chairman of the Hong Kong Baptist convention.

Meanwhile, David had some decisions to make. What did he want to do with his life? It didn't take him long to conclude that he should finish his education. Lingnan University had returned to its old campus in Canton. Its buildings had not been damaged, and the faculty and students were returning. David decided to rejoin them. He put the money he had made into mortgages in Hong Kong, which allowed him to attend the university without asking his father for financial help. For the next two years he remained at Lingnan, studying for his Bachelor of Arts degree which he received in 1947.

Normally, David might have been expected to follow in the steps of many of his contemporaries, who, having completed their degree, returned home to enter whatever business they could. Like a minority of his fellow students, however, David wanted to do graduate work, to get a Master's degree or even go further for a doctorate. He also had a strong desire to see more of the world. He was twenty-four years old and felt that once he entered the business world he would be tied down. The time to go was when one was young and single, and what better place to go than the United States?

Selecting a university to attend was a problem. Tens of thousands of young American veterans, recently discharged from the armed services, had flocked to American universities and colleges to further their education. Every campus was crowded and admission was by no means automatic. Fortunately, David wanted to study at the graduate level, where the pressure on enrolment was less intense. After many enquiries, he managed to gain acceptance at Temple University, an institution which had been established by the Baptists in 1884.

David's desire to travel to the United States was coupled with an urge to enjoy more control over his own life. Looking back on it, he says, "It was a sense of trying to gain a freedom from family restriction and the way everybody had to conduct themselves in the family structure." In the years since he had first gone to Fort Bayard in 1942, he had been home a total of only eight months. For a considerable period, therefore, he had been away from the strong traditional family controls typical in a Chinese household. During that time, he had become accustomed to making his own decisions without consultation and without needing to ask anyone's permission. He enjoyed that and felt all the more keenly the invisible web of custom when he came back from Lingnan.

Getting to the United States was not easy. Eventually, he booked passage on board a Norwegian freighter, the *Lidvard*, which was bound first for Los Angeles and then for Philadelphia via the Panama Canal. The ship had room for about ten passengers. It was an exciting trip for him and he enjoyed it to the full. Gregarious by nature, he mingled easily with the other passengers. As he recalled the voyage, "It was a long trip, and on the way, I met with people such as a recently retired businessman from Shanghai, or a young Catholic father who tried to convert me. I met with all different kinds of people. I was very keen to improve my English so I kept talking. Whenever I had any free time I would do a lot of reading and a lot of singing too. I would go to the bow of the ship, watching the waves, and sing "Don't Fence Me In." That reflected my state of mind at that time. I wanted to break out and be on my own. It was not so much just the family that I tried to get away from; it was the whole social system, the whole Chinese society. I wanted to try something totally new."

When he arrived in Los Angeles, where the ship was to remain for a couple of days, David telephoned a friend he knew from his church in Hong Kong, who was living in the city. He met David and showed him the sights of the city. That evening they went to the Hollywood Bowl where David heard beautiful music played under the stars. It was overwhelming. If this was America, he must see more of it. When his friend suggested that he might prefer to go to Philadelphia overland, he thought it a good idea and transferred from the ship to a hotel the same day.

Meanwhile he made another telephone call to a Lingnan University classmate in San Francisco. The classmate invited him to come up—an easy day-long bus ride—and stay with him for several days. His friend was anxious to show him as much of San Francisco as he could and it was here that for the first time David encountered the cultural shock of living in a non-Chinese country.

David found Americans to be very outgoing, frank and sincere. He was surprised at how friendly they were, even if they did not know you. The Chinese, in his opinion, "are very reserved and very quiet. They would rather not talk, and wait for you to talk. They will always tend to agree, and you must try hard to get them to share their own feelings." He found the Americans almost overwhelming with their friendliness and warmth. Sometimes, this warmth seemed almost to reach a point when, to the Chinese, it bordered on being uncomfortable and they were unsure how to handle it. The Americans tended to treat a new acquaintance almost as a long lost brother and would be on a first name basis in minutes. American society, David concluded, was very different from the one in which he grew up, and it would take more than a little mental adjustment to become accustomed to it.

Another example of the cultural difference encountered by David in San Francisco emerged when he met two young cousins of his friend, one a singer and the other a dancer, who worked in a night club. They took David with them to see the show. After the performance, David went with the singer in his car. "We were driving out," he recalls, "and all these people were coming out from the night club, ladies included, and they all wanted to touch him—his face, his hands. He was like an idol. I was sitting next to him and what I saw just shocked me!"

Visiting San Francisco was an enjoyable experience, with its broad boulevards, gardens, the Golden Gate Bridge, Chinatown and all the other attractions. It had been years since he had visited a large city which did not show the scars of war. The cleanliness and the spaciousness of the city impressed him, as did other features of the American scene such as drive-in restaurants and fast-food outlets. It was all new and exciting.

His university friend was also en route to an eastern American university, so David proposed that they travel together. His friend already had an airline ticket, but David suggested he trade it in and join him on a Greyhound bus. Travel by bus was much cheaper and they would be able to see more of the United States from the road. David's brief bus journey from Los Angeles to San Francisco had been pleasantly comfortable and he envisioned something of the same on the way to Philadelphia. His friend agreed, but after seven days and nights of almost non-stop travel, both were heartily tired of that mode of transportation. They did see a lot of the American countryside, however, and became experts in snatching quick meals at the various brief bus halts. There was probably no happier person to arrive in Philadelphia than David.

He found the city to be "a wonderful, gorgeous place." The suburban area was clean and filled with nice houses, the city centre pleasant, the people rather conservative and the weather very agreeable. The colourful leaves in autumn and the crisp winter days were a novelty, and he loved to go walking in the snow and then to Chinatown for a hot bowl of rice.

Since his Lingnan University friend had gone to a university in New York, David was determined to make new friends at Temple University. When he arrived there, the housing administrator said to him, "I suppose you want a single room or a double room."

"Wait," David replied, "what is the largest room you have?"

"I have a room for seventeen people. It's like an army barracks."

"Put me in there," he replied, "because I would rather be with people than be by myself."

There was another reason for his choice. His English was relatively good, but he knew he had to improve it a great deal if he was to get the full advantage of the lectures from his English-speaking professors. He also had to improve his skill in verbal communication to take part in serious conversations on various academic topics, and improve his knowledge of English jargon and slang for more casual talk. With this in mind, he became active in the university's International House, an institution started by the Rockefeller Foundation to encourage American and international students to meet and mix. He joined the fellowship of the local Baptist church and became a member of the university's Chinese fraternity. Whenever the opportunity offered, he travelled to nearby towns and cities, interested in everything and wanting to know what made America tick.

Most of his time, naturally, was taken up by lectures, research, writing and study. His priority was to obtain a Master of Business Administration degree. Before he left Hong Kong, he had watched his father becoming involved with an entrepreneur who had a gift for manufacturing a variety of products. David wanted to help his father when he returned. He was eager to find out what made the Americans so successful in their commercial endeavours and then apply it when he got home.

His time at Temple passed all too quickly and in the spring of 1948 he received his Master's degree. To complete the degree in one year was a considerable achievement. It reinforced his self-confidence to the point where he began to think of trying for a doctorate, also at an American university. There was still so much to see and learn in the United States, and since he was there, what better time to do it?

David's good luck continued after his graduation. He wanted to meet Americans and he wanted to earn some money, so he was delighted when his application to work at a YMCA camp as a waiter was accepted. The George Williams College Camp was located at a beautiful spot on the shores of Lake Geneva, about midway between Chicago and Madison, Wisconsin. The camp hired a lot of students during the summer and was a popular spot, well run and featuring many activities for family members of all ages. David lived in a dormitory with the other students and soon found himself immersed in camp life. He found that he loved the work because he got to meet all kinds of people and serve them. He remembers, "I still had a lot of time on my hands so I asked for more jobs. They said, 'Okay, you get yourself trained as a lifesaver. You can become as high as a lifeguard.' I said, 'That's fine.' So I got my certificate and I became a lifeguard. I went out with a whistle, white helmet and a cross on my swim suit. I would patrol the docks where the kids and everyone was swimming and that was good. I participated in the camp choir and also in the employees' stunt nights putting on shows."

Shortly afterwards David took on a third job, driving the camp's station wagon to the local railway station, meeting incoming guests and taking them and their luggage to the camp. With the three jobs he was kept fairly busy. Yet he still found time to learn to play golf. A nearby golf course allowed the camp employees to play without paying a fee, and when he heard about that, he decided he would try it. The golf pro sold him an inexpensive half-set of golf clubs and David bought a book called *Power Golf* by the well-known professional golfer, Ben Hogan. Accompanied by a fellow waiter as new to the game as he was, David set out for the golf course. First, one of them would hold the book and read aloud the instructions, then the other would do so while the first one practised. Helping each other in this way, they made their way around the course, thoroughly enjoying themselves. David admits now, however, that this self-taught method completely ruined his swing. "When I played in Hong Kong," he laughs, "people would say, 'Hopeless, absolutely hopeless, a terrible swing.' I was a hitter. I was hitting the ball instead of swinging."

The summer of 1948 passed pleasantly. Despite his several jobs at the summer camp, David did not make a large salary. Occasional weekend trips to Madison, the state capital, or to Chicago were not too expensive if he was careful, but he had to watch his finances since he was paying his board and tuition from his own pocket. Spending the summer at the camp helped a great deal and he made arrangements to return the following year if at all possible.

Having received his MBA, David had to consider his next move carefully. He decided to continue his studies and try for a Ph.D. degree in economics, having found he was more interested in economic thought and philosophy than in industrial management. He applied for entrance as a candidate for a doctorate at the New York University and was accepted. At that time, New York was unsurpassed as a centre for trade, commerce and finance. David felt he might be able to get involved in some business venture as he had in Macao. In any event, it was worth a try. If he could make some money and carry on with his studies, so much the better.

During his time at NYU, David stayed at International House on Riverside Drive in upper Manhattan. New York, he found, was almost overwhelming. The university was much larger than Temple, but as a graduate student he received more attention from his professors than if he had been packed into a large undergraduate class. It was a fairly uneventful year for him—many seminars, a lot of studying and endless hours in the library doing research. He did not find any opportunities to get into business so in the summer of 1949 he went back to the summer camp at Lake Geneva.

When he returned to New York in September, he found a marked change in the number of Chinese students at the university. This was the year when the Communists gained complete control of the Chinese mainland. Even before this time, there was a tremendous exodus from China and many wealthy families were sending their sons to the United States to complete their education. David met and befriended many of them. He had two years' experience at American universities, his English was very good and he was familiar with American customs. It was natural that they should seek out his company, and David soon found himself involved with them socially. His new friends, however, had far more money than he. Some of them lived in apartments on Fifth Avenue, or in New Rochelle or Long Island. Their lifestyle demanded an income which David didn't have, and he had no desire to go out with them without paying his own share. It was not a comfortable feeling.

One way to get around the situation was to make it more difficult for them to find him. He started to go to different libraries, for example, and stayed away from familiar haunts. At the same time, he decided to try and get a job to make some money. With his experience as a waiter for two summers at the YMCA camp behind him, he decided to apply for a job at a Chinese restaurant in Brooklyn. None of his new friends would ever go there so he could work on the weekends, earn some money and avoid being invited to activities he really couldn't afford.

He found a waiter's job at a Chinese "dine and dance" restaurant called the New Fulton Royal. There he really got to know American manners and customs. While waiting to have his order filled, for example, he learned not to drum his fingers on the counter when one of the cooks slammed a cleaver within inches of his hand. For a while, he brought a book with him to read when there was a slack period, and this brought another lesson. Some of the less-educated waiters resented such conspicuous studiousness, and one or two occasions they threw his book in the garbage pail. He stopped bringing any books to work. The path could have its bumps and potholes, but David soon learned what to avoid and concentrated on his job.

The salary of a waiter was not high, but that could be made up by tips. Service was expected and David did his best. Whenever possible, he would do more than the customers expected and that was always appreciated. While some people regarded waiters as no more than instruments, others wanted to be very friendly. "For someone from a different culture," he reflects, "it's not easy to handle at times. How friendly is friendly, how warm is warm? How much is hot air and how much is not? As a waiter, it was the best education about people and society."

The money he made as a waiter was more than welcome as David recommenced his studies in 1949. This would be his third year at an American university which, following his two years postwar study at Lingnan, was a considerable stretch of academic pursuit. He had paid for all of it himself. Now and then he would receive a small gift of cash from his father, but he never wrote home for money. He was proud of what he had been able to accomplish on his own, but his resources were drying up rapidly. He was also beginning to experience academic burnout. Work on his doctorate was beginning to get harder and he noticed during the winter of 1949-50 that he was slower to achieve the objectives of his studies. There were no complaints from his professors, but he knew in his heart the old enthusiasm was lacking.

Left: Young David in Hong Kong, about five years old.

Above: Full house at Number 7, Grampian Road. David (bottom step) poses with a group including his maternal grandparents (in traditional Chinese clothes), his father and mother (middle of back row), his father's sister and two younger brothers, and seven of David's siblings.

Above: Care-free days before the war: David on his fire-engine red Harley-Davidson.

Top right: David (foreground, with Hawaiian guitar across his lap) and his Sunday school musical group. The group included David's brothers Alex (seated with guitar) and Daniel (accordion).

Bottom right: East meets West: David's father, Lam Chi Fung, on the day he received the Order of the British Empire. Here he chats with Governor of Hong Kong, Sir Alexander Grantham, and one of the colony's most respected citizens, Sir Shouson Chow.

Above: Graduation photo from Lingnan University, July 7, 1947.

Top left: After the shipwreck, December 1944: David (left) and his uncle had this photo taken as soon as they returned safely to Hong Kong.

Bottom left: Baptist Sunday school teachers in 1940, with David standing in back row, far right. He remains friends with some of these teachers to this day.

Right: David (right, with his brother Daniel) was a volunteer in Hong Kong's Civil Aid Services from the early 1950s until he left the colony in 1967.

Below: A friendly pose with fellow waiters from the YMCA summer resort in 1948.

Facing page, top: The family firm: David (third from the left) stands with his father and six brothers.

Facing page, bottom: David and his father with representative of the French coal company, Charbonnages du Tonkin, in 1955. David was by this time handling much of the family's business operations on the South China Coast.

Dorothy and David Lam on their wedding day, October 1, 1954. Dorothy's dress is the one she wore when she met first met David, at the ball for the Duke of Kent.

In the summer of 1950, he returned again to work at the summer camp, and it was there that he decided to go back to Hong Kong. There were several reasons behind his decision, among them the belief—widely held at the time—that Hong Kong might be overrun by the Communists. The long conflict between the forces of Chiang Kai-shek's Nationalist government and Mao Tse-tung's Communist Party had resulted in victory for the latter. In 1949, mainland China became the People's Republic. With two huge land masses now under Communist control, and with Eastern Europe under Russian domination as well, the Cold War was beginning to warm up, particularly as the Russians had just exploded their first atomic bomb. At the time when David was settling into his job at the summer camp in 1950, North Korea invaded South Korea. This led President Truman to promise American military help to halt the aggressors while the United Nations gathered more forces to assist this effort. The Pacific coast of Asia seemed to be bursting into flames, and in 1950, as in 1941, Hong Kong could not defend itself if the Communists decided to take it.

As danger mounted at home, David and other Chinese students at the university received a letter from the U.S. State Department informing them that the government would be willing to pay for their ocean passage from San Francisco to Hong Kong should they wish to return. The reason behind this unexpected offer was not given, but it was a stroke of luck. David had received a letter from his father saying that he was not well and wanted David to return. This, on top of the other reasons, made him decide to go back even though he had not received his degree.

By the summer of 1950, David was the proud possessor of a second-hand car. When he finished work at the summer camp, he decided to drive through the United States to California, going by a zigzag route which would take him to almost all the major tourist attractions in the American West. To help defray costs, he brought two female companions with him, one a nurse and the other a kitchen assistant whom he had met at the camp. Both wanted to go to the West Coast and both were as eager to see the tourist sites as well. It was a long but pleasant journey, far better than the original bus ride he had taken to

Philadelphia three years earlier. Arriving in San Francisco, he sold his car and then boarded the SS *President Cleveland*. He found that by adding a bit more money to the price of the government's ticket, he could get a second-class passage. Remembering his trip on the Norwegian freighter, he decided it was worth it.

Two weeks later, after a brief stopover in Hawaii, David leaned over the ship's rail to watch the ship ease towards the dock in Hong Kong. A new phase of his life was about to begin.

FOUR

Return to Hong Kong

WHEN DAVID DISEMBARKED from the *President Cleveland*, he had to go through the usual queue for customs inspection. When the customs official found out he was returning to the colony he expressed considerable surprise. "Why are you coming back? Everyone here wants to leave," he said. It wasn't exactly the kind of greeting he expected on the dock, but the official was expressing a common feeling at the time.

Hong Kong had changed dramatically since David had left. The civil war in China had brought a flood of refugees. The fall of Canton to the Communists alone added an estimated 700,000 mouths to those the colony somehow had to feed, according to Nigel Cameron's *Hong Kong: The Cultured Pearl*. By the time David returned, there were 2.3 million people in the colony, a fourfold increase in the short period of five years. Formerly, entry from China into Hong Kong was unrestricted but in 1950 entry at the border was restricted to a daily quota. Even so, the population continued to grow.

This tide of both legal and illegal refugees created a great many problems. Naturally, it caused a tremendous housing shortage, and with it a sanitation problem. There was constant danger of fire in the tinderbox tenement buildings erected to provide shelter for the newcomers. Water, always a problem in Hong Kong, had to be restricted.

On top of it all the rate of crime, especially among the young unemployed, was a constant worry to the authorities.

British officials were also concerned about the war in Korea which had broken out a few months before David returned. In October 1950, Chinese "volunteers" were identified as fighting with the North Korean army against the forces of the United Nations. The United States decided to impose an embargo on Chinese trade in December. This prevented Hong Kong from exporting a wide range of goods from the People's Republic of China to the United States. In May of the following year, the United Nations imposed an embargo of its own on the sale of strategic commodities to China and this had an even worse effect. According to Robert Elegant's *Hong Kong*, "It drastically undermined Hong Kong's traditional standing as an entrepôt, or trading port. Furthermore, the United States embargo created a period of stagnation during which Hong Kong had to adjust to its unnerving position in a limited war."

In the initial postwar period, however, Hong Kong's economy had been given a boost by the great demand for new housing. This spurred the growth of industries allied to construction, including the manufacture of cement, paints, plumbing fixtures, furniture and metal products. Textiles soon became important as well. Hong Kong began a thriving export trade of its own manufactures, which was soon to outvalue its former source of income as a trading station between China and the rest of the world. Among the postwar swarm of Chinese refugees into Hong Kong were many talented people who brought their skill, expertise and commercial knowledge. With their drive, energy and entrepreneurial spirit, they created new business in the colony, and in time, they were able to overcome—indeed even take advantage of—the restrictions put on trade owing to the Korean War. One such refugee was Y. C. Cheng, who was to play an interesting role in the fortunes of the Lam family. He became a close friend of David who, in turn, became one of his greatest admirers.

When he returned to his father's house in Kowloon, David was twenty-seven years old. For the past three years he had lived an independent life, supporting himself on the money from his share of the cargo of salt imported from Macao and the profits he made on buying the "new" Hong Kong dollars. He had experienced individual freedom both in the United States and in the two-year period attending Lingnan University in Canton. For several years during the war he had assumed the position of number one son in the Lam household. Within traditional Chinese families, the eldest son was looked upon as the *primus inter pares* among the children. Although the father held the ultimate authority, the eldest son would assume his role, should he be away or incapacitated. A certain deference to the eldest son was expected from his younger brothers because he was older, and presumably wiser. This was an old Chinese tradition and David's father strongly supported it. David, upon Daniel's return from the Philippines, had found it difficult to readjust. The first and second sons of Chi Fung had led two quite different lives over the past nine years, and when they met again in 1950 they were almost strangers.

David's father had continued to work in his coal importing and distribution business after the war, but in these years the demand for coal began to slow down. Kerosene was being used more and more for home cooking, and diesel oil began to replace coal as a fuel for generating electrical power and in the factories. Oil was cleaner, easier to store and generally more efficient. As the coal business began to wind down, however, Chi Fung had the good fortune to become engaged in another venture which was to be far more profitable. This was his partnership with the Cheng brothers, who had come from the same village as he had near Swatow.

The four brothers were not well educated and none spoke English, but they did have creative minds and a mechanical talent for making things needed in the village. Opportunities in the village were minimal, however, so they moved first to Canton and then to Hong Kong before it was captured by the Japanese. The brothers knew Chi Fung and contacted him looking for business opportunities. Chi Fung introduced them to various people and soon they were making a number of items ranging from barrack-room bunks to steel helmets for the Hong Kong military authorities. When the Japanese attacked the colony they left for "free" China by way of Fort Bayard, where David had met them when stopping over. The third brother, Y. C. Cheng, had established a small factory making copper wire from Chinese copper coins, but the advancing Japanese army overran this lucrative if short-lived venture.

After the war, the four Chen brothers returned to Hong Kong, where they lived on the fourth floor of a tenement building. They had little money, but they still had the skill and drive to turn their hands to anything. Once more, they met with Chi Fung, who loaned them money on a short-term basis so they could engage in various small enterprises. They always repaid the loans promptly and finally Chi Fung suggested they should operate on a more organized basis. He felt it would be best if a limited company was formed. He would put up the money and instead of the Cheng brothers repaying him, he would own one-third of the company stock. The four brothers would own the remaining two-thirds. The brothers agreed, Chi Fung became the chairman, and the basis was laid for the Chiap Hua Manufactory, a company which was to eventually make many millions of dollars.

The company soon began to expand in a number of directions. Hong Kong had no mines or mineral deposits but, after four years of war, the South Pacific had thousands of tons of metal ranging from spent artillery shells to sunken ships scattered among the islands. When collected or salvaged, they furnished brass, copper, steel and aluminum which the company melted down in its factory and shaped into a variety of products. Empty shell casings were remade into a variety of items from thermos flasks to hurricane lanterns. Scrap aluminum was gathered from wrecked aircraft all over the Pacific, brought to Hong Kong, cut up and the metal melted down to make window and door frames for construction companies. In one example of ingenuity, the catapult machinery used to launch aircraft from the flight deck of an American aircraft carrier was taken out and reassembled on shore, where it was used to help shape frames from the molten metal.

One of the company's ventures was the purchase of naval and supply vessels declared surplus after the war. These were brought to Hong Kong, broken up for their scrap metal and a good profit realized. When the aircraft carrier mentioned above was brought into port, the ship was found to contain great quantities of material the navy had not removed. Several hundred sets of dishes, knives and forks and other items were promptly resold at a profit. One locker contained a number of scuba diving suits complete with all the appropriate equipment. Some of it had never been used. David heard of this find and, with one of his brothers, decided to try the scuba equipment out. Fortunately, even though they had no instruction on how to use it, everything went well.

David had been pleased, on his return to Hong Kong, to find that his father's health had improved. Chi Fung drove himself hard and it was difficult for him to realize that he could not do as much as he did formerly. From a financial point of view, he was doing well. The company he had formed with the Cheng brothers was producing everything from flashlights and cigarette lighters to clocks. He was devoting more time to endeavours associated with the Baptist church and his dream of building a Baptist college in Hong Kong. This would cost a lot of money, but he was never deterred by such obstacles nor discouraged by slow progress. He felt he was doing God's work and his faith was strong. He would pursue his goal to the end.

Chi Fung had a job for David. While Daniel, who was working in the Chiap Hua Manufactory, had studied engineering, David had studied business administration and economics. This was a good background for what his father had in mind—to take charge of the Ka Wah Bank.

The bank had its origins in Canton in the early 1930s. It was started by a group of Chinese businessmen who had strong connections with the city's Baptist community. Using the bank's money, they began to speculate in real estate. Unfortunately for them, the market began to go down rather than up. As a result, they came to Hong Kong with the intention of opening a branch there to seek more deposits. They were land-rich but cash-poor. Since they were leaders in the Baptist church in Canton, the bankers worked through the Hong Kong Baptist churches and talked to the leaders. David's father was one of the junior leaders but he had one thing the others did not. He was from Swatow. As David explains it, the Swatow people were a very hard-working and successful minority in Hong Kong, and that gave Chi Fung a lot of connections. Knowing that Chi Fung was a young, up-and-coming respected businessman, the bankers got him to support a branch bank in order to attract Swatow money.

Chi Fung had no reason to suspect the motives of the Cantonese businessmen. In retrospect, he probably should have investigated them more closely, but his doubts, if any, were dismissed by their Baptist connections. He entered into the scheme, encouraged his friends to patronize the new branch, and put some of his own and his company's money in it. In Canton, the money in the Hong Kong branch was siphoned off to continue speculation in real estate. The end result was that the central bank went bankrupt and the depositors were left holding preferred shares rather than cash. The outbreak of the war and the Japanese occupation did nothing to improve things. After the war, however, the situation changed. Freedom brought with it an improvement in real estate prices and the bank's properties rose rapidly in value. The bank was reopened, including the Hong Kong branch. A few years later, when the Communists seized control of mainland China, the main office in Canton closed again, this time permanently.

The Ka Wah Bank in Hong Kong remained open, however. It had been authorized in Hong Kong and, in essence, it was no longer a branch but an independent bank in its own right. It was shortly to come under the sole direction of its majority shareholder, Lam Chi Fung.

When David first went to the Ka Wah Bank, it was small in every way. The bank's assets totalled about a quarter of a million dollars. Its premises were the size of a small coffee shop. An older man named Tam was the bank's manager and David was to be the sub-manager. The bank was neither thriving nor aggressive; indeed, it was only puttering along, with deposits coming mainly from Baptist churches, chapels and schools which put their trust in Chi Fung.

David was not particularly impressed with his new job. He felt he either had to build it up or he would not want anything to do with it. As it happened, he was to be with the bank for over sixteen years, most of the time as its chief manager. During these years, he was to bring about a great many changes in the firm.

One of the first things David wanted to do was to have the bank located in a building owned by the bank itself. With the backing of the family he secured loans, bought several shops, tore them down and constructed a fourteen-storey building. The bank occupied the ground floor and the upper floors were rented. Once the building was completed, more people noticed the bank and came in off the street. Deposits went up.

David was involved in almost every phase of the work. Selecting an affordable site, buying the shops, tearing them down, getting permission to put up a new building, hiring an architect, arranging a loan and all the rest of it took a long time to complete. Nevertheless, it was very good experience for him. He got a sense of the value of real estate, construction costs and the relationship between income from rental property and the repayment of capital and interest to the bank.

David also decided to bring in more clients to the bank by hiring a couple of men to go around drumming up business. One service they offered was delivering cash to shop owners in the morning and collecting cash after the stores had closed.

After he was appointed chief manager, David decided to build more branches of the bank in order to reach out to more potential clients. He had to be very careful, however, because even though the bank's capital was increasing, he did not want to have too thin a margin between income and expenditure. After all, the bank was comparatively new, the competition was keen and he was well aware of the limitations of the bank's resources.

It would be an understatement to say that David was a conservative banker and very cautious about his loans. His studies in economics at New York University had made him very aware of what happened to banks in the United States in the Wall Street crash of 1929. He was also mindful of the fact that the "mother" bank in Canton had gone bankrupt through speculation. On the other hand, he realized that the path he was taking would not lead to a rapid increase in the bank's balance sheet. Looking back, he reflects, "It would be kind of impossible if I went into speculating in stock or in real estate. Then I would be duplicating what the original partners did to get the bank into trouble. Hindsight now tells me that if I had gone into speculation, the bank could be worth billions of dollars. However, I knew too much. I studied too much. I knew the consequences. My principle was I cannot speculate with other people's money. That was my limitation, so my frustration was that I could not expand and have it grow as rapidly as other banks."

Although the Ka Wah Bank prospered only modestly, if steadily, it kept him out of the trouble besetting some of the other Hong Kong banks in the 1950s and 1960s. At times, for a variety of reasons, some of them experienced runs on their reserves. Those who had speculated too heavily in real estate found themselves facing a financial crunch and had to be bought or bailed out. Eventually the government had to enact stricter rules to curb such speculation. David, who was gaining respect in Hong Kong banking circles, was very much in favour of it.

David's reputation as a man of principle and solid integrity led to his appointment as a member of the powerful Banking Advisory Committee in the 1950s. This committee, which decided on interest rates and on the classification of banks, was comprised of leading members of the major banking houses in the colony, some of them with assets in the billions. It was quite an honour for David and gave him entry into the upper echelons of Hong Kong's financial circles. The Ka Wah Bank was in the Class C category because it was small.

David's position as chief manager of the family bank did not mean he was enjoying an opulent lifestyle. When he started as a sub-manager he was paid the equivalent of about CAN$150 a month. He was living in the family home in Kowloon and continued to do so for almost a decade. When he was appointed chief manager after the new bank building was completed, his salary was increased. At no time during his entire career was it more than CAN$750 a month. To supplement his earnings in the early years, he sometimes indulged in a modest stock purchase on the Hong Kong Exchange. Better still, when he had a few dollars saved, he would invest money in Y. C. Cheng's shipwrecking business. "Y. C." was the third of the four Cheng brothers, and David and he were fast friends. David was able to make a few thousand dollars now and then from this venture which, years later, would allow him to buy his own house. He had started this association with Cheng just as the Korean War was grinding to a halt and Hong Kong's economy was beginning to turn around. "That was pure luck," he admits now, but it allowed him to start a small nest egg of his own.

While David was working to learn the banking business and to improve the position of the Ka Wah Bank, the Lam family's chief source of revenue was the company Chi Fung owned with the Cheng brothers. It was doing very well and showing a good profit in its various enterprises. Although he was chairman of the board, Chi Fung did not take an active part in the actual running of the company. He had decided to rearrange his family interests and create a private family company in which both parents and children held shares. Each son had an equal share, while the two daughters each had half that of the sons. Chi Fung and his wife also kept shares but not a controlling amount. He might dominate decisions as the head of the family and chairman of the board of the family's enterprises, but he was becoming ever more interested in church affairs. This left his first son, Daniel, more influence at the family board meetings when decisions were made. Dividends from the business went into the family "pot," and all shared in the ownership of it. This treasury, however, was built up and used to expand the business rather than distributed to family members. Money from this source, for example, helped to build the new Ka Wah bank. The latter was a good investment, but David's share in it would be no more than one of his brothers who was attending college in the United States, or one who was earning good money as a medical doctor rather than working for the family firm.

The organization of the family company was done in a traditional Chinese way. It called for a considerable amount of harmony among family members if it was to work smoothly, but Chi Fung had stressed harmony all his life and had impressed it on his children. The concept of the members of the family looking after and supporting each other had deep roots in Chinese history. The hierarchy within the family was also customary and accepted. The parents expected and received deference from their children, whom they liked to have near them. They expected the children to look after them in their old age since they could not expect support from any other source.

The Chinese family, in sum, was a tightly knit unit, shaped by the traditions of an agricultural society and the experience of centuries of turmoil and uncertainty. Beyond this inner citadel of family were more distant relations, personal friends, village acquaintances and, much further removed, people from the same province. Chi Fung, for example, always had a soft spot in his heart for people from the Swatow area where he himself had grown up, and whose dialect he spoke. When David had received his first university degree he had been taken to meet some of his father's friends from the Swatow area. He could see his father was almost embarrassed that his number two son could not speak the dialect. He resolved to learn it in order to please his father, and duly did so.

It was at a family business meeting that the decision was taken to make an amicable separation from the Cheng brothers. The company was flourishing and Daniel had been working in it for many years. As the company expanded and the years went by, however, sons from the families of the four Cheng brothers joined the firm as well. Looking into the future, the Lams felt it might be best if they took their one-third interest in the company in kind rather than in cash or stock. David carried out most of the negotiations and both parties agreed that the Lams should have complete ownership and control of the factory making flashlights. This represented about one-third of the value of the group's enterprises and both sides were satisfied. The company had made flashlights of every conceivable type for American firms which distributed them worldwide.

In 1954 a deal was struck to make flashlights for a large American firm called Ray-O-Vac. This turned out to be so successful that the Lam family decided to expand its manufacturing capabilities. Once again, David was called upon to help. Land was needed to build a large building in which the factory could be located. Fortunately, he was able to negotiate the purchase of land from Imperial Chemical Industries whose directors, apparently, felt that Hong Kong did not have much of an economic future. As a result, David was able to acquire the land at a good price.

Since David had more experience with banking than anyone else, he was also asked to arrange for the financing of the factory. As it was a family affair, he could not—nor would he want to—use the Ka Wah Bank. Instead, he got backing from senior officials in the Hong Kong and Shanghai Bank. David also made arrangements to hire an architectural firm to plan the building. Ten storeys high and located on the waterfront, it would contain not only the most modern machinery for making flashlights but a large cold storage area, an ice-making plant and a large warehouse.

The opening of the new building housing Chiap Hua Flashlights Ltd. took place in November 1962. It was a major affair and the guests included two American businessmen who were more than a little interested in the new plant: the president and vice-president of Ray-O-Vac International. Both had come from the United States expressly to attend the opening ceremonies. By this time, the Lams were not only making flashlights for them but flashlight batteries as well.

The Lam family became involved in the battery manufacturing business partly because of the Vietnam War. Ray-O-Vac had been manufacturing a leakproof, all-steel battery which was not only popular with the general public but widely used by the United States Army. When the army became increasingly involved in Vietnam, the demand for the batteries soared and the company calculated it would be profitable to manufacture them closer to the conflict. They decided not to build in Hong Kong since, in the late 1950s, there were still some reservations about its future. Instead, the company decided to establish a battery factory in Bangkok, Thailand. To assist them in this project, they suggested the Lams come in as junior partners. The American company would provide the machinery, the building and the factory overseer; the Lams would look after all the details preparatory to erecting the building. The deal was agreed upon and the Raylam Battery Company came into existence.

The question that arose next was which of the Lams would be sent to Bangkok to make all of the arrangements. The fingers pointed to David. He was the one with wide travel experience, a banking background, a sprinkling of languages and a degree in business administration. It also helped that David was a gregarious person. He liked to meet and talk to people, and his years in the United States had reinforced his outgoing nature at the expense of the customary Chinese reserve. He tended to be more direct and outspoken than his brothers when negotiating a business deal. The responsibility was placed on his shoulders and he set off for Bangkok.

Although he had no personal friends in Bangkok, he had some contacts among the sizable Chinese community in the city. By this time he was married, and his wife had some cousins living there. These were the first people he met. David had no knowledge of Thai, but the cousins did. Through their network of kinship he was able to get information he wanted while avoiding their wishes to become involved in the deal.

David remained for months in the sweltering heat of Thailand's capital. He had to decide whether to buy or lease the land, a question which depended on such factors as the best location for the factory, proximity to transportation, availability of labour, and supply of water and electricity. He also needed to know and work within Thailand's rules governing the establishment of a foreign enterprise.

All of this involved a great deal of work for David. He stayed at a hotel, borrowed a cousin's Volkswagen to get around, learned how to find his way throughout the city and picked up a few helpful Thai words and phrases. He learned how to ignore or avoid the ever-present question of "cumshaw," pleading that the American majority owners knew nothing of this practice in business dealings and expressing his own preference to avoid bribery if at all possible. Most of the time this approach worked, but not always.

Once everything was in place, Ray-O-Vac decided to ship from the United States a prefabricated structure called a Butler building. David had never heard of it and only when it arrived and was put together did he realize it was unsuitable. Quite simply, it was far too hot. "It was a North American building," he remembers. "Even when we put more windows in the Butler building it was too hot and stuffy. It taught me a lesson—don't take other people's advice too quickly and say to yourself, 'Oh, they must know.' I was the man on the spot in tropical Thailand. I should not have let myself be persuaded and moved by the thinking of people ten thousand miles away."

When the new building was opened, David left Bangkok as quickly as he could and returned to Hong Kong to assume his responsibilities in the bank. Daniel, representing the family, was to be appointed a director of the Raylam Battery Company; David had nothing to do with it when his job was done. He received no bonus for the work he had carried out in Bangkok but had to be content with the fact that he had added to the family's assets. In one way this was a comforting thought, but for an individualist like David there were drawbacks as well. The family's assets were controlled by a private company with the adult males of the Lam family serving as its board of directors. It was not possible to sell one's shares on the public market—they had to be sold to another family member or to the family as a group. This had all sorts of implications. Using shares as collateral for a loan, for example, or cutting away from the family business and using shares to set up one's own enterprise would be difficult to do without the family's approval, and this really meant without the sanction of the board of directors. David did not wield the greatest influence on the board and for years he had to curb his spirit of independence in order not to upset the traditional way in which the family's business affairs were managed. If it had been a public company, he would have had no problem. But, as he reflects now, "The worst thing that can happen is to own shares as a minority shareholder in a private company because there is no market for them. While I was working for the company, I was willing to work for almost nothing to build it up. When it was built up, I could not turn my shares into cash."

The only way he was going to build up a bank balance over which he had sole control was to invest some of his small savings outside the family business. He had already started to do so through Y. C. Cheng in the shipbreaking business, and this was beginning to pay off. David needed the money, for by the mid-1950s he was married. It was the best thing that ever happened to him.

Dorothy Tan was born on Christmas Day, 1929. Her father, the educated fourth son of a mandarin, was a Baptist. Her mother's father was a minister in the Seventh Day Adventist Church, however, so Dorothy attended religious services with the latter. Both parents were born in small villages close to Swatow. Her mother, a clever and determined woman, had had an arranged marriage. When she had children, she vowed that they would never have to submit to such a thing. Moreover, she felt strongly that both her sons and her daughters should receive the best education possible. Coming from small, poor villages, the Tans saw education as the key to breaking away from poverty and opening the door to opportunities otherwise beyond their grasp.

Like many others from the Swatow area, the Tan family moved to Hong Kong. There they renewed acquaintances with Lam Chi Fung who, years earlier, had thought of marrying into the Tan family himself. Dorothy's father became the Far Eastern manager of an American chemical company, a position which disappeared when the Japanese attacked in 1941.

Dorothy was a schoolgirl when the Japanese bombs fell on Hong Kong. After the colony was captured, the Japanese seized the Tan's house and gave them three days to collect their belongings and move out. They went to Kowloon, where Dorothy was able to continue her education for a short time, though she had to substitute Japanese for her English classes. Her uncle, who like Dorothy's father worked for an American firm, had been arrested by the Japanese and had suffered greatly in prison. When he was released and told Dorothy's father about the cruel treatment he had undergone, the Tan family decided to leave for mainland China. After a harrowing trip, they eventually made their way back to Swatow and remained there, living in primitive conditions until the end of the war. When they returned to Hong Kong, Dorothy's father regained his former employment. This enabled him to send Dorothy to the Diocesan Girls' School to complete high school while her older brother and sister, Gilbert and Edith, went to the United States to attend universities there. Dorothy's high marks gave her entry into the University of Hong Kong, and it was while she was still a student there that chance brought her and David together. The occasion was a ball given in honour of the Duke of Kent who was visiting the colony in 1952.

The relationship between the Lam and the Tan families went back many years. Dorothy's father and Chi Fung had been schoolmates in the same village near Swatow, and both had moved to Hong Kong. The two families kept in touch, visiting each other during the celebrations surrounding the Chinese New Year. When David was attending Lingnan University during the war, Dorothy's older brother and sister were students there also. Although there were no shared business relations between the two families, theirs was a longstanding friendship. However, since Dorothy was six and a half years younger than David, their paths crossed only infrequently. He hadn't realized she had matured into a beautiful woman until they met at the ball.

The young Duke of Kent was not married. The governor of Hong Kong made a special effort to ensure there would be plenty of guests in the Duke's age group at the ball, and arranged with the University of Hong Kong to have ten female students invited. Dorothy, then in her second year of studies, was among those selected. David was well known and received his invitation separately.

The young duke was more interested in military affairs than in balls and spent a great deal of his time in Hong Kong with the garrison. On the night of the ball he had only one dance and then left the floor, claiming he had a headache. Young bachelors like David and the various aides-de-camp swept in to propose dances to the unescorted females. Spotting Dorothy—"a very charming, very beautiful young lady"—David asked her for a dance and, to the tune of "Star Dust," they rekindled the old family friendship. He managed to have three more dances with her before the ball was over, and resolved to get to know her better. For the next two years, they went out together until Dorothy obtained her university degree. David then asked to marry her. The engagement was announced on September 9, 1954, and both began to prepare for the wedding in a leisurely way.

Towards the end of the month, however, the wedding plans accelerated to a terrific pace. David's mother had suffered a severe stroke, so severe that her doctor felt she would die in a matter of days. That tragic news was made worse by the Chinese custom that if a parent died, there should be no joyous occasion held by a member of the family for three years. A wedding was certainly a joyous occasion and neither David nor Dorothy wanted to put it off that long. The only thing to be done was to have the marriage immediately.

Both families agreed to the proposal, and the rush began. Although she had bought the material to make one, Dorothy still had no wedding dress. She decided to wear the lovely long white dress she had worn at the ball for the Duke of Kent. There was no time to buy a wedding ring so the engagement ring was taken off and reused at the ceremony. David also had much to organize. He had been given a room with an adjoining bathroom in his father's house where the newly-weds would live. At the time of his mothers's stroke, he had only started to redecorate the room and there was hardly anything in it: no bed, no pillows or bedsheets. He dashed out and bought what was needed for a next-day delivery.

There was no time for a formal reception, nor to arrange for a church wedding, and the ceremony was held at home on the first of October. As David remembers the wedding, "The pastor came with his wife, and a few friends came. The pastor's wife wanted to play the wedding march on the piano. We said no because Mother was upstairs. She was in and out of a coma and if she should wake and heard the wedding march, what would she think? Then the pastor said, 'Let us sing then.' I said no, don't sing. If Mother heard singing, she wouldn't know what was going on. 'So let us read the hymn then,' said the pastor. 'No,' I said. 'If everyone reads the hymn, there will be too much noise.' The pastor said, 'Then I will read the hymn.' I said, 'You will have to do it in a very low voice.' "

It was probably the quietest wedding prepared in the shortest time that ever took place in Hong Kong. There was no honeymoon as David's mother was so ill. She recovered slowly, remaining partially paralyzed so that she had to use a cane to walk.

With his small salary from the bank, David was not able to rent an apartment of his own. This had important implications for Dorothy. As the wife of the most senior son living at home, she was expected to take over the duties of her mother-in-law. It was quite a task and continued for several years. She remembers her housekeeping duties quite well: "I remember I took care of the food bills, the salaries for the nurses and for the doctor, for every servant, the chef, the gardener, the general *amahs* and the baby's *amah*. I looked after guests coming to the house. Grandfather and mother also lived with us. It was a big house, four storeys high with four generations in it.

"The next year, the younger brother got married. Mother-in-law wanted them to live in the big house also. Then when number five sister-in-law got married, Mother-in-law wanted her and her husband to live with her so we had another family come into the house. David's younger brother number six married an American girl and they also moved into the house. At that time, I was taking care of everything. Most of the servants lived in the house. It was an old-fashioned way, but the Lams ran the household in that style. I was very submissive because this is the Chinese way."

The in-laws kept her busy: "I was upstairs whenever Mother-in-law called and downstairs whenever Father-in-law called." Because she had studied English, Chi Fung would also call her whenever foreign missionaries came to the house.

Fortunately for Dorothy, she got along well with her in-laws. In turn, she was considered an asset to the family. Her parents were well known and respected. She had a university education which was not that common for a Chinese woman at the time. From a cultural point of view, she was equal to anyone. She played the piano, she could speak English and she had won a prize for her knowledge of Mandarin. She could also speak and understand the Swatow dialect, which pleased her father-in-law. Like David, she also had a strong sense of independence, probably passed on by her mother who was opposed to such customs as arranged marriages, concubines and the accepted superiority of men over women in Chinese culture. Except for the lack of privacy and the constant duties placed on her, Dorothy found living in the Lam household a comfortable experience. She found it easy to talk and discuss things with her sisters-in-law, all of whom were on friendly terms with each other. And it was as easy to communicate with David. He was not the type of man to come to a decision and expect his wife to agree automatically. He discussed things with Dorothy, appreciated her opinion and generally reached a consensus before taking any action. It was to be a good foundation for their marriage.

David and Dorothy had their first children while they were still living in the Lam family home. The first child, Deborah, was born on July 17, 1955. Unfortunately, David was not at home for the birth, having accompanied his father to the Ninth Convention of the Baptist World Alliance in London, England. It was there that Chi Fung was elected vice-president of the alliance in recognition of the tremendous work he had done for the church in Hong Kong and Macao. He had been working for years to establish a Baptist college in Hong Kong and planned to use the return trip to meet numerous Baptist groups in the United States in order to raise funds for the college. Given David's three years of experience in America, it was natural Chi Fung would ask for his son's help. Their trip lasted for weeks and overlapped Deborah's birth.

When David returned, he found Dorothy had not had an easy delivery and was under increasing strain. Renovations in the house had resulted in his mother being moved to the same floor as David and Dorothy, and the nearest bathroom to her was the one they used. To reach it she had to go through their bedroom. This routine during the day bothered no one but during the night, especially in the early morning hours, it was hard to get a good night's sleep. Moreover, since she was feeling better, his mother was beginning to entertain more and she expected Dorothy to be in attendance when she had guests. When their second daughter, Daphne, arrived in August 1956, a second room was allotted to them, but David realized that somehow he had to find new quarters where they could live a life of their own. A third daughter, Doreen, was born in 1960.

It was about this time that David's next youngest brother, Alex, got married. This carried with it the implication that the newly-weds would move into the family home and the new bride could take over Dorothy's role. This made it easier for David to move out. But, as David puts it, "We had no money, and we really didn't know what to do or where to turn. As luck would have it, the Anglican bishop of Hong Kong, Bishop Hall—a great guy—out of the blue invited us to his home for tea. He lived in the New Territories, up in the hills beyond Shatin, then just a village. His house sat on a piece of level ground. There was a small lawn, a garden full of flowers, a little swimming pool and a Chinese-style cottage. I stood on the lawn and looked down to the green valley of Shatin. I looked to see the trees and the flowers. I saw on the other side of the bamboo growth thirty or forty turkeys and in a compound many goats, all belonging to Bishop Hall.

"In the hustle and bustle of Hong Kong, I had not been to a place which would give the kind of tranquillity I had always longed for. I literally touched the flowers, walked the garden, looked at the scenery and the house and shed tears. I told Bishop Hall that this was the best place I have ever been to in Hong Kong. This is Heaven!"

The good bishop must have been impressed with David's praise. A week later he wrote to him saying that he and his family were going to England on a year's furlough. He would be happy if David would take over the house for a very modest rent while they were away. They would leave all the furniture, the kitchenware, everything they would need. A caretaker would remain to look after the goats and turkeys. All the Lams had to do was to walk in with their suitcases.

David and Dorothy jumped at the opportunity. Since there was someone to step in and take over Dorothy's responsibilities in the Lam household, and since it appeared the move would only be a temporary one, there was no opposition from the senior Lams. David, Dorothy and their two young daughters moved in as soon as the bishop left. Once there, surrounded by green grass, flowers and the quiet of the countryside, they knew they could not go back.

FIVE

Working for the Family

From the time he returned to Hong Kong in 1950, David set out to rekindle old friendships and make new ones. One group he always enjoyed meeting was the Lingnan University alumni, those students who had shared good times and bad when the university had to move to the interior of China. Another important group in his circle of acquaintances was the people from the Swatow area where his father was born. A closely knit community known for their hard work and entrepreneurial spirit, over the years they became a force in the economic life of the colony. Many of them had settled in Vietnam, Thailand and Malaysia, creating a commercial and cultural network which stretched throughout Eastern Asia.

David also became involved with a group of young men like himself who grew concerned about the future of Hong Kong during the years of the Korean War. The embargo placed on trade with China had a devastating effect on the colony's trade and many people were predicting Hong Kong's collapse. American banks started to pull out and many foreign banks began to scale down their offices. "There was doom and gloom everywhere," remembers David. "At that time there were groups of serious younger people who wanted to do something to bring about a change. One group, consisting of men in their thirties, belonged to the Chiu Chow [Swatow] community. We met once a month for lunch and talked." One of the group's members was Li Ka-

Shing, who years later would be one of the biggest players in the global real estate market.

David remembers telling the general manager of a French bank that the salvation of Hong Kong would be to turn itself into an industrial centre. The Frenchman replied that David was "absolutely crazy." There was no protection for Hong Kong industry since the colony was a free port. There were no anti-dumping laws. Land was expensive and raw materials were nonexistent. And there was no trained labour because there hadn't been any industry. The Frenchman thought the idea a big joke.

Certainly there were problems that had to be overcome, and the group David met with was determined to change the downward economic trend many saw in the colony. "Luckily," David says, "there were a lot of these people in Hong Kong at that time. They became the salvation of Hong Kong."

David widened his circle of friends in all of these groups, and saw many of them become very successful businessmen in the colony. They got to know him also, and their respect for his business acumen and integrity was to be extremely important to him in later years.

David also expanded his network of acquaintances by joining the Rotary Club. The Hong Kong Rotary Club had over two hundred members from all over the world, but for some time David tended to remain with members whom he knew rather than mix with others at luncheon meetings. Slowly, he realized that he was "like someone who went to a gourmet buffet with a small plate. I was like someone walking through a gold mine without picking up a few nuggets." Feelings of racial discrimination were as common among the Chinese as they were among other nationalities in the colony, but David took deliberate steps to overcome them. His decision to get to know men from non-Chinese origins is one he never regretted. "When I look back," he reflects, "it has totally widened my world and enriched my life. Suddenly I would look at people and I would say to myself: 'I will not look at the difference any more; I will look at the commonality. What do we have in common? What can we do together?' And I started building partners and I've never gone back. It has helped me all through my life."

David's desire to travel beyond the colony was sometimes gratified by his father. In 1952, Chi Fung asked him to go to Saigon, in the southern part of Vietnam. The French were still in control but a strong Communist element was determined to throw off colonial rule. Although the Vietnam War had not yet broken out, conflict periodically flared in the countryside. Even in the cities, a careful watch was kept to prevent acts of terrorism or any movement which might be interpreted as disloyal to the government.

In Saigon, David got caught in a situation he would never forget. He and a friend were being conveyed through the streets in a motorized, three-wheeled taxi. The driver was going fast and hit a French military truck pulling from the curb. David's leg was badly cut and his friend was bruised and lost a few teeth. With blood pouring from his leg and a growing crowd of spectators gathering around, David asked someone to get a doctor. Nobody moved. He asked them to call an ambulance. Again nobody responded. Finally, his friend managed to get another tricycle taxi which took them to a nearby community hospital.

"We went in," he says, and asked for a doctor. "I was faint and losing blood. They said, 'No. Nobody can touch you until they get the police.' So the police came in due time and asked for my passport, where I came from, why I was there, what was I doing, who did the damage, what made the wound, what hotel I was staying in, how many days had I been there. After going through all that interrogation, I said, 'Now, do I get a doctor?' They said yes. The doctor came and started to sew me up. He didn't do a very good job. Even after seven days the cut wasn't healing. They asked for a military doctor from a French army barracks nearby. He came in uniform and didn't say a word to me. He put his hands on both sides of the wound and, without saying anything, just tore it open. I could have killed that guy. In this poorest, low-class hospital with its humid heat, mosquitoes and flies, I was just a nothing.

"Then the doctor put his nose close to the cut, smelled, stood up and walked out. He didn't say a word. It wasn't healing so they had to do it again. So they wheeled me in to the operation room, gave me an injection which knocked me out, and carved more rotten flesh from the wound and cleaned it." As soon as he was able to hobble about on crutches, David made airplane reservations to return to Hong Kong and arranged to be met by an ambulance. The large scar on his leg would be a constant reminder to him of that particular business trip.

A few years later, as we have seen, David accompanied his father to England and the United States to help raise funds for a Baptist college in Hong Kong. Eventually, the Southern Baptist Convention, through its Foreign Mission Board, agreed to help the college get started, providing that Chi Fung could raise substantial funds in Hong Kong. At this time, the Korean War was coming to an end and the Vietnam War was warming up. Relations between China and the United States were getting worse, and Christian missionaries were being forced out of China. Chi Fung asked the Foreign Mission Board to send as many of these missionaries as possible to Hong Kong, where their knowledge of China and their experience would be of greater benefit than if they returned home. His advice was heeded and a large number came to the colony to continue their work. Among them were many scholars, and from them a small number were selected to form a faculty for a Baptist college. It started in a couple of rooms in the Pui-Ching Middle School. Chi Fung was principal of the school and in time he became the founding president of the Hong Kong Baptist College.

David couldn't help but be impressed by his father's drive and determination to get a college established. Chi Fung had worked for years to establish better schools for children, and saw another college in Hong Kong as a necessity, given the population's tremendous growth in the 1950s. David says of his father: "His greatest asset was that once he was convinced that this needed to be done, he convinced himself that it was God's will. He truly believed that he was an instrument of God, a worker for God, so therefore any setback, any failure, didn't faze him at all. It was nothing."

"When he was raising money in Hong Kong, he and I would travel across the ferry every day. If he saw someone whose face was familiar, he would ask, 'Do you know that fellow?' I'd say, 'He is the manager of a bank I know.'"

" 'Let's go,' Father would say. I would take him over and introduce him. He would pull out his donation receipt book and say, 'Would you like to donate some money for a Baptist college?' My father would shake him down right on the street. After a while I said, 'You embarrass me. The minute I introduce someone to you, you pull out your donation book.' But he totally believed it had to be done."

His father served as a good tutor to a son who would raise a lot of money for charities in years to come.

Most of David's trips were made to further family interests or to assist his father. In 1960, however, he was asked to go to the Middle East as part of a three-man trade delegation promoting Hong Kong's manufacturing industries and tourism. The delegation, which included a senior representative from the Department of Trade and Commerce and a high official from the Hong Kong and Shanghai Bank, visited Iran, Kuwait, Saudi Arabia and various small countries around the southern rim of the Arabian peninsula. They met many of the rulers and government officials in these countries, frequently in huge tents with floors covered with thick rugs. At times it was almost like a scene from the *Arabian Nights*, with deals made over innumerable cups of hot coffee. David also took the opportunity to visit Israel while he was in the area, seeing not only the major cities but also many of the smaller places he had read about in the Bible.

The colonial government later tried to interest him in appointments to other government bodies. This, David knew, could lead to more powerful positions in the colonial administration, but he turned them down. His priorities lay elsewhere.

When David and Dorothy rented Bishop Hall's house in the hills of the New Territories, they found that they enjoyed the peaceful life in the countryside more than either one had imagined. The hillside view from the house was marvellous. The gardens provided all the flowers and vegetables they could want. They had to drive up a twisting narrow dirt road to reach the house, but the forty-five-minute journey from Kowloon separated them from the roar of traffic and noise of the city.

Knowing they had use of the bishop's house for only one year, David began to look around for a piece of land where he could build his own house. He found a site a little lower down the hill, but also found that purchasing it was far from simple. The land could not be bought outright; rather, one purchased a lease. The government's method of selling such leases was by weekly auction, with the "upset" price and date of auction published in the *Hong Kong Gazette*. David had made some money in the stock market and this, coupled with his savings, provided enough to buy the lease and construct a house.

The auction was a public affair with competitive bidding. At the beginning of the auction, a man came to David and said that if David did not give him $3,000 he would compete at the bidding and drive up the price of the property.

"It was just against my principles," David recalls. "I said, 'No. I don't succumb to blackmail.' So he kept bidding it up. During the auction it became just him and myself. Finally I turned around and said to him, 'If you bid again, you can have it.' The auctioneer was not happy to have communication between bidders, but that's what I said. He stopped and I bought the land and engaged an architect."

David had a good idea of what he wanted. The situation of the house was to be determined by the view, rather than the traditional principles of *feng shui*. The location was on a steep slope, but the architect felt that a series of firmly embedded columns would easily take the weight of the two-storey house. The contractor agreed to build it, and fortunately for David, Bishop Hall decided to stay in England for an extra four months.

When work began on the house, everything seemed to be going well. The contractor, however, was busy building high-rises in Hong Kong and sent his young son to supervise David's house. The son was a clever, likable young man, but he tried to cover up some errors made when anchoring the columns of the house. The house was completed to the roof when David invited his brother-in-law Herbert Cheng and his sister Alice and a few friends to see it. They roamed around it, admired the view, saw where the swimming pool would be, and then went to Kowloon for dinner and a movie. When they returned, the house was gone! The columns had buckled like a camel kneeling down, and the whole house slid down the hill to the bottom of the valley. Had this happened a few hours earlier, David and his friends would have crashed down with it. Once again, someone was looking after David since nobody was hurt when the house went tobogganing down the hill.

The whole house had to be rebuilt by a different contractor. David managed to recoup his costs from the contractor who had made the error and, fortunately, the bishop's delayed return made it possible for him to move directly into his new home.

Being a homeowner gave David free rein to garden to his heart's content. He planted hundreds of rose bushes, Chinese sweet oranges, papayas and bougainvillea, a bamboo grove and dozens of flowers and vegetables. The new house provided David with far more than fresh flowers and vegetables, however. For the first time in his life, he was in complete control over his own household. He and Dorothy could do what they wanted when they wanted, and could manage their domestic affairs as it suited them, rather than have to coordinate them with the larger family.

Contact with the family remained a big part of their lives, however, with much of each weekend spent at the house of Chi Fung. Saturday mornings began in the big house with a prayer meeting. Then Dorothy and her sisters-in-law would prepare a western meal for the whole family, often using recipes from *Good Housekeeping*. As Dorothy remembers it, "The whole morning was occupied with prayers and preparing the meal. After that, the men would have a business meeting during the whole afternoon. Then, the daughters-in-law would have a good time together while waiting for their husbands to complete their business, and then we would go home. On Sunday we would go to church, and the children had to be in Sunday school. We had to take them out at half past nine. Then everyone went to lunch at the Lam family home after which we would return home."

Sunday afternoons, or what was left of them, were spent in a variety of fashions. Gardening pleased both parents, but as the children grew older, there were other activities in which everyone took part. Hiking and swimming were favourites, frequently followed by a picnic. David had bought himself a large scooter, so sometimes he piled the entire family on board and went for a ride along the dirt roads that criss-crossed the hills in the New Territories. The area still was partially wild at the time, and on one occasion, a cougar or mountain lion made off with one of the bishop's goats. In the 1960s, David purchased a small motorboat, and it was pleasant to get out and sail around the numerous islands in the vicinity of Hong Kong.

Although he enjoyed boating and swimming with his family, there were other activities which they could not share. One was flying. He trained on a Stinson L-5, a monoplane with an engine, according to him, like a lawn mower. He learned quickly and soon obtained his pilot's licence.

Dorothy was normally ready to go anywhere or do anything with David, but she was a bit apprehensive about flying. One day, she and the children were out near the Kai Tak airport where the flying school was located. As she recalls, "He was up there trying to make loops with a Tiger Moth biplane. A lady, an acquaintance of ours, said she also had lessons making loops and that it was quite safe. She told me not to worry, because once she had fallen out, but she had a parachute and it was fine. Then she asked me, 'Of course, your husband must have a parachute?' That started me thinking, trying to remember, and worrying. I hadn't asked him if he had a parachute with him. For hours I was there biting my lip, waiting for him to come back safely." As it turned out, David was wearing a parachute.

But even when he got his licence, Dorothy worried. "At that time," she says, "if you crossed the boundary into China and came down, the Communists would put you in jail. If a strange plane flew over Chinese territory, they would shoot at it."

By the 1960s, Hong Kong's economy was beginning to thrive. Some of David's entrepreneurial friends were becoming millionaires, especially those in real estate. David's investments with Y. C. Cheng helped to supplement his salary, as did his periodic forays into the stock market. The latter investments were on a small scale but they could pay off handsomely. It was as much the money he received from these sources as his salary that permitted him to live in the style he did. He had a lovely house with a swimming pool and gardens. There were four servants to look after the house and the three children. Both David and Dorothy owned their own cars. Dorothy liked to drive so it was she who drove the children down the dusty road to the highway and then on to school in the outskirts of Kowloon.

In those years there were very few Chinese families living close to the Lam residence. David was the first to build a house on his street and although there were other houses in the neighbourhood, most of the families there were Caucasians. Some of their children would come over to play, but as Daphne says now, "It was like a duck and a chicken trying to communicate. Yet we could somehow manage to play with each other. We couldn't talk, we just played with Barbie dolls together and did the best we could." It was a lot more fun when the girls' cousins paid a visit because then they could chatter away to their hearts' content.

In addition to raising a family, building a home, working for the bank and getting himself involved in various other activities, David launched himself on a project which was to occupy a considerable amount of his time and effort for years to come. It began in 1954 at a monthly meeting of leaders of the Hong Kong Baptists. At the meeting, "for absolutely no reason," he recalls, "I stood up, opened my big mouth and put my foot in it. I said, 'When I was a student in Canton, there was a well-run and well-respected Baptist hospital. When we look around here, we see refugees by the million. We see poor people who need medical help. We really should have a hospital with Christian missionary doctors willing to help.' No sooner had I made my little speech when I could see the elders sort of smiling, with a little bit of snickering. But they didn't want to discourage this young man so they sort of made eyes to each other. I saw that too. They said, 'Let us form a Baptist medical board.' I said, 'Wonderful. At least we will have a group to study about it seriously.'"

A board was formed and at the first meeting, David was elected chairman of the board. Had he known the difficulties he would have to overcome he might have refused the chairmanship. Yet, on reflection, he has no regrets: "Sometimes naiveté is an asset. Knowing too much can be a liability in life." Besides, there was Christian work to be done and that was sufficient motivation.

One of the first things he did as chairman was to drive around Hong Kong with Dorothy. He said to her, "If the whole of Hong Kong was given to us and we could put a Baptist hospital anywhere we would like, where would we want to put it?" After looking around they agreed the best place was at the end of Waterloo Road on the slope of Lion Rock Mountain.

In the following year, 1955, David accompanied his father to the Baptist Convention in London, and later to the United States. While his father raised money for the Baptist college, David spread the word that he was looking for a volunteer missionary doctor to come to Hong Kong to serve in his hospital-to-be. He received a positive reply from Dr. Sam Rankin, who had been a medical missionary in Canton for two years before being forced out when the Communists took over.

While awaiting Rankin's arrival, David scurried around to find a clinic for him. As the doctor remembers, "A first-floor apartment on Waterloo Road, just in front of Pui-Ching Baptist Middle School, was secured, which could be converted to office space. David helped plan the renovation of the apartment for medical work. A large waiting room, a combined pharmacy and registration office, bathrooms, rooms for *amahs* and three examination and treatment rooms were completed. He also helped secure a staff including one of his cousins, Allan Chan, who was an efficient registrar, treasurer and dispenser of medicines."

The official opening of the clinic on January 2, 1956, was the occasion for a big celebration. David had taken Rankin to various Baptist churches to introduce him and when opening day came there were flowers, prayers, speeches and hospitality—but no patients. That afternoon, however, the first patient arrived and had to be led into the clinic from the street. She was a Chinese woman who had a severe allergic reaction to lacquer she had used on her hair, a common practice at that time. Her eyelids were swollen shut. After treatment, she was able to return the next day, able to see, for further care from Dr. Rankin. In the weeks and months that followed, the clinic was to treat hundreds of patients.

The arrival of Dr. Rankin was very fortunate for the Lam family. For several months, David's father had been in St. Theresa's Hospital with severe jaundice. He was kept alive by blood transfusions, intravenous fluids and antibiotics. David and three of his brothers came to Rankin's apartment a few weeks after he arrived in Hong Kong. They had secured numerous X-ray plates taken of their father and asked

Rankin to look at them and give his advice. Their father seemed to be going downhill rapidly. After examining the plates, Rankin observed that Chi Fung had a nonfunctioning gall bladder. His advice was to operate, or their father would die in a few months. The family agreed on an operation, which was performed by one of the best surgeons in Hong Kong. It gave their father nearly seventeen more years of a very productive life. David and Dr. Rankin became close friends, and the doctor was to deliver a number of David's nephews and nieces in years to come.

The clinic was a first step, but it was not a hospital. David knew where he would like to build it, but he had neither land nor money. He had become very friendly with Tony Petty, a young Englishman who worked in the colony's land department, and who had helped him find the piece of land on which to build his house. In confidence, Petty showed him a map on which was marked certain areas the government was reserving for special purposes such as schools, hospitals and parks. David noted one reserved area was exactly where he and Dorothy felt a hospital should be built. With Petty's help, he prepared a letter for the Crown Land Office proposing it be given for a non-profit Baptist hospital. All he could do then was wait.

At the end of the year, Daniel and David escorted their father to Government House in Hong Kong. For his many services to the community, Chi Fung had been made a Member of the Order of the British Empire, and the governor was to present him with the medal. David took the opportunity to approach the governor, Sir Alexander Grantham. He told him about his plans for a hospital and his need for a specific area of crown land, and let him know how grateful he would be for his help. He concluded by handing the governor a piece of paper with the description of the property on it. The governor, dressed in his official uniform, had no pocket in which to put it. Instead he borrowed David's pen and wrote on his shirt cuff the information he needed. In due course the property was set aside for hospital use. As Dr. Rankin describes it, "No more strategic piece of land could have been found in Hong Kong. It would be easily accessible by bus from Hong Kong, Kowloon and the New Territories."

With the site reserved, the next task was to decide the location of the hospital on it. There were a number of good architectural firms in Hong Kong, but none had recently built a hospital. Dr. Rankin had secured the plans for a 100-bed American public service hospital which spread out over several acres, but with land so expensive and with a limited projected budget, David had to rethink his strategy. A very good friend of Dorothy had married a young architect, Stanley Kwok, who worked for a well-established architect named Eric Cummin. Cummin was asked to take on the task. He solved the problem of land usage by building the hospital as a high-rise rather than spread out.

The hospital now took about one-third of the five acres the government had put aside, and David feared that if he did not use all the proffered land, the colonial government would withdraw part of it. David knew that his father's Baptist college board was looking for land where they could build a college, and he offered them the land adjacent to the hospital. They gladly accepted, and David could now claim all five acres from the Hong Kong government for good cause. The college board was so delighted that it persuaded David to join them, and he later became vice-president of that institution.

During the next several years, David and his board of directors were busy raising money to build the hospital. Rather than wait for all of the money to be collected, they decided to start erecting the hospital while the money was still coming in. Several floors were left empty, and provision was made for additional floors to be added when funds became available. An elevator shaft was built but the elevators would be installed later.

When the hospital was opened in 1963, David became chairman of its board of trustees. He continued to be involved in its development for years to come, seeing it grow from fifty beds to over seven hundred. Dr. Rankin remained with the hospital until 1971, and his friendship with David continues to the present. Both could be proud of their role in developing what was to become the largest private hospital in Hong Kong.

The 1960s were busy years for David. Aside from his banking business, he had been deeply involved in building the family's flashlight factory, the plant in Bangkok and now the Baptist hospital. This had given him considerable knowledge about real estate and the cost of developing it. With Hong Kong now beginning to develop at a quickening pace, he suggested that the family go into real estate development, particularly rental or condominium structures. The family agreed to invest some money in them, and again gave David the task of overseeing the venture, which proved successful. He also built another house with his own money, which he sold at a profit.

There were two other enterprises in which David was engaged outside the family business. One was a flower shop. He had several friends who loved flowers, among them the CEO of the Hong Kong and Youmati Ferry which ran from Hong Kong to Kowloon and various islands in the New Territories. They and two other friends got the idea over lunch one day and decided to start the flower shop, not just for money but, as David remembers it, "for the joy of owning a flower shop." David was given the task of making all the arrangements. He found a place at Ocean Terminal where all the large ships docked, selecting a vacant shop with the space and location he wanted. Inside he planned a waterfall as the background for the flower display which included everything from orchids to daffodils. With two expert florists on staff, the Green Fields Flower Shop was a success almost from the beginning, and became one of the best flower shops in Hong Kong. The shop provided a small but tidy amount to David's income. He was so delighted with it, however, that he would have been happy if it merely broke even.

The second enterprise also came out of a circle of friends with whom he had lunch on a regular basis. One was Chan Chak-Fu, a close friend who was to own hotels in Hong Kong, Thailand and the United States. A second was Sydney Leong, a Hong Kong lawyer who owned substantial properties in downtown Hong Kong and later in Vancouver. A third, Dr. Chan Shun, was in the garment business and doing extremely well manufacturing shirts for companies in North America. Robert Li, the fourth, was a property owner in Hong Kong.

One day Dr. Chan mentioned to David that he was planning to start a bowling alley with Chan Chak-Fu, and asked if he would be interested in a small shareholding. David agreed and soon found himself arranging finances, organizing construction and acting as the manager of the enterprise which became known as the Star Bowl. This, again, turned out to be a successful venture which added a bit more to his income.

It was in the 1960s that David began to feel the burden placed on him by working for the family rather than for himself. His entrepreneurial spirit was being confined by the Chinese tradition whereby the profit from the family business went into the family treasury with the expectation that all would share equally. Whatever profits the Ka Wah Bank made went to the family, and whether he worked four or fourteen hours a day, his salary remained constant. The problem, from David's point of view, was that no provision was made for exceptional hard work, talent and creative ideas. There was some resentment among one or two of his brothers that he involved himself in some enterprises which were making money for him rather than for the family. On the other hand, David felt this was the only way to make some money over which he had sole control.

Another frustration for David was the difficulty he experienced in having the family make quick decisions to take advantage of the opportunities presenting themselves in Hong Kong. David found that his outlook and that of his older brother were growing further apart with each passing year, and he knew a point would be reached when there would be open confrontation between the two. This, he knew, would be extremely painful to his father and because of that, David came to the realization that it would be better if he eased himself out of the situation rather than have a battle in the boardroom.

Dorothy and David usually spent their annual vacation travelling. In 1961 they decided to take an extra long vacation and spent two months travelling to Australia, New Zealand, the United States and Canada. They wanted a break from the pressure of work in Hong Kong and, at the same time, they were looking for a country where they might settle, should they decide to emigrate. They had thought of Singapore, Taiwan, Thailand and Indonesia, but upon reflection felt they might do better in an English-speaking country. A democratic country with the freedom to use one's own initiative was what David wanted, one that had a good record of tolerance and was free of the excesses of racism which blighted many of the countries they had visited. Religious freedom, of course, was a necessity, and if the place had a small Chinese community, so much the better.

They came to North America via the polar route, spending a few days in Anchorage before flying south to Seattle. While there, David telephoned Paul Lam, a friend from his student days at Temple University. Paul persuaded them to come to Vancouver, only a few hours of train travel to the north, and picked them up when they arrived. The train station was on the edge of the city's Chinatown, which is one of the most colourful in Canada. Paul and his wife spent the next several days showing them around Greater Vancouver.

Even before coming to Vancouver, while still in Seattle, David and Dorothy had gone by ferry to Victoria. There they visited Butchart Gardens, world famous for its acres of flowers and trees. "We couldn't believe there was such a place in the world," Dorothy says of that visit. "Everywhere we turned, people were so nice, so friendly, and we were very happy."

David was equally impressed with Vancouver. Driving in the suburbs he noticed the lawns and gardens surrounding the well-kept houses, the numerous parks, beaches, the tremendous views of the mountains across the harbour and the cleanliness of the bustling city core. "We fell in love with the city," he says. "Dorothy and I looked at each other and said, 'Let us look no further, this is the place.'"

When they returned to Hong Kong, David began to make enquiries about the possibility of immigration to Canada. At that time, the chances of being accepted were slim. There was a long waiting list, a quota system and high demand for immigrant status. This was discouraging, but Paul Lam agreed to let him know if any changes in Canada's immigration laws occurred, and David decided to be patient. He had to consider how to break the news to his family since they were unaware of his long-range goals, and there was also the question of his position at the Ka Wah Bank. If the rumour went around that the chief manager was planning to emigrate, it might engender a damaging loss of confidence among the bank's clients.

Several years passed before David decided the time was ripe. In 1966 he met the superintendent of Canadian immigration in Hong Kong, Robert Wales. After some casual talk, David raised the subject of immigration and the possibilities of immigrating to Canada. Wales remembers, "He knew who I was and what I did. He wanted to know what sort of people we were looking for and what were the difficulties and various things involved. We had quite a long chat about that. I encouraged him because he was the kind of person that Canada was looking for in the mid-sixties. We needed people with managerial expertise and people who had the kind of background that David had." Among other advantages, David spoke English well, and his children were the right age to ease into the Canadian school system.

One of the points Wales raised had a considerable impact on David. He suggested that David should not put off his decision for too long. If he moved to Canada soon, he would meet more people, get involved in Canadian society and have time to become adapted to their new circumstances. The longer he delayed, the more difficult he might find it.

It gave David and Dorothy a great deal to think about. Canada was still their favourite choice. They had considered Australia and New Zealand, but both countries seemed to be outside the mainstream of world commerce at the time. Britain held many attractions but David had the impression that the business community would be difficult to break into. There seemed to be as much emphasis on who you were as on what you could do. The United States was very attractive, but its restrictive immigration policy meant David would have to wait for many years before he could hope to gain entry. Canada had relaxed its immigration laws several years earlier. Wales put forward a strong case: "You keep telling me how you love Canada. I think you should go, and if you don't like it, you can always come back. But be an immigrant now. You are only forty, you have twenty or more years before retiring. In those years you could establish something, and therefore when you do retire in Canada, you won't be retiring among strangers."

It was time to make a decision. Dorothy was willing to go anywhere with him. She had every confidence he would succeed in whatever he tried. Emigrating to Canada meant that she would no longer have servants to help her in the house, but her daughters, now aged six, ten and twelve, all volunteered to help their mother. The girls only spoke a few words of English, but they were young enough to learn a new language without any great difficulty. Besides, it would be something of an adventure, since they had never left Hong Kong.

Chances of acceptance by Canada were good. The immigration authorities had recently been experimenting with a point system which judged applications on criteria such as health, education, ability to speak English, age, profession and financial security. David, Dorothy and the girls passed all the hurdles easily. With the assistance of Robert Wales, David was allowed to go through some procedures privately, since as chief manager of the bank he did not want it known that he was planning to leave Hong Kong for good.

The thing he dreaded most was to tell his father, fearing Chi Fung would not understand his reason for leaving. From his father's point of view, David had a nice family, a good home and a salary which allowed him to live in some comfort. Chi Fung had leaned heavily on David for advice ever since the exchange of old Hong Kong dollars after the war, and David had been very helpful as well in church matters. The two worked well together, but Chi Fung was probably not aware of David's strong streak of independence, nor his son's increasing desire to throw off the restrictions imposed by the family's traditional way of conducting business. If there had been harmony at the board meetings, everything might have gone smoothly, but there was only the appearance of harmony. Tension was growing and David was finding it increasingly difficult to reach agreements with others on the board about how the business should be conducted and expanded.

He had to consult his elder brother about his plan and told him frankly about his intention to emigrate and his desire not to upset his father. Daniel suggested that he should apply to the bank for a three-month vacation in Canada which, in due course, could be extended. This would allow their father to become gradually accustomed to his son's absence and make it easier for his father to accept the idea. David agreed. At the next bank board meeting, however, the plan was brought into the open. David had been granted a three-month leave but was then accused of using this as a cover to leave permanently.

This shattered David's hope of departing quietly in a way which would not upset his father. He offered there and then to resign from the Ka Wah Bank, but not to change his plan to go to Canada. His brother Alex, who had worked under David as manager of the bank, could step into his shoes. David would sell his house and his other possessions and start anew in Canada with only the money he had accumulated through his own personal efforts. No financial grant or bonus was offered to him by the family for his seventeen years of service on the various family enterprises. He could not sell his share of the family business on the open market, and there was no offer by the other shareholders to buy him out. He would be on his own. One thing he did not lack, however, was self-confidence and a strong belief in God's help. When times were tough, there was a hymn he used to sing to himself:

> Guide me, O thou great Jehovah,
> Pilgrims through this barren land,
> I am weak, but thou art mighty,
> Hold me with Thy powerful hand.
>
> When I tread the verge of Jordan,
> Bid my anxious fears subside,
> Bear me through the swelling current,
> Land me safe on Canaan's side.

He was to hum this tune to himself many times in 1967.

SIX

Arrival in Canada

DAVID HAS NEVER forgotten his reception when he arrived at Vancouver airport, May 29, 1967. As he tells the story, "Our youngest girl was heavily asleep. No matter how I tried to wake her, she remained asleep so I carried her. The other two girls were half asleep and Dorothy was holding on to them. We had no one to help carry our luggage, but we managed to struggle up to the Customs and Immigration counter. They said 'Welcome to Canada!' They shook hands with us and our girls. I could see our girls' surprise because, to their minds, people in uniform are not usually friendly, and how was it these were so nice? Then they said, 'Let's give you a hand,' as they grabbed our suitcases and took them and us outside the airport. People were so nice."

Once out of the airport, they were taken to the Cove Motor Hotel at the corner of Pendrell and Denman. It was owned by Dorothy's sister and her husband, who had emigrated to Canada over two years earlier, and David had reserved a small housekeeping suite there. The following day, they set out to start getting familiar with their neighbourhood and the city.

Although warmed by the reception at the airport, David knew that getting established in Canada would be an uphill battle. He knew only two people in the city—Dorothy's sister at the hotel and his old friend, Paul Lam, who had an antique shop in Chinatown.

He did, however, have a letter of introduction to the manager of the main branch of the Bank of Nova Scotia, Paul Coombs. The Canadian bank had branches in the Far East and David's reputation was known to them. The bank was interested in widening its presence in the area, and it was particularly interested in buying the Ka Wah Bank if the sale could be negotiated. Although small, it was well respected and it would give the Bank of Nova Scotia a foothold in Hong Kong.

David was unaware of the bank's intention, but he was happy to meet people in the banking community in Vancouver. Banking was his profession, but he knew he could not merely knock on the door of a Canadian bank and ask for a job. He did not know the local conditions nor was he familiar with Canadian banking regulations.

He and Coombs took an immediate liking to each other. David talked about the surge in trade and commerce across the Pacific which he foresaw. He expressed the opinion that Vancouver was particularly well located as the major port on Canada's West Coast to take advantage of the coming economic upturn, and that it would be wise for the Bank of Nova Scotia to position itself now to reap the benefits later.

Coombs wrote to his head office about David, stressing his wide knowledge of business affairs in Asia. At Coombs's suggestion, David was invited to fly to Toronto at the bank's expense to meet some of its top officials. He was there for several days, meeting, among others, Cedric E. Ritchie, then head of the bank's international division, and later its president and chief executive officer. After a series of meetings, lunches and dinners, David returned to Vancouver. In due course, he had a telephone call from Paul Coombs. He had made quite an impression in Toronto, and the bank wanted to hire him as their representative in Hong Kong.

David could not accept their offer. He had not left Hong Kong in order to return to it. The freedom he was experiencing in Canada was too precious to him, and he did not want to be in a position where he might be competing with his family's bank. The Lam family did not wish to sell the Ka Wah Bank. Much as he appreciated the offer, he turned it down. The Bank of Nova Scotia had no other position open, a situation Paul Coombs regretted as he was aware of David's potential value. Despite the outcome, the two men were to remain close friends.

As the weeks went by and the summer sun warmed the beaches of Vancouver, David's enchantment with the city grew. Years later, when asked by *Vancouver* magazine why he selected the city over many others he had visited, he said, "I go by philosophy and feeling. When I go to a place and I love that place, I love it usually for its natural beauty. And I love it more so if there are good people there. Now, where there are people, there is business. If I make a dollar, my bottom line increases threefold because I gain on the people and I gain on the beauty. If I am to be taken to a place that I dread, that I don't like, then if I make a dollar I really get only thirty cents."

While David was out looking for business opportunities and employment, Dorothy spent a considerable amount of time looking for a suitable house. Both felt they should avoid looking for a place in Chinatown. David enjoyed the people he was beginning to meet there, but if he was going to immerse himself in Canadian society, then he should try to find a house in a pleasant district where they could absorb the Canadian way of doing things.

They found a house which suited them on Ash Street in the Cambie district. It was on a corner lot, had a lovely garden, and the price was $43,000. It also had a full basement which, with some work, could provide a few more bedrooms. They moved in July, furnishing the house with inexpensive items from Sears. David was aware that payment for the furniture would come from his dwindling capital. He would borrow money if he knew it would generate an income to pay off the debt, but furniture was a consumer item and paid nothing.

David and Dorothy were welcomed by their neighbours to an extent that almost overwhelmed them. They were the first Chinese family to move into the neighbourhood, but that made them more an object of interest rather than suspicion. "Our neighbours," David says now, "were just out of this world." Next door lived a retired British major, Maurice Law, and his wife Nancy. They had no children but had a swimming pool. The Lams were invited to use it and soon they were close friends. A few houses away lived Allan McEachern, who was later to become the Chief Justice of British Columbia. He soon invited the Lams to his house and sometimes took the girls up to Whistler for skiing. Nearby lived Dr. James Smith and his wife Mary. Smith was a Scotsman. On New Year's Eve, the Scots celebrate Hogmanay, sometimes with more enthusiasm than Christmas. And so it was that one cold evening, with snow on the ground, the Lams heard a peculiar, penetrating sound on their front lawn. Looking out the window they beheld Smith, dressed in a kilt and jacket, playing the bagpipes. As David remembers, "We didn't understand what was going on. We went outside. When he was finished playing, he said, 'I thought of you and your family, your three young girls. I thought you may be sort of lonely in a new place, and I thought I would dress up and play the pipes to entertain you.'"

Another group whom David found very supportive was the members of the Baptist church. The Oakridge Baptist Church welcomed the Lams with great warmth and, David says, "was extremely important to help us feel we belonged. The people were just completely overwhelming in their welcome, not only during the service, but during the week." David's Christian faith gave him strong support during those months in Vancouver when he was looking for employment. He was sure God's hand would guide him and, confident in His judgement, he slept soundly every night.

One thing David learned quickly was that Canadian house owners tended to look after their property themselves. David had had a gardener in Hong Kong, but on Ash Street he was his own gardener. Dorothy used to have servants, but now she was the housekeeper, *amah* and chauffeur all rolled into one. There was a lot of available space in the basement, so David decided to start taking courses offered at a local high school, including one on building construction which covered everything from plumbing and wiring to woodwork. After several months of courses, he bought an array of tools and was ready to start. With the advice and help from friends, he built a recreation room, office, storage room and an additional bedroom over the next few years.

Meanwhile months had passed, and with no money coming in, David considered the possibility of opening a flower shop or establishing a bilingual limousine service catering to visitors from Asia. Both ideas called for capital he did not possess and which, with his share of the family business tied up, he was unlikely to get.

The break in his fortunes came unexpectedly. One day, David was at the airport awaiting the arrival of a friend. There he saw another person apparently doing the same thing, and struck up a conversation with him. Fung King-Hey had also come to Canada recently looking for business opportunities, and the two found they had a lot in common. Always willing to widen his circle of friends, David invited Fung to lunch with a little group he had formed called the Hong Kong Merchants Association of Vancouver. The association at that time consisted of four or five people who met for lunch once a week, much like a Rotary meeting. The membership was unique in that they were a minority group attempting to either establish or improve their position in a foreign land. It was an opportunity to meet people who were encountering similar difficulties and get advice and encouragement from others who had overcome obstacles in their own business. Fung King-Hey came to the lunch and to many others. He liked David and soon they were close friends.

Fung's knowledge of English was very basic, to be generous. He was a well-established entrepreneur in Hong Kong and had managed to make a small fortune there without having to learn a second language. To establish himself in Canada as well, however, English would be a necessity. David steered him to an English teacher, and then helped him get into an English immersion course at the Berlitz language centre. Before Fung had completed his full course, however, he had to go to New York to attend to important business matters. Knowing something of David's background, he asked David to come with him and serve as his interpreter. Again, David was willing to help, and the bond between the two men grew stronger.

Fung was aware that David was still looking for employment and had not yet found what he wanted. One day he said to David, "You are still thinking like a chief manager of a bank. You must realize that you are in Vancouver. Nobody cares whether your background is as a chief manager. They don't know you, and you have got to make a living. You are thinking big, but you don't have the cash or the capital." He added, "If you permit me, I think you should be a salesman."

Arrival in Canada

"In what?" David asked.

"In real estate, of course," came the reply. "Think about it."

The appeal of real estate at this stage was that one required no capital to become involved in it, and by the summer of 1968, David's reserves were becoming low. His options were running out.

It was during that summer that David had occasion to have some documents notarized. Wanting to avoid the expense of going into the city core to have a lawyer do the task, he looked in the telephone book to see if there was a notary's office within walking distance. There was, but when he arrived there, the notary had left. A secretary in the office told him there was another notary across the street who was a partner in Newcombe Realty.

When David went to the realty office, he met Sid Newcombe, who had the authority to notarize his documents. When that was finished, he began to talk to Sid's brother, Edward, and they had a long conversation. David told him about his work in Hong Kong, his experiences so far in Canada, his desire to stay in Vancouver, and that he thought he would try looking for a position as a real estate salesman. Newcombe was impressed with David's story and suggested to him that he would be welcome as a salesman at Newcombe Realty. David was delighted and rushed home to tell Dorothy.

"I've got a job," he said.

"How much does it pay?" she inquired. "I was so happy I didn't ask," David had to admit.

Reality hit on Monday morning when he returned to meet Ed Newcombe. David told him he was ready to work immediately. That was acceptable, but Newcombe told him he would have to obtain a realtor's licence. That would take time, not only to study all the rules and regulations, but David would have to sit for an examination. The next question he asked was about his salary. There was no salary involved, Newcombe explained. A salesman worked on a commission basis. If, for example, he sold a house for $10,000, he might expect to earn $600. Of that, the company got half, since it had to pay the rent, the staff and similar expenses necessary to serve the clients. Nevertheless, Newcombe went on, if David made a sale without a licence, the company would credit the commission to him. David agreed to this and, still thinking like a chief manager, asked, "Where is my office?" Pointing to an outer office, Newcombe said, "There are several desks in there."

David went in and found a desk a little wider than his two legs put together. On top was a telephone. He remembers thinking, "I've got to put the phone on the floor to create more space." At one time, he stood up quickly and the whole desk collapsed.

The first months were difficult and sales were few and far between. David worked hard to prepare for his realtor's licence which he obtained early in 1969. The first sale he made before he obtained his licence was to his friend Fung King-Hey, who bought a house on Churchill Street. David received $400 from the sale. It was not very much, but it was the first money he earned in Canada. To celebrate, he decided to take his family and his friends Eddie and Lily Kong and their three boys to dinner. They all went to Mr. Mike's, a popular but inexpensive steak house. It was so long since he could afford a steak that he almost had forgotten what one tasted like. When the waitress asked if he wanted dessert, David said no. Instead, he piled the group into his car and went to a Peter's Ice Cream drive-in where he bought everyone an ice cream cone. It was the end of a perfect day.

During David's one and a half years with Newcombe Realty he did not sell many houses. "Every time I came home," he recalls, "the whole family—the three girls and their mother—would look at me like someone with a shotgun who had gone out hunting and brought home nothing. Or had gone fishing but came back with no fish." Nevertheless, he was by no means idle. If he was going into real estate, he wanted to master the topic. He found out that at the University of British Columbia, one could take a diploma course on real estate appraisal. He did not want to be an appraiser, but he knew he could gain valuable insight by taking the course. It was given at night. He would leave the office and go to the university campus, stopping at the Varsity Grill for bacon and eggs, which he could buy for less than a dollar. He got to know the part-owner of the coffee shop, Bing Leung, and they were soon friends. Leung would bring him soup and pie he hadn't ordered and tell him, "You are going to succeed. Work hard and believe in yourself." David recalls with considerable emotion, "He gave me so much love and help when I needed it."

David continued to visit the coffee shop for a long time. For five years he went to night school two or three times a week, taking every real estate course the university offered including mortgaging, financing and agency work. He gained all the diplomas necessary to become a member of the Real Estate Institute of British Columbia, and later was admitted as a Fellow of the Real Estate Institute of Canada. For someone in the profession, it was admittance at the highest level. Despite the time and effort, David felt it well worthwhile. Certainly, it was to pay dividends as well as enhance his reputation.

During the summer and autumn of 1968, though house sales were abysmally slow, David kept busy. He still had at the back of his mind that he might be able to interest his family in investing some money in Canada, but the reaction to his suggestions was negative. He kept up-to-date with the real estate market, and he continued to expand his contacts with local people and Hong Kong immigrants. Nonetheless, he was beginning to feel the route he was taking was not the right one. He was not going to make his fortune selling houses. He was interested in real estate and the more he studied it, the more fascinating he found it. But it appeared to him he had to operate on a much higher level. He remembers, "I suddenly came across one word—matchmaker. You have money and I have opportunity for you. I have got to know you before I know what kind of properties or opportunities I want to matchmake for you."

Instead of listing houses and waiting for someone to come and look at them, David's idea was that he would try to find real estate which had potential for development and would attract investors and buyers. At the same time, he would try to establish himself as a real estate broker. Once he found out what a potential investor in real estate wanted, he would look for a property which matched the investor's need.

His first venture in this direction came when he noted an old house sitting on a large property on North Road, which forms the boundary between Burnaby and Port Coquitlam. He had driven all over the Lower Mainland looking for a lot of this size which could be developed. In front of the house was a large, stately Douglas fir tree. David took photographs of the site and enquired about the zoning regulations. He concluded that it would be suitable for a two-storey building, with offices upstairs and commercial outlets such as a grocery store, credit union or insurance agency on the ground floor.

Having found a site with good potential, David went to see his friend Fung King-Hey. Fung found the idea attractive and suggested that the two of them contact friends in Hong Kong, propose that they each invest three or four thousand dollars in the venture and proceed from there. If David and Fung each got fifteen friends to invest and invested $10,000 themselves, the property could be bought and developed. It was a sound approach, but David did not have money to invest. Fung immediately offered to loan him that amount, and the deal was made.

Both men made their separate approaches to their friends in Hong Kong. The economy in the colony was beginning to thrive. Both men were well respected, the proposal was well prepared, and to many in Hong Kong, the price of the land seemed very inexpensive. As the money came in, David decided to incorporate the investors. Since Vancouver had a reputation for being located in a wet climate, David decided to name the company Sunnyside Estates. He followed the same idea in many subsequent companies, using names like Sunnyhill, Sunnyvale and Sunnyland to assure his investors that the West Coast climate was one of the most favourable in Canada.

Although David owned only a small percentage of Sunnyside, it was up to him to get the company in operation. He was appointed president and immediately set to work while continuing as a salesman at Newcombe's. One of the first things to do was hire an architect and explain what he wanted done. When the plans were first presented, the architect had placed the building in such a way that the Douglas fir tree would have to come down. David replied, "No, it's too beautiful." The only alternative was to move the building behind the tree, giving the building less exposure to traffic. When he balanced exposure to traffic with retaining the tree, David opted for the latter. The completed building was nominated for a design award by an architect's organization, and though it didn't win, David was so pleased with the letter citing its nomination that he had it framed and hung in his office.

During this period, he also interested Ed Newcombe in several ventures. In December 1969, he and Newcombe formed Sunnyhill Holdings, a company which continued to make profits for a number of years. David was also involved in Newcombe Developments and one or two other companies. Newcombe remembers his new salesman as, "very, very thorough. When he would make up a listing on a building, everything was done properly on it. The detail was thoroughly investigated. He was excellent on figures, planning up the expenses and the income."

As the end of the 1960s approached, David began to build up a clientele of people in Hong Kong who were interested in investing in Canada. It was not that he avoided Canadian participants; rather, he had far more friends in Hong Kong than in Vancouver, and his reputation there was very high. At this time, too, there was considerable uncertainty about China's future moves and a feeling in Hong Kong that it might be wise to invest money overseas as a safety measure. Canada seemed a country with a good growth potential where investment was welcome and business opportunities good.

Just as he was renewing contacts with Hong Kong, David had the opportunity to visit the colony with Dorothy and the children. His father and mother were celebrating their golden wedding anniversary in 1970, and they decided to gather all of their children and grandchildren together.

Although David had left the colony in 1967, Lam Chi Fung had by no means forgotten him. In 1968, while in the United States on his annual fundraising trip for the Hong Kong Baptist College, Chi Fung decided to visit David to see how he was progressing. It was a joyous reunion. David was not yet making money but he assured his father he was happy with the move to Canada, and that he was sure, with God's guidance, his situation would improve. He wanted to show his father something of the country beyond Vancouver, but couldn't afford to take the family and his visitors very far. Instead, he bundled everyone into the car and took them up to Harrison Hot Springs, a few hours drive from the city. The Lams wandered all over the resort and Chi Fung especially enjoyed a swim in the sulphur hot springs. The family was back home on Ash Street by late evening. Chi Fung was pleased to see everyone in good spirits. On leaving, he told David, "I have no more concern. If you have thanksgiving in your heart, although you have not made money, you will be all right."

When his father called in the entire family to help celebrate his fiftieth wedding anniversary, he paid for the travel costs of those who were living in North America. This was fortunate, for at this time David could not afford the airfare for himself and family to fly to Hong Kong. During his time in Hong Kong, David visited a great many friends and former business acquaintances. He was able to talk to them directly about the potential he saw for investment in Vancouver and there was little doubt about their interest.

As far as his own family were concerned, there had been little change in the three years since David left. The bank and the flashlight manufacturing business continued to show a good profit, but there was no attempt to expand into other fields. Although he had severed his ties with the Ka Wah Bank, David could not dismiss the feeling of wanting to help the family and bring to its notice some of the opportunities he saw in Canada. For example, some time earlier he had met a senior official and part-owner of Security Trust, a Calgary firm which wanted to expand to the West Coast. The company had a considerable number of oil land leases in the Prudhoe Bay area in Alaska which looked promising, but it was short on cash. David had suggested that the Ka Wah Bank might be interested in buying half the trust company for an exchange of shares. This would allow the company not only to expand to the West Coast but to have a branch in Hong Kong as well. He spoke to his father about the scheme when Chi Fung was in Vancouver and he was in favour of the idea. It happened that Daniel, David's older brother, was in the United States at the time, and he was persuaded to come to Vancouver on his way back to Hong Kong. After explaining his scheme to Daniel, they drove to Calgary for direct talks with officials in Security Trust. Daniel returned home without making any commitment.

Shortly after his return, David was informed that the family was not interested in the deal.

It was a speculative venture, but over time the oil leases became very valuable property. The Ka Wah Bank would have made large profits. On the other hand, if the scheme had gone through and David had assumed a high position in the restructured company, he would have been regarded as working for the family once again. "Looking back," David reflects, "the family's refusal was the luckiest break for me." This was the last attempt David made to have the family company diversify its interests beyond Hong Kong. As a shareholder in the family company, he stayed aware of what was going on but concentrated on his own affairs without any expectation of support from the family board of directors.

By this time, David had left Newcombe Realty. The move was made at the suggestion of Fung King-Hey. "There was nothing against the Newcombe brothers," says David. "They are honourable, above board and very knowledgeable. It is a matter that they belonged to the older school of playing safe and being cautious. There's nothing wrong with that, but you can overkill on being cautious. You end up by making no mistakes but with doing no deals. You have got to be more aggressive to make things happen."

David decided to join an aggressive firm called Wall and Redekop. He was persuaded to do so by Robert (Bob) Lee, a Canadian of Chinese parentage who already worked at the firm and had money invested in it. Lee had first met David through a mutual friend, Dr. Chan Shun, one of the partners in the bowling alley David was involved in before he left Hong Kong. David and Lee saw a potential for partnership in their mutual business interests. As Lee describes it, "I was doing business with people from overseas already and had successfully negotiated a large amount of real estate for two families. When David joined our firm, I thought it would fit well because I was born here and knew most of the owners, and David had the buyers."

The changeover meant more than merely moving David's real estate licence from one building to another. Dr. Chan, his brother and another associate were investors in one of the "Sunny" companies,

Sunnyvale Development. Chan was chairman of the firm and David was its president as well as an investor. As part of David's move, it was arranged that Sunnyvale would loan Wall and Redekop half a million dollars in return for stock options and other considerations.

When he joined with the firm, David was given the somewhat grand title of President of the International Division. In reality, he was simply a real estate salesman with a small cubicle of an office and a secretary shared with Bob Lee. When the listing of new properties were passed around, he received his at the same time as the other salesmen. He had no salary, but like the others, would receive a commission for any sales made. On the other hand, David's position was a special one in several respects. Wall and Redekop was indebted to Sunnyvale, and some of the properties which David had acquired through other "Sunny" companies had been turned over to Wall and Redekop to manage. These properties, of course, were owned by various groups of clients to whom David was responsible. With the backing of his overseas contacts, he could form his own companies and buy on the market as an individual without involving Wall and Redekop, as could Bob Lee. In a sense, David was wearing several hats—one as a salesman, one as a client of Wall and Redekop's property management business, and a third as an entrepreneur who kept a sharp eye on the market.

During the early 1970s, the real estate market in Greater Vancouver was beginning to boom. David had been fortunate to enter the field when he did, and in the decade which followed he was sometimes surprised at his own success. In the late 1980s he told a reporter, "I was totally ignorant of my shortcomings. The bumblebee shouldn't be able to fly because it is out of proportion. But the bumblebee is ignorant of the scientific data. Isn't it wonderful when people refuse to accept that they don't have a chance and give flying a good try anyway?"

If he was ignorant about the Vancouver real estate business in the beginning, each passing year in Vancouver gave him greater expertise and more knowledge about the potential of the city. At the same time, he was fully aware of the valuable asset he had in his friendship with a growing number of investors in Hong Kong. He knew that he dare not make an error so he had to be cautious. Caution had to be balanced with risk, but the risk to be taken on any given property or development could be minimized by careful study of all the factors involved when evaluating its worth. David's judgement was rarely wrong and this did not go unnoticed in Hong Kong.

Generally, the Hong Kong investors liked to form a separate company on each new venture, with David as a junior partner but playing the role of the company president. Looking back, he comments, "This has been a magic formula. I would say, 'I want you to buy this shopping centre' and explain why. They would say, 'Sure. What's the best way to do it?' I would say, 'Form a Canadian company and buy it.' They might reply, 'Fine. Would you join the company?' I might say, 'No, I'm really asking you to buy that. I will look after it for you.' So some would just go ahead and buy it, which is fine. It makes life simple. But 90 per cent or more would say, 'All right. Let's form a company and you be the president and you put in some money.' This so-called 'some money' can be from 10 per cent to 50 per cent."

The annual meetings of the "Sunny" companies were frequently held in Vancouver. It was a good excuse for the investors to have a combined business and pleasure trip away from Hong Kong, and often they brought their wives with them. David looked after everything, from making hotel reservations to arranging spare time leisure activities. "It was always a joyous occasion," David says. "There would be feasting on Chinese food. There would be a weekend trip perhaps to Harrison Hot Springs for swimming, hiking, golfing or the hotel's health club massage. People came, they liked Vancouver, and on their own, they would end up investing personally through me—not necessarily setting up a company—and introducing a lot of friends. That's how I got my connection circle to grow and grow."

He had the investors' trust and this was his most valuable asset. At directors' meetings, he sometimes made business proposals which were accepted before he had finished. "I probably had gone about half way," he reflects, "and they would say, 'Done. You do it. Go ahead. That's it.' If they don't trust you, you could make a double presentation, but they're not listening."

One of the features of David's "Sunny" companies was the variety of people he dealt with and the different objectives they had in mind. Some sought short-term gain, while others wanted an opportunity for a tax writeoff. A few would make an all-cash payment on a property that was showing no returns but would produce a large capital gain in later years. Some would not tell David exactly what they wanted but asked him to show them what he had for sale. "These I did not serve too well," David recalls, "because I'm a matchmaker and I have to know as much as possible."

Around this time, his friend Fung King-Hey returned to Hong Kong and became active again with his two partners, Kwok Tak-shing and Lee Shau-Kee. With them, he formed Sun Hung Kai Securities. Fung wanted David to come back to Hong Kong and join them in their enterprise. He offered him not only a very good salary but also 10 per cent of the shares of the company. He was very persuasive but David preferred to stay in Canada. He remained on very friendly terms with Fung and his partners, however, and when their company expanded and their profits multiplied into the millions of dollars, Fung used to tease him about his refusal to join them. The three partners were eventually among the ten richest men in Hong Kong.

But Vancouver had its own attractions, and David was a person who preferred to make one dollar in an attractive environment than ten in the energetic, cutthroat economy of Hong Kong. He had seen the lovely valley below the house he had built in the New Territories fill up with high-rises and industries. He did not want to go back to that, nor live in so restricted an area whose population was steadily growing. David had burned his bridges. Hong Kong would always remain for him an exciting place to visit, meet friends and catch up on what was going on in the colony. Vancouver, however, was now his home.

SEVEN

Lift-Off

David's house on Ash Street was to give him years of pleasure. Its steady rise in value was not as important to him as the fact that he had a home in a pleasant neighbourhood and that he was made welcome by his neighbours. He was determined to become a Canadian citizen in the shortest time possible. Being a Canadian meant more to him than merely getting his citizenship papers. He wanted to immerse himself and his family in the Canadian way of doing things and become knowledgeable of and comfortable with Canadian customs.

One of the first things David and Dorothy had to consider was having someone help the children learn English. They enrolled them in a school which had a "New Canadian class" for children not accustomed to English as a working language. A kind lady they met at the Oakridge Baptist Church, Mrs. Eva Williams, volunteered to help them learn English and reinforce what they were learning at school. Although their progress was good, it was not as fast as the parents wished. School would start in September, and after a visit to the School Board, they were advised to enroll them in the Annie B. Jamieson Elementary School only a few blocks away. "The best way," they were told, "is just put them in the class and let them struggle, and in no time they will pick it up."

Each of the children faced a challenge in their own way, but they managed to overcome them without too much difficulty. Doreen, the youngest, was put in grade one but found it boring, so her mother persuaded the school authorities to promote her to grade two. However, the teacher quickly realized that Doreen was simply mimicking the other children, smiling and trying to do what they did, but not knowing what was going on. One day, the teacher asked her to stay behind. Doreen did not know why and thought she would be punished for imitating. She started to cry.

"The teacher hugged her to show her she was a friend and wanted to help," David recalls, but Doreen didn't stop. "At that point, the teacher really felt for her because she also began to cry. Doreen then stopped crying and felt very accepted. She came home and told Dorothy and Dorothy cried, and she told me and I cried. It was a very touching thing. That's why I always say you have to accept people. On the one hand, it is so easy to reject people. It costs you nothing. The decision is up to you. But accepting someone can change both lives." In a few years Doreen got a first prize in public speaking and was later elected vice-president of the student council at Sir Winston Churchill high school.

Daphne, the second daughter, was put into grade five. Her English improved rapidly and she remembers enjoying the more relaxed atmosphere in Canadian schools. "The class sizes were much smaller," she reflects, "and the teachers seemed so much fun. They were light-hearted. They all looked like friends, bright-eyed, so totally different from the strict ones I had in Hong Kong." Even on the first day at school, she did not feel in the least rejected. "By grade seven," she says, "I felt like a Canadian kid."

Deborah was twelve years old when she started attending school in Canada, and found it more difficult to adjust. She was just learning the rudiments of English when she left Hong Kong. It was not easy to overcome the barrier of language, and for the first year or so it was a relief to return home where Chinese was spoken.

For Dorothy, fitting into the Canadian mainstream was easier than it was for her daughters. She had learned her English at high school and, later, at the University of Hong Kong. While she could understand and speak it, she was not yet fluent in it. For her, the initial

Lift-Off

major adjustment was to a different lifestyle. In Hong Kong, she drove a Jaguar, and the Ka Wah Bank had provided David with a chauffeur-driven Mercedes Benz. Now they had a small, second-hand Datsun. In Hong Kong, they had four servants. Now they had none, and only after David made a couple of sales could they afford a part-time gardener to help once a week.

Dorothy never lamented the loss of servants. She took over the chores of the household without complaint and had the children help her so they would get used to the idea as well. She had always liked to drive and was quick to adjust to driving on the right side of the road. She was soon able to spot an empty parking space as quickly as any native Vancouverite. She even became a volunteer driver with the Meals on Wheels program, providing hot meals for elderly people. Later, when David's investors and their wives came to Vancouver for meetings, Dorothy would take the wives on a tour of the city and act as their interpreter when they went shopping.

When they lived in Hong Kong, David and Dorothy sometimes flew to Japan, Taiwan or elsewhere on vacation, leaving the children at home in care of their *amah*. In Canada, there was no money available for them to travel in the summer of 1967. Early in 1968, David was told that when the children went back to school in the autumn, they would be asked by their friends where they went on their vacation. If they said they stayed at home, it would be a bad reflection on the family. This observation had an element of truth in it, enough for David to consider what he might do to take the family on vacation in the least expensive way. He could not afford to spend money for hotels, meals and air travel for a family of five. The answer was to buy a trailer. Staying overnight in a trailer park would cost only three or four dollars, and usually the parks were within a short distance of lovely vacation spots.

One day, on a drive south to Bellingham, they spotted a second-hand trailer which was being offered at a good price. David bought it. It was small—only seventeen feet long—but to David it looked huge. He had never driven a car with a trailer and wondered whether he could manoeuvre it. The salesman gave him a five-minute lesson, showing him how to put his hands on the wheel at the twelve o'clock position, then at the three o'clock position to turn the trailer one way, and at the nine o'clock position to turn another. The first time he had to back up in a restricted area was in Portland, Oregon. David remembers, "It was at noon, the sun was shining, and there were thirty or forty office workers sitting about munching their sandwiches. They looked at me and almost shook their heads. My wife said, 'There's no way you can get in.' I said, 'I've just got to try this twelve o'clock, three o'clock thing.' Then, with everyone watching, I made just one reverse drive, brought the trailer and car perfectly into the curb, turned the key off and walked out. Everyone clapped. They were betting I couldn't do it."

During most of the 1970s, travelling with the trailer became the family's way of going on a vacation. As David's income increased, he bought a larger trailer and then a Winnebago motorhome. Being able to take the family to a place like the Okanagan, park the trailer beside a lake and spend the weekend swimming was one of the things he liked about Canada. To those born in British Columbia, it was a natural thing to do. For someone accustomed to the restricted confines of Hong Kong, it was an overwhelming experience.

It took little encouragement for Deborah, Daphne and Doreen to blend into the Canadian scene. Learning English was a necessary first step, of course, and the language was all around them—at school, in the church, at play with the neighbourhood friends. Singing familiar Baptist hymns in church in English helped, and joining the church's Pioneer Girls widened their circle of English-speaking friends. Had the Lams lived in Chinatown, the girls' progress towards bilingualism would doubtless have been slower. At the same time, David and Dorothy did not want them to forget their Chinese culture. They spoke Cantonese at home. When David's father and mother came to visit them, the three girls were able to talk to them easily in Cantonese. Some years later, when they visited Hong Kong, they could use either language with ease.

None of them were ever subjected to racist remarks and there were no doors closed to them because of their Chinese origin. Decades earlier there had been anti-Oriental riots in the city, and it was only after the Second World War that Chinese-Canadians obtained the right to vote and the right to study at the university for any profession they wished to enter. By the late 1960s, however, Vancouver had experienced great change. It provided an atmosphere of tolerance in which the Lam family could thrive—and thrive they did.

In the early 1970s, there was probably more studying going on in the Lam household than in any other in the neighbourhood. The three girls spent an hour or more each evening on their homework. David went to the university several evenings a week for his courses in real estate and spent his "free" evenings studying at home. He had an advantage, in a way, in that he was learning the theory of the real estate business while at the same time being involved in it.

He continued to attract clients from Hong Kong, and the number of his "Sunny" companies multiplied. Not all of his properties requiring management came under the supervision of Wall and Redekop. With some, he kept the same management the premises had at the time he bought them. Using several management companies meant more supervision on his part, and he began to look for a company which could supervise all or most of the properties. He found one in McKenzie Management, having met its general manager, R. L. Richards, through a mutual acquaintance.

By this time David had decided to leave Wall and Redekop. Richards remembers David telling him that he did not want to stay with the large company. "He wanted to be with a smaller group and he made it quite plain his objective eventually was to go out on his own," says Richards. "He said that his research satisfied him that we had a good reputation. We would be a good place for him to be while he considered whether we had a long-term relationship or whether he, in fact, set up on his own."

After several meetings, the two men agreed that David should move to the new firm. The deal arranged was fairly typical for a senior salesperson. He was not an employee and therefore had no salary. That was agreeable to David who felt that if he was paid a salary, it was his duty to work solely for whomever was paying him. Nor was he a partner since he invested no money in the firm. As vice-president of McKenzie Management, an acceptable title for the type of client he was dealing with, he was an officer of the company but not a shareholder. "With hindsight," Richards admits, "we should have asked him to become a shareholder right early."

McKenzie Management, of course, was interested in providing the services for any of the properties David and his clients bought. Typical properties were apartment buildings with thirty to seventy-five suites, or neighbourhood malls with a Safeway and twenty or thirty smaller stores. David did a lot of looking for commercial properties, often unlisted ones for which he produced purchasers to make offers. "He became known as a purchaser," remembers Richards, "maybe not for his own account, but as one in contact with people with money. These owners and other salespeople tended to seek him out and say, 'I know that so-and-so can be bought. Do you have a purchaser?' And then, after being a buyer's representative for a long time, he too became a seller's representative because some of his clients didn't keep the real estate forever. He was in a position then, when he wanted to sell, that maybe he would have a formal listing, or maybe just a suggestion from the owners, that they would like to get rid of their properties. So he did some very successful agency work both sides."

David was allocated two small offices, one for himself and one for his secretary. He paid no rent, partly because any sales he might make with a listing put out by the firm would mean splitting the commission with it, and partly because he had placed a number of his properties under its control for maintenance. When he was involved in a private deal, however, he did not have to share any of the commission with the firm.

It was while he was associated with McKenzie Management that he and Bob Lee arranged to buy two major Vancouver buildings, which gave them both a handsome commission. The deal started with a chance meeting with Geoffrey Lau. Lau was born in southern China, moved to Hong Kong in the 1950s, and then went to study architecture at the University of Melbourne. After he graduated, he worked in Australia and Hong Kong and later moved to Malaysia to work in the family business. His uncle, Datuk G. P. Lau, had built a large commercial empire in the postwar period. During the 1970s, however, China's support of Communist activities in Southeast Asia convinced the Lau family that it would be prudent to invest funds overseas. Since

Geoffrey Lau was well educated, spoke English and had professional experience as an architect, it was agreed he should go to Vancouver.

He arrived early in 1974 with a letter of introduction to the Chinatown branch of the Royal Bank of Canada. The bank's assistant manager, Bill Ma, invited David and Bob Lee to meet Lau at a Chinese luncheon, and it came out that Geoffrey's family also came from the Swatow area. When David learned that Geoffrey was looking for employment in an architectural firm, he decided to do what he could to help him. Through his old friend Stanley Kwok, who was now a practising architect in Vancouver, he helped find Geoffrey a position with Romses, Kwan Architects, where he spent his first year in Canada.

David and Geoffrey met periodically in the following months. During this time, David also met Lau's elder brother, C. K. Lau, who made frequent visits to Vancouver. He and David got along very well together, and as they became more familiar with each other's interests and background, they found there was potential for matchmaking. One such opportunity arose when Geoffrey heard through contacts in the architectural office that the Board of Trade and Baxter buildings in downtown Vancouver were for sale. C. K. and he concluded that they represented a good investment opportunity and decided to ask David to assist in negotiating the purchase.

David was delighted to take up the challenge and quickly called in Bob Lee to share the task with him. David would handle the offer from the Vancouver end while Lee would negotiate with the owners in Toronto whom he happened to know. Working for Lee at this time was a young man named Andrew Grant, who had recently graduated from UBC with a Bachelor of Commerce degree in urban land economics. He did a lot of work directly for Lee, gathering information on properties and acting in a fashion comparable to an articling student in a law firm.

The preparations involved in the purchase of two buildings of this nature took a lot of time. Both buildings produced revenue from leased office space, and this revenue had to exceed the expenses of maintaining the building and pay a reasonable return on the initial capital investment. There were taxes to consider, along with factors such as the costs of heat, light, water, security, cleaning, painting and decorating, fire protection, repair and maintenance work. There were also the tenants to think of: How long were their leases and what were they paying per square foot? How did their rates compare with other buildings in the area? What were the parking charges? What was the quality of the construction of the building, and when was major upgrading anticipated? These and many other questions had to be answered before a serious offer could be given. Payment would be made in cash once the deal was struck, giving the contract fewer clauses than normal.

David and Bob Lee worked for months, examining the information Grant dug up for them and using their combined experience to find more. By 1975 they had made an offer, assuring the owners that the principals they represented were serious about the offer and had the hard cash available. Nevertheless, the negotiations began to falter. Someone else approached the owners with a much higher price saying he had a buyer, and was able to obtain a month's option on the buildings. Actually, the rival agent intended to sell them to Geoffrey Lau at an inflated price. Bob Lee found out about this in Toronto, however, and through his and David's efforts, Geoffrey Lau and his family were finally able to buy the two buildings at a fair price.

The sale attracted considerable attention in real estate circles as it was one of the largest Canadian deals outside Toronto. The price of the two buildings was around the $20 million mark, one of the largest purchases of its type to have originated in the Far East. David and Bob Lee's commission was handsome. Since they had saved the buyers a considerable amount of money, C. K. Lau invited them and the buildings' former owner to visit Southeast Asia.

David's recollection of the three-week trip gives a vivid idea of Lau's generosity and appreciation. Arriving in Tokyo after the long flight, the group was informed that Datuk G. P. Lau, Geoffrey's uncle, was waiting for them. The airline hostess led them to a waiting room where G. P. Lau was standing with a group of high officials from the Japanese trading house Nissho Iwai. As David describes the scene, "They were all standing there with interpreters bowing. We didn't know what was happening. G. P. Lau said, 'These are my friends in Japan. They want to take and show you around.' We had jet lag and actually I was very tired, but he persuaded us. So we got into the limousine. Each of us had a limousine with the host talking on the way. They took us to a hotel. At the hotel, I said, 'Thank you, good night.' Lau said, 'No, we have arranged for you to go to dinner.' I said, 'We already had dinner on board.' He said, 'No, no, you must come.' "

The group went to a sumptuous and expensive dinner party where each guest was attended by a geisha. Comments David, "The geisha girl is never what people imagine she is. She is not a prostitute, she is a professional entertainer. They would pour drinks and put food in your mouth, but nothing hanky-panky."

After that, David was dead tired but the party moved on to a nightclub. "Cabaret girls kept coming and going to our table," he remembers. "When they sat down, they would pass around a plate of almond or rice cookies, or they would pour tea or a drink. Then they would make a little excuse and move away. I asked, 'Why are they coming and going?' and G. P. Lau replied, "Every time they come they charge $100.' I said, 'You must be kidding!' "

The next day, the group flew to Hong Kong, accompanied by G. P. Lau. David was surprised to find that Lau had come to Japan expressly to meet and welcome them, with no other business to attend to. It was, he reflects, "a very Chinese tradition of respect."

In Hong Kong, David, who knew the business community very well, was able to return some of the hospitality by introducing the Laus to some of the leading figures in the city. The party went on to Borneo where, at his main base near Kota Kinabalu, G. P. Lau had arranged receptions, more entertainment and tours of the family's plantations and timber concessions. From there, the party went to Singapore and Kuala Lumpur. David had business associates in both places who showed the group the local sites and wined and dined them in regal fashion.

All in all, it was a trip none of them would ever forget. There would be other business affairs with Geoffrey Lau later, but this first one was the largest and affected the careers of both men.

With the commission he received from the sale of the two buildings, David was now able to achieve his ambition. He was going to strike out on his own.

He had been with McKenzie Management for only a short time when he began to feel that he should make a move. McKenzie was a good company with an excellent record, but it wasn't set up to serve his target market with the highly personalized service he wanted to give his clients. A further consideration was his position as a real estate salesman. For tax reasons, his "take-home pay" from a $10,000 commission was far less than that from a $10,000 capital gain made through one of his "Sunny" companies.

There was also the question of getting the very best deal for his clients. If he was representing a client on the purchase of a commercial property listed with another firm, the listing salesman would anticipate having to share the commission with David. Faced with sharing a commission on the one hand, or hoping a client would turn up so he could make the full commission, the salesman would naturally put David's offer on hold until an option was about to expire.

In David's words, "I was preventing myself from getting the best deals. When I cannot get the best deal, my reputation suffers because my clients look to me not as just any salesman, but as someone who could find a deal for them." He decided, therefore, that in any sale of this nature, he would no longer expect to share a commission and would ask sellers to treat him as a client, or at least an agent working for clients. Realizing the impact this would have on McKenzie Management, he had early on informed the firm that for his own peace of mind he wanted to pay rent for his office as well as the salary of his secretary. It gave him a feeling of greater independence and eliminated a sense of obligation he felt for not providing these split commissions. But now it was time to move on.

One more factor influenced his decision to strike out on his own. In the six years that had passed since he formed his first "Sunny" company, he had attracted so many groups of clients wishing to invest in Canada that he had run out of "Sunny" names to incorporate. Maintaining a close watch on about two dozen companies while at the same time seeking further opportunities was becoming a strain. He

Previous page: David, in full uniform, with Dorothy at Government House.
PHOTO: JEFF BARBER

Top left: Summer vacation: trailer camping in a British Columbia park ground in 1969.

Top right: Government House in Victoria, the Lams' official residence while David served as lieutenant-governor from 1988 to 1995. PHOTO: J. MICHAEL ROBERTS

Right: The Lams in their New Territories house in Hong Kong around 1963, with Lion's Rock Mountain in the background. The mountain is now covered in highrises.

Above: The Lams in their first Canadian home, a bungalow in Vancouver's South Cambie area, with daughters Debbie, Daphne and Doreen.

Above: The popping of flashbulbs accompanies David's entry into public life. With Chief Justice Alan McEachern at the swearing-in ceremony.
PHOTO: NOW NEWSPAPERS

Top right: Arrival by Canadian Forces helicopter during the vice-regal visit to B.C. coastal communities in 1989. Left to right: J. Michael Roberts, secretary to the lieutenant-governor; David and Dorothy Lam; Lieutenant-Commander Charles J. Hierons, honorary aide-de-camp. PHOTO: J. MICHAEL ROBERTS

Bottom right: Official duties: ribbon cutting at the 1994 opening of Valleyview Elementary School in Courtenay, B.C.

The Queen, David and Dorothy Lam at the opening of the flower garden at Government House. PHOTOS: RAYMOND K.K. CHAN, MING PAO

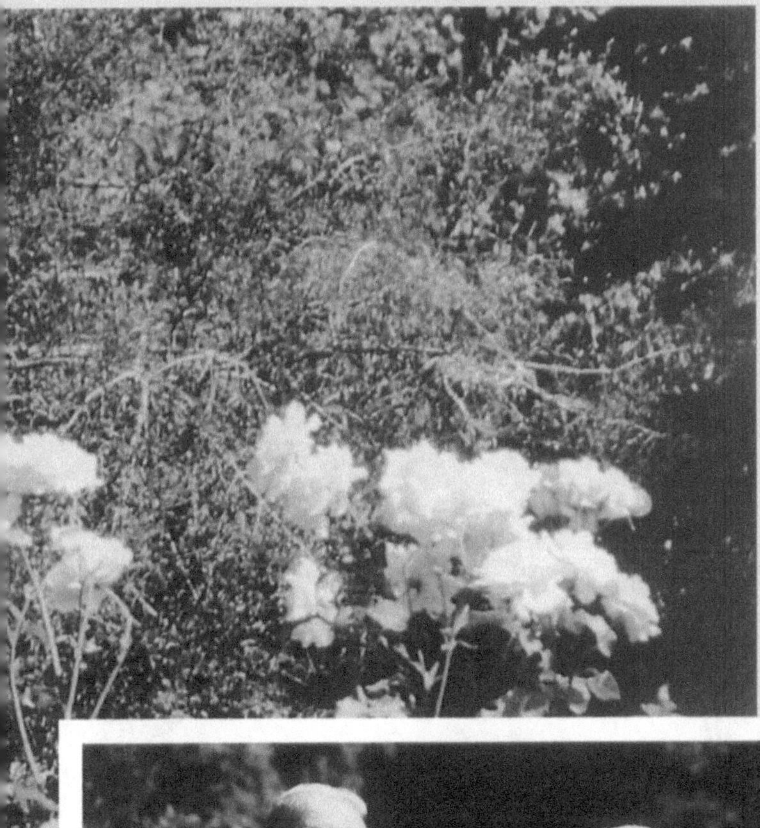
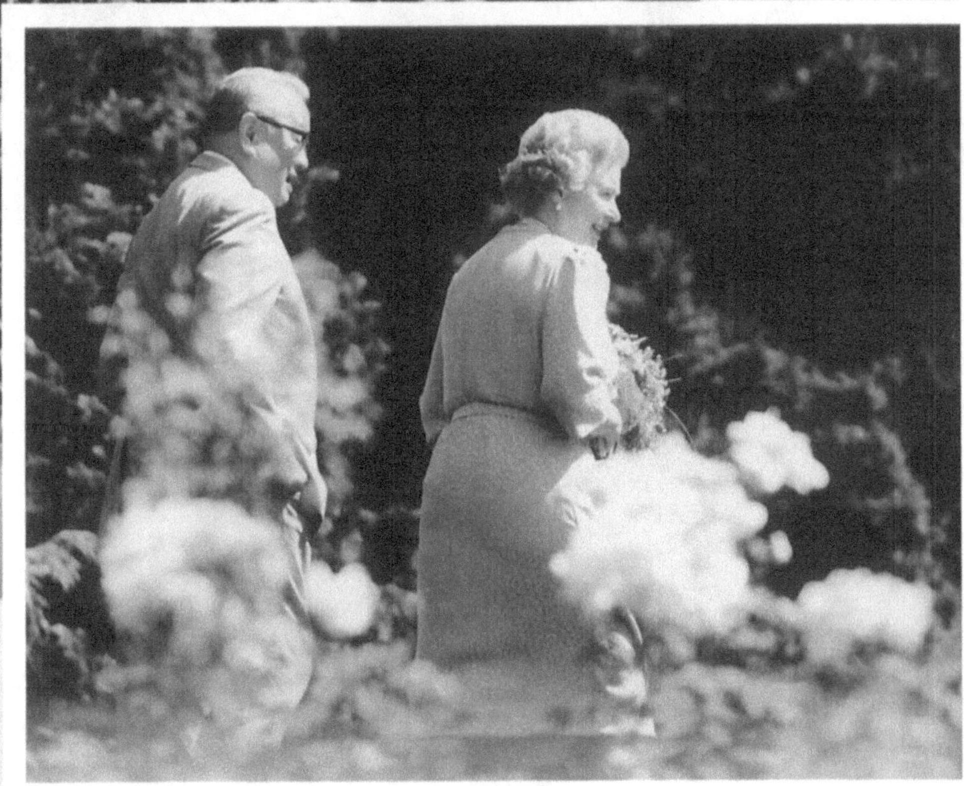

Above: David Lam in the Victorian Rose Garden at Government House. PHOTO: BETTY WRIGHT

Right: Three generations of the Lam family celebrate together in Vancouver. PHOTO: PHILIP LAU

needed help and found the man he wanted in Andrew Grant, the young man who had been working for Bob Lee at Wall and Redekop.

Grant had been working at Wall and Redekop for almost a year. One of his major tasks had been acting as Lee's assistant on the sale of the Baxter and Board of Trade buildings. David had found him a conscientious and hard-working young man, and told him that if he left Wall and Redekop he should let David know. Grant informed him that he had already served his notice as he wanted to widen his experience. Not wanting to appear to be luring someone from his friend, David suggested Grant should see Lee first and find out if he wished to employ him privately. Grant made the enquiry, but Lee, who was to remain with Wall and Redekop for another two years, had no objection to his transfer.

When Grant reported back that he was free to join the new venture, David realized that another serious change was in order: "We had no place for him to sit down so I got a chair and he sat next to the typist. I said, 'Andrew, we have just got to leave this place. It's too cramped. I have about two hundred square feet in the office for the three of us. Let's go and find an office.'"

Shortly after, David went to see an architect friend named William Tong and asked him to come with Grant, himself and his secretary to look for an office. The four of them visited several different buildings. After they had looked at the available space, David then asked each one to state his or her preference. The result was unanimous: the IBM Tower in Pacific Centre. Located in the heart of downtown Vancouver next to the Four Seasons Hotel, it was close to everything, including the major hotels where David's clients would be staying when they came to visit.

By this time, David had already incorporated his new company, which he called Canadian International Properties. When the vice-president in charge of allocating space in the IBM Tower examined David's card, he thought at first he was dealing with a major company which would rent the entire twelfth floor. David brought him down to reality with a request for a corner office with a total of five hundred square feet. Somewhat shaken, the vice-president readjusted his thinking but pointed out that a corner office of that size did not allow easy access to the corridor. David settled for larger space and better access, at ten dollars per square foot. Although the normal contract was for five years, David opted for the long-term lease of ten years.

It was a risk, but he was an optimist. With the commission from the sale to the Lau family, he felt he could afford the costs of his own office and small staff. For the first time, he would be completely on his own, but as he put it, he was determined to "do or die." It was a far cry from his first venture as a young teenager in Hong Kong, selling flowers from the garden he created in the family's yard, but the same entrepreneurial spirit still shone brightly. His confidence that with God's help he would succeed never wavered.

He moved into the new office at the end of 1975. He remembers, "After a month or so, Andrew Grant came to me and said, 'David, I have had the opportunity to go through all your companies and all the interlocking and intertwining relationships, your bank loans and your loans from the various people. I appreciate your hiring me to be your assistant but, honestly, what do we do for money?' I said, 'That's not my department. That's your department.' He couldn't believe his ears. I said, 'Andrew, I was joking. I was just telling you that I have faith and confidence that if I keep providing sterling quality service and trustworthiness, we cannot fail. I cannot afford to make one wrong deal. I cannot afford to take anyone for one dollar. I will fly because people will seek me out, and we will grow. I will struggle to pay the rent and keep you and the secretary.' "

David was well aware that the maintenance of an office and staff would be a drain on his income. There had been no overhead while he was working for the other firms. Now, aside from rent, there were telephone bills, office supplies and many other expenses. With two dozen companies to look after, he needed an accountant on staff and also a receptionist. With this added burden of salaries to pay, David decided he had to have additional income. It would be best if the income was steady and reliable, rather than money which came in an erratic manner like commissions. The best way to achieve this, he felt, was to go into property management.

During his time with Wall and Redekop, and even more so with McKenzie Management, David had learned a good deal about the management of properties. If the property was small, it could be a simple affair; if it was large, it could be complicated and might start at the construction stage. David's colleague at McKenzie Management, R. L. Richards, describes what was involved with a large office building that was handed over to the firm following construction: "We staffed the building. We put in the building engineer and the assistants. We hired the janitors. We negotiated the maintenance contracts or trained people to do maintenance in the building. We operate that building 365 days a year, 24 hours a day.

"That's just the physical maintenance of the building," he adds. "Then you have to see that the tenants perform according to their covenants. You have to collect the rent. You have to bill the extra rent. You have to do the accounting . . ."

Firms that provide maintenance receive an income for their service over and above the actual cost of maintenance itself. The payment of these services is usually made periodically throughout the year, providing a steady source of revenue which is not affected too much by the ups and downs of the real estate market. If the management venture is to be profitable, however, there must be a sufficient number of properties available to manage. Quite a few of the "Sunny" properties required management, and David gradually put these under his own control when their contracts came up for renewal. Moreover, his clients in Hong Kong, Taiwan, Singapore and elsewhere continued to trust his judgement, and each year he added two or three more companies to his portfolio.

Until David was able to hire some property managers, however, it was Andrew Grant who looked after that side of the business. As he remembers that period, "It was not a fun side of the business. It's the collection of rent, fixing the roof, leasing of the space—those kind of things."

Still, working with David was an education in itself. Grant admired the way his employer conducted business and his ability to make friends, but soon realized that David also had the vision to see the potential of a property and the patience to follow the detailed work involved in turning it to more profitable use. The business he was generating in Hong Kong was not something that was just falling into his lap. Although David was fortunate to get into the real estate business at a time when overseas clients were becoming interested in Canada, they were investing in many places as well as in British Columbia. It was David's business acumen, integrity and the force of his personality that led him to become a trusted conduit for their investments.

"He was the true matchmaker," Grant reflects. "That means there is an interest on the part of the buyer. But just like any buyer, the buyer has to be convinced. Let's say there is a building that may have some good and bad features. What you have to do as a matchmaker is recognize what the good points are, be able to deal with the negative ones and put that combination together with somebody who wants to buy it. In many cases, one of those buyers was David. He was an investor in the deal too. He made much of his money as a principal, not as an agent."

In the seven years since David had started at Newcombe Realty, his income had increased from zero to a healthy six figures. With this had come certain changes in his lifestyle. His first car in Vancouver was a second-hand Datsun. As clients began to come from overseas, he traded in the Datsun for an Oldsmobile Delta 88. When he made some more money, he bought a Mercedes 450 SLC sports coupe for himself as a runabout and a Mercedes 450 SEL to drive potential clients or partners in his companies around the city. The latter was not strictly necessary, but it projected a certain image.

David often took his clients to his home for dinner, and at one point he considered moving from Ash Street. One house he particularly liked was in the UBC Endowment Lands looking across English Bay at the North Shore mountains. "It had three and a half acres and a huge garden," he remembers, "so I was kind of keen on that particular one. I tried to talk Dorothy into taking it. Dorothy, being a very practical housewife, felt it would cost a fortune to hire someone to look after the garden. Also, she would have to make some changes because the house was designed for entertainment. The living room and dining room were very large, but the bedrooms were very small. It was almost like a clubhouse. Her values were not on entertainment and socializing, so she said no. I said yes. She said no. Naturally, it was no."

Having a luxurious car and a lovely office was one thing, moving into a huge house was another. David had at first thought that a luxurious home would provide the right ambience for potential clients to meet and work on million dollar deals. On reflection, he considered it might be unnecessary. "If I have all this glitter and gold trimmings," he asked himself, "will they give me a million dollars each? No. They will still have to go through their grapevine to check. I have to have a totally unblemished record because even if I am a little bit suspect, people will take no chances. They will go somewhere else. I cannot afford to make one small mistake, because the gossip grapevine, the rumours, the checking behind the scenes always go on. When the word comes back that 'this guy is 100 per cent,' they will sign the cheque right away. That record and the reputation is far more important than a large house with a view."

During the years when David's income began to increase, Dorothy's way of life changed very little. When they had first settled into their house on Ash Street, she managed her budget of three or four hundred dollars a month like any other frugal housewife. As things got better, she was able to enjoy some of the small luxuries which were noticeable by their absence during their first two years in Canada. She could now afford to send the girls to take piano and tennis lessons. She never had a taste for expensive clothes, but it was nice to be able to buy a new dress without calculating its impact on the budget. She loved to drive a car and enjoyed driving the new Mercedes rather than the old Datsun. Earning more money also allowed the Lams to give more, not only to the church, which remained a very important part of their life, but to a variety of other institutions they felt should be supported.

As David's real estate deals began to involve more and more money, Dorothy never became apprehensive about the amounts involved or the possibility of failure. She had complete confidence in his ability and rarely saw him unsure or uncertain. "David seldom worried, even over a weekend when millions of dollars had not come over from Hong Kong to confirm a deal," she recalls. "He would say, 'We'll just go to bed. There's nothing we can do, and remember, people who worry cannot go to sleep.' He wasn't the worrying type, so maybe that influenced me."

In all probability, Dorothy had as much influence on David as he had on her. She never complained about the innumerable evenings he was away from home while he was studying at UBC, nor did she ever suggest during those first hard years in Vancouver that they should return to Hong Kong and resume the comfortable life they had left. She was quite sincere in her offer to go to work herself and contribute to the family income, had things not improved. Even when David's finances surged upward at a dramatic rate, Dorothy kept both feet firmly planted on the ground. Theirs was a happy and harmonious marriage. From the beginning, David found her a "gung-ho sort of girl," willing to travel anywhere he wanted to go and sharing his zest for new adventures. She was always supportive of his plans to widen his business ventures. Best of all, they enjoyed each other's company and shared a strong Christian outlook on life. It is little wonder that they made friends easily.

EIGHT

In Full Flight

If the first half of the 1970s had been good for David, the second half was to be even better. The real estate business continued to flourish, and the lower mainland of British Columbia maintained its attraction for investors from Hong Kong, Singapore, Taiwan and elsewhere. There was investment money coming in from Europe as well. The rate of inflation was rising, and this led to increased speculation in the market. Immigration to Canada was continuing at a steady rate and British Columbia benefited not only from immigrants from Asia but from other parts of Canada as well.

David had long passed the period when he was interested in selling houses. He had sold only five or six during his entire career, and that was during the time he was with Newcombe Realty. His interests were in commercial and revenue-generating properties, and he continued with them until he retired. Although he gave little thought to moving outside real estate, he was once approached to invest in an Alberta oil exploration venture at a time when world oil prices had shot sky-high. He gave it considerable thought but decided against it. Reflecting on his decision to remain in real estate, he says, "We learn that one must diversify, but we have seen a lot of people get into big trouble because they know only the word 'diversify.' They really don't know what they are diversifying into, so it's just a poke in the dark, and it got a lot of people into trouble. If I diversify, I've got to diversify into something that I have a feel about. I have a feel about real estate."

With almost all his assets in real estate and his business dependent on it, David was constantly thinking about liquidity and not overinvesting. In his courses at UBC on real estate, "location, location, location" was always stressed as the key to success in the business. There is no doubt that location of a property is a most important factor. But David would add "timing, timing, timing."

"Inflation," he says now, "was the greatest saviour of dumb investors." David was very conscious of the impact that inflation or deflation could have on the market. Some businessmen in Hong Kong, where the economy was booming, invested heavily in the Vancouver market and were badly burned when growth rates turned out to be lower than they expected. David did his best to look ahead, balance risk with caution, and would generally enter into a deal only after a very thorough investigation of the property involved.

There were times, however, when he had to act quickly and on instinct. A good example of that occurred in Calgary in 1972. Jack Poole, a friend of Bob Lee, had his eye on a large building site there. He had plans to develop it, but he needed financial assistance. There were others interested in the property and he had to act quickly. Poole phoned Lee to see if he would come in with him on the deal. Lee telephoned David who was interested, and both flew to Calgary immediately. They drove to the site where Poole met them and told them, "You have to make a decision before twelve o'clock." There was a possibility another buyer would offer a larger price that afternoon, but having made the initial approach to Lee, Poole felt an obligation to offer him the first choice. Both David and Lee were aware of the price per square foot of commercial property in Calgary, and after examining the site, they made an immediate decision to participate in the deal. The decision was made within hours of landing in the city, and it turned out to be a very profitable one.

David found a particular pleasure in making a good deal. Such transactions, he says, are "more for joy, for happiness, not as much for money. Money is keeping the score. It's just like golfing. You play golf, you look at your ball, you look at the situation, you know the challenge facing this coming stroke, and then you decide which club to use. Now, all the feasibility studies and appraisals in the world are not going to help you until and unless you decide which of the dozen clubs you are going to use. You must decide. You have to pick up the right club."

During the 1970s, David's ability to "pick up the right club" continued unabated. His trips to Hong Kong became more frequent and his circle of friends and clients widened. Despite his obvious success, the Lam family business never approached him to become a partner in one of his companies or take a share in one of his ventures. An exception was his brother-in-law Herbert Cheng, who had married his youngest sister Alice. Herbert was the son of Y. C. Cheng with whom David was associated in the 1950s in the shipwrecking business. Like David, Herbert was educated partly in the United States. The Cheng family was well-to-do and Herbert joined David in several ventures, one of which was a company called Honada. At the time it was formed, David had run out of "Sunny" names. When a Hong Kong friend suggested Honada, a combination of Hong Kong and Canada, David accepted it. The company started with capital of $500,000, with David receiving a loan of $50,000 from his partners so he could have a 10 per cent share. When wound up, Honada's capital had grown to about US$14 million after successful deals both in Canada and the United States.

David's first venture into American real estate was a personal affair. During his travels, he became aware of a development in Sudden Valley, just across the border from Vancouver in the state of Washington near Bellingham. Adjoining the development was a lovely golf course, and Lake Whatcom was nearby for sailing and swimming. David bought one of the lots and decided to build a house there. It would serve as a retreat from his active business life in Vancouver and was close enough for him to drive there in a couple of hours.

His next purchase of property in the United States was in San Francisco. David liked the city from the time he first visited it as a student en route to Temple University. He had friends and Dorothy had some cousins living there, but there was a more pressing reason which led David to look to the city for real estate investment. In 1972, the

New Democratic Party had won the provincial elections in British Columbia. This represented a tremendous political change in the province. For twenty years the Social Credit Party under W. A. C. Bennett had dominated the political scene. Despite its name, the party was conservative in its outlook and capitalist in philosophy. The new premier, David Barrett, and his party were at the opposite end of the political spectrum. Among other things, their socialist view of government meant placing greater controls on business.

David remembers the coming of the new party scared away a lot of Hong Kong money, particularly when it introduced rent controls. He explains, "It was controlling income without controlling the expenses. So with the increase of expenditure, before you knew it, the expenses are going to catch up and overcome the income to the point where the property will have a negative income. My clients' investment will completely evaporate when the property becomes zero value. So this is the time when my clients walk away from ownership. They would rather go to some other places, and those places are totally up to me."

San Francisco seemed a logical place to go. As it happened, he had signed up for a seminar on real estate there and took Dorothy along. As they looked around the city, he began to think that he should spend time there and really get to know it. The only way to do that, he decided, was to buy a little condo and start living like a San Franciscan. "I said to myself, I must take the attitude always that every condo, every apartment, is for sale. They're not, of course. Just assume that they are for sale and if they were, which one do you like?"

After driving around the whole city, they decided to try the Nob Hill area, which was close to Chinatown and to the downtown area. David recalls, "I would walk up to the doorman of a building and say, 'I'm looking to buy a unit. Do you have any available?' He might say, 'No. This is a rental building. There's nothing for sale here.' I would say, 'Do you know of any around here that's for sale?' He might say, 'Oh, you should go down to this one or that one. Those are condos. This one is not.' So I would slip him a few dollars. I started working like that as if every one is available. Finally I found one. It fit my bill just perfectly so I bought it. It was a one-bedroom condo with a most beautiful view. I sent my interior decorator from Seattle down there to fix it up, bought a car and kept the car there, and I started to live like a local."

When David's associate, Andrew Grant, came down to visit, he found him established in a classic San Francisco building, one of the first high-rises on Nob Hill. Located on the eleventh floor, with a sweeping view of the city, the apartment was the perfect base of operation for Canadian International Properties. Instead of dashing in and out of hotels, David could talk to prospective clients in an atmosphere which was both homey and stylish. The interior decorator had done a magnificent job with everything from the colour scheme to the furniture. Having performed the same task for the Lams' retreat in Sudden Valley, he knew their tastes, and David was to employ him on other occasions for similar jobs.

Since he was spending more time away from Vancouver and his daughters were old enough to look after themselves, David sold his house on Ash Street. He no longer had time to look after his garden, and rather than leave the house empty while he and Dorothy were away, he decided to become a renter.

Around this time builder-developer Frank Stanzl began to build a twenty-four-storey rental apartment at the end of Comox Street, on the border of Stanley Park. Bob Lee was interested in the building and had tried to buy it without any luck. Later, when it was completed, Lee mentioned it to David who liked the location and felt his Sunnyvale Development company would be interested. They made another approach to Stanzl, who agreed to sell half of the building. When David's partners in Sunnyvale came from Hong Kong, Singapore, Kuala Lumpur and elsewhere to see the property, they said they much preferred to buy an entire building rather than part of one. Nevertheless, David convinced them it was a very good deal and they bought half.

When David and Dorothy left Ash Street, they moved into the top floor of the Comox Street building. It had a magnificent view over the park, the harbour and a good part of the city. Sundecks on both sides provided space where he could tend flowers and vegetables in window boxes and other containers. Later he also rented the floor beneath him, and in time the whole building would come under his sole ownership. That, however, was some years down the road. In the meantime, David's attention was drawn to the American market.

Going to San Francisco was one of the best decisions David ever made. He started there in the same way he had in Vancouver, with two goals: to become better acquainted with the city itself and to make more contacts. He immediately began to attend weekly meetings at the Rotary Club, and went out of his way to talk to the members who represented a cross-section of San Francisco's business community. Finding that rental prices in the city were considerably less than in Vancouver, David speculated that costs would likely increase. The decision of the Arab states to place an embargo on oil exports in 1972 had increased fuel prices almost four times. This had hurt many building owners whose rents had been fixed, sometimes for years, on the basis of low fuel costs to heat their buildings. David scanned the real estate pages of the local newspapers and visited local firms involved in the market.

One of these visits was to a chartered accountant who, knowing David's interest in real estate, mentioned he had just received a sales presentation and gave it to him. When David went over to view the property, it was a case of love at first sight. The Insurance Exchange Building, located at 433 California Street, was twelve storeys high with classical Roman pillars on the facade. The location on one of the city's main streets was good, and the view from the upper floors lovely. The building itself needed some renovations, however. The elevators worked but were slow and creaky. The foyer needed a facelift, and many of the washrooms were overdue for renovation. Nevertheless, the building was sound; it had character, good location and, David thought, considerable potential. More important, he felt it was underpriced.

The asking price was $4.3 million. There was a mortgage of about $3 million, so by assuming the mortgage, David could get it for $1.3 million in cash. He did not have that much so he thought of bringing in three partners, each putting up $300,000 with himself putting in the remainder. He immediately began to telephone prospective clients, and though initially he thought he had the money, at the last moment one of his clients backed out. This caused a delay, and in that period an American named Ernie Meiger stepped in to buy the building. David was disappointed, but he was not one to bear a grudge or be pessimistic. Instead he went to see the new owner and congratulate him.

He asked Meiger, "What is your intention? Do you intend to keep it, hold it, speculate to sell, to flip it?" Meiger replied that he and a group had bought it for tax purposes. They intended to put in some money right away, lease it out at better rates and then sell it. "When you want to sell it," David said, "let me know." Meanwhile, David tried to socialize with him. "I took him to Chinese meals," he remembers, "and he took me to his golf club, so it was good."

During the remainder of the year and on into 1977, David divided his time between Vancouver, San Francisco and other parts of the United States. Some nine months after he had lost his bid to buy the California Street property, he had a call from Meiger. He and his group now wanted to sell and were offering David first choice. Meiger said he wanted to make a million dollars on the deal, so the price would be about $5.4 million. David wasn't too surprised since he knew a lot of money had been spent fixing up the building, and didn't dispute the price. Instead, he suggested that the profit Meiger wanted to make would be acceptable if he would agree to take it in the form of a loan, payable at 7 per cent over a seven-year period. "Why all these sevens?" the seller asked. "Because I'm Chinese. I like sevens," David replied. (During the first half of the 1970s, Canada's inflation rate was 7 per cent, and this may have affected David's decision. By 1981, Canada's inflation rate had reached 12.5 per cent.) Meiger agreed, but that still left David with the problem of raising the money to fill the gap between the seller's profit and the $3 million mortgage on the building. This represented a sum of about $1 million.

David at first intended to seek out some clients who would be interested in forming a company to raise the money. At this point, however, Dorothy entered the picture. David valued her advice and always discussed matters with her. "When are we going to have a building we can call our own?" she asked him. "Maybe starting with this one," he replied.

The more he considered the idea, the more he liked it. It would mean borrowing money from the bank, but he had done that for years. The previous loans had all been for ventures in which several wealthy overseas clients had been involved and the bank, appreciating their financial resources if a deal went sour, had never turned down his request. The loans had always been paid in full and on time. David assumed there would be no problem with financing this time, and sent his assistant, Andrew Grant, to check on the building and the final details of its purchase.

As Grant remembers that trip to San Francisco, "It is a sophisticated city and hence we had fancy lawyers, estoppel certificates and all sorts of things that both David and I had never heard of. But you could never admit that to the other side so we became experts in this very quickly. I conducted the due diligence period, read the leases and verified the income." It was a good deal, he concluded. The rents in the 120,000-square-foot building were very cheap relative to those in Vancouver.

With Grant's work completed, David went to the manager of the Royal Bank of Canada with whom he had been doing business for eight years. Since the loan was close to the million dollar mark, it had to be referred to higher authority. To the manager's chagrin, he had to report to David that the loan had not been approved despite his repeated assurances that the loan was a sound one.

A short time later David attended a reception on the thirty-sixth floor of the Royal Centre, where the bank has its Vancouver headquarters. There, he met a vice-president of the bank who said, "David, I don't know what you have been doing to my managers, but they have been coming to me for two days on their knees, kissing my ring on your behalf." David remembers replying, "You are saying your managers are kissing your ring on my behalf; that means you think I should be the one on my knees kissing your ring. I'll tell you one thing: I don't have to deal with you anymore. I've got thirty accounts with your bank, all with wealthy people in them. This is the first time I wanted a loan for myself without partners, and you are taking such a sticky approach to it, I don't have to deal with you." The vice-president started to laugh, but David said, "This is not very funny," and turned around and left.

Having been a chief bank manager himself in Hong Kong, David knew how to speak to other bankers. After that encounter, there was no more talk about "kissing of rings." David got his loan approved speedily, which allowed him to complete the deal. For the first time, his company, of which he and Dorothy were the sole proprietors, owned a building without any involvement of partners.

It was an excellent purchase—in fact, the best he had ever made during his career in real estate. Business in San Francisco was picking up, and the oil embargo was beginning to break down. Many leases in the building began to come up for renewal, and more realistic rents could be negotiated to make up for rising costs. When David bought the building, rent was $10 dollars per square foot. When he sold it, less than a decade later, the rent was $27 per square foot.

The purchase was only one of many real estate transactions in which David was involved during the next five or six years. Sometimes they involved only one of his own companies; other times, he would team up with Bob Lee, who several years earlier had left Wall and Redekop to establish his own company, the Prospero Group.

The California deal was highly illustrative of David's way of doing business. Once he had made a careful assessment of a property, he could act very decisively. When he felt he should sell, it did not matter if he was offered $250,000 or $500,000 less than the market price of the property if that was the only way he was going to sell it. The same principle held true when he wanted to buy. When Ernie Meiger first bought the building in San Francisco, David was very aware of the building's price, since he had been on the verge of buying it himself. Nine months later, when Meiger offered to sell it to him at a million dollar profit, David did not try to beat down the asking price. He had in fact cultivated a friendship with Meiger so that when he decided to sell he came to David first. That was a very important step. Accepting the price allowed David to finance the purchase according to his own terms with no protest from Meiger. That was important too. David explains, "When I want to sell, I sell regardless. When I want to buy, I buy regardless. The little difference of a half a million here or there doesn't matter." Recently, in an interview with the *Chinese-Canadian Community News* of Ottawa, he expanded on this point. "Don't go for the last dollar," he advised. "I always felt that I would rather lose a deal than lose a friend. Many of my clients are now my friends, and many of my friends are my clients. I always pay slightly more than the market and charge slightly less, so I always seemed to have waiting lists for my buildings."

David liked to travel, and since he kept a car in San Francisco, he and Dorothy frequently set out on long drives taking them from one end of California to the other. Often, they would travel in other western states as well. The sun and warmth of Arizona was far more attractive in winter than the cloudy skies and chilly weather in Vancouver. They began to spend the spring and summer in Vancouver, the autumn in San Francisco and the winter in Tucson, Arizona.

In Tucson, they bought a spacious townhouse next door to the El Dorado Golf and Country Club. It was so close that it was not unusual for them to find golf balls in their backyard or sometimes in the gutters of their roof. Once or twice, the balls shattered a pane of glass. Both he and Dorothy enjoyed the game, joined the club, and whenever they could they went there to relax and soak up the sun. Once again, they had an interior decorator make all the preparations, so that when they assumed occupancy, it was a matter of walking in with their suitcases. When they were not using it, they frequently offered it to their friends in Vancouver for several weeks at a time, just as they did with their house in Sudden Valley. David also found a number of business opportunities in Tucson over the years, including a shopping centre in which his Honada company invested.

During the late 1970s and on into the 1980s, David continued to do some lucrative business in the United States. His main base was San Francisco but some of his investments were in Seattle, Dallas and elsewhere. In fact, by the time he retired, David was to make more money in the United States than in Canada.

Although David was making a great deal of money as the equity of his real estate investments increased in the United States, he never neglected his interests in Canada. The market was rarely static, and it always seemed that one or another of the companies required attention. Sometimes, it was a matter of selling a property and moving on to another. If a company was particularly successful, its revenue might be used to buy a second or third property. All of them needed maintenance, and Canadian International Properties looked after that task with a small but efficient staff.

David also learned to delegate more authority as his holdings increased, but when necessary, he could do the detailed work as well as any member of his staff. In that respect, he may have been influenced by his long involvement with Hong Kong businessmen. Speaking about their tremendous success in the 1970s and 1980s, he comments, "I think the Hong Kong people's success can be boiled down to a great love and belief in what they are doing, so much so that they themselves will spend all their waking hours thinking about their own business. They do almost non-stop research. They go into minute details, very shocking minute details, and all the successful people I have dealt or been associated with have been invariably so concerned with detail it's not funny. You may think, 'By golly, he is so high-powered and wealthy that he probably left a lot of things to others.' Yes, but their minds have already covered everything they delegate in minute detail. The ability to delegate is supported by another characteristic: they will try to get hold of talent at all costs. By doing so, they are not abdicating their empire; they are fortifying it."

Finally, he notes that many successful people have one thing in common: "On their bedside, in the bathroom next to the toilet, in the dining room, everywhere, is a little pad of paper with a pen. They could be at home, wake up in the middle of the night with an idea, and then they will write it down. Detailed understanding of their business—that is the key."

David himself had several notebooks scattered about his home in which he could write down an idea he did not want to forget. When it came to detailed research and attempting to handle every item of business himself, however, he found a middle way between that of his Hong Kong friends and the approach he had learned as a student in the United States. He knew how to delegate responsibility. His vice-president, Andrew Grant, was surprised at the authority David gave him when Grant had first joined the firm. Although David kept an eye on the progress of a deal as it developed, at the same time he did not want to appear to be looking over Grant's shoulder at every move he made. He wanted to encourage Grant's self-confidence and gave him as much leeway as possible. Sometimes Grant made decisions which surprised David, perhaps over some point where Grant was better informed than he was. That did not annoy David, who never felt he knew everything there was to know about real estate. He sometimes quoted Confucius on these occasions: "When you are among three people, remember you can always learn from at least one of them." If Grant had a better way of doing something, David supported him fully. When Grant had done a good job, David responded immediately with his praise. If something went wrong, David would suggest they sit down, discuss the matter, analyze the decision that led to failure and learn from the mistake or setback. Since he was the boss, David would accept the blame for the error. If, on the other hand, it was a success, he believed in sharing the glory.

Aside from the buying and selling of commercial and apartment buildings, David was interested in development work as well, especially on the commercial side. In the 1960s and 1970s, increasing pressure was put on developers who wanted to build rental or condominium buildings in Vancouver. The city began to demand that a greater portion of the site be devoted to open spaces with lawns and gardens. Building codes were imposed respecting enhanced fire protection and reinforcement of buildings to sustain the shock of an earthquake. Building height limits were instituted and a certain proportion of rental units in major developments was required to be put aside for low-income families. As more and more regulations were placed on developers, costs went up to the extent that some were unwilling to involve themselves in building rental units at all.

David preferred to develop commercial properties where there was less hassle with municipal officials. Better still, he enjoyed buying a shopping centre, improving it and perhaps selling it. The decision to sell would be based in large part on his own feeling which, he admits, was "not very scientific." Once he bought a shopping mall for his clients, he made a point of visiting it periodically to walk around and talk with people. "You see which merchant is doing well," he explains, "and which one is just struggling. You get a sense of the health of that shopping centre. When I observe all this, I have to make a decision. In order to make it better, I have to get rid of below-par tenants and give the space to successful ones. I also need to find a way to renovate and make it beautiful, repave the parking lot and everything. That doesn't mean I can increase my income, because tenants have leases. But when they need more space I might buy space from some tenants and offer it to more successful tenants. Then I can cancel the existing lease and write one at the market rate, so I increased the income to justify my spending a few million dollars to upgrade the shopping centre."

That done, he would then tackle the tedious process of getting rid of the below-par tenants. If they were struggling, they would usually be willing to go. David would just buy them out, tear down their space and rebuild. Sometimes the process would involve renting several mobile huts to provide temporary accommodation. Even that required careful thought. "People don't mind going to a mobile home to buy liquor," he comments. "They're the best tenants to move out there. So suddenly there is empty space. You move some tenants in and out, tear down and build up. You are juggling, juggling. By the time everything is finished, the centre is improved."

"I bought a shopping centre for about $800,000," he recalls. "I put in $5 million for renovation and rebuilding, using money borrowed from the bank. Suddenly, you have a brand new shopping centre. One thing I knew is that the location was perfect. I knew it was going to be good. After the renovations, the income increased and we sold it for $11 million."

Deals like this were not unusual, and with two or more each year, David's income began to increase rapidly. The inflationary trend in the late 1970s and early 1980s added more value to real estate properties, and the declining value of the Canadian dollar against the American dollar gave the properties in the United States yet an additional boost to his increasing wealth.

His overseas clients were more than happy. He had established with them a reputation for success which was key to his entire business career. Their trust reached extraordinary levels. He remembers telephoning a potential client about a good property outside Vancouver, but being unable to make the client understand the name of the place where it was located. In the end, the client said, "Never mind, just go ahead and buy it."

David thoroughly enjoyed what he was doing, far more than his earlier banking career in Hong Kong. He was his own boss, and although it carried many responsibilities and called for serious decision making and risks, at least it was he who was making the decision rather than the family members. His friend Richard Chong recalls, "To him, business was fun; it was a game. It wasn't solely to make money. Money didn't really mean that much to him in those days. It was the challenge of making it, and he always looked on the optimistic side of life. If he had a loss of one or two deals, it didn't bother him that much. He just went on to the next one."

In a speech to the United Way in the late 1980s, David reflected further on the general theme of his friend's comments: "I was told by a well-known economist that the only business of business is to make a profit. I pondered on this saying and was shocked by it. What a horrible world ours will become if the only business of our business is to make money. I would say the business of business is to serve, to make a better world for everyone, and in the process, hopefully, you will make some money."

David's growing eminence in the business community led to his being viewed as one of its philosophers, and he was increasingly asked for general advice to business people. In 1988 he told the Vancouver weekly, the *West Ender*, "Number one: put a lot of emphasis and importance on people. Number two: if you want to make a lot of money, try to have a philosophy of 'try not to make a lot of money.' Without that . . . you become tense. Nobody can work without peace of mind. That peace of mind comes when you say, 'I don't have to do it.'" He added, "Everything is people. Nothing else matters in the world—only people. When one places a lot of value on human relationships, I think one is getting there."

Whenever he had the opportunity, David would try to convince others that there was far more to life than merely amassing wealth. He was well aware of the value of money as such and the benefits it could bestow on those fortunate enough to have accumulated a great deal of it. But he did not feel it should be the driving force in a person's life. He was fond of quoting the adage, "If you have two loaves of bread, sell one and buy flowers. One will feed the body and the other, the soul."

Sometimes he tried to bring the same message to his friends in Hong Kong, many of whom had become very wealthy in the late 1970s and 1980s. As a businessman himself, he applauded their success but to those who seemed driven to pile million upon million, he suggested that they take time to look beyond the business world, to relax a bit and to seek out values beyond the bank vault. He felt that many of them had become so dominated by the drive to become financially successful that they were missing things in life. Their goal was to become better, richer and smarter. That "er" suffix would kill them, he felt. No matter how rich they were, there was always someone richer. No matter how smart they were, there were others who were smarter. Take time to enjoy life, he urged them. Spend some of your money to make the world a better place. Don't measure yourself by the number of dollars you can accumulate. Sell one of your loaves of bread and feed your soul.

It was not an easy message to get across, especially while Hong Kong's economy was racing ahead at a remarkable rate. The British colony was becoming one of the world's financial centres and with the establishment of full diplomatic relations between the United States and the People's Republic of China in 1978, there was a possibility of renewed trade with mainland China. The repossession of Hong Kong by China was still two decades down the road, and in those twenty years, the colony's economy was to gain even greater momentum. It is interesting to speculate on what David might have accomplished from a strictly financial point of view had he returned to the colony and re-entered business there. As it was, he preferred to remain in Canada. He was content with his life and happy in his new home.

NINE

Expanding Horizons

FROM HIS OFFICE in the IBM Tower in the Pacific Centre complex, David had a good view of the downtown core of Vancouver. In some ways, it reminded him of Hong Kong. The skyline seemed to be constantly changing as old buildings were demolished and new office towers were constructed in their place. Behind boarded sites, jackhammers and drills dug out foundations for new hotels and banks. It was becoming more difficult to obtain a sweeping view of the harbour and mountains, and if one had such a view, one knew that the rent would go up when the lease was renewed.

Working downtown meant there was a wide selection of restaurants where he could have lunch. Chinatown was close enough for him to walk there for lunch with the Hong Kong Merchants Association. This group, of which he was a founding member, had grown tremendously but it still provided a marvellous meeting where he could catch up on all the Chinese community gossip and collect snippets of news about events on the other side of the Pacific. The association had grown beyond its original purpose of being a social meeting for former Hong Kong residents; more and more it was assisting new immigrants with advice about matters such as language, education and taxation. David was all in favour of this and did what he could to help.

He and Dorothy received their Canadian citizenship in 1972. For the first time in their lives, they were able to vote for a politician who was going to play a role in governing a country in which they lived. It was a marvellous feeling. Although David never thought of running for office himself, he was pleased to make a financial contribution to one party or the other. He tended to assist the person rather than the party, contributing "in bits and pieces of $3,000 here and $1,000 there." Later, in the 1980s, he was known to contribute more to the Progressive Conservatives than to the other political parties.

In their early years in Canada, Dorothy and David, of necessity, sought out the least expensive forms of relaxation. David had always liked to read, and when Dorothy went shopping with him, she found that the best way to avoid impatience on his part was to arrange to meet him in a bookshop. David loved to browse and could spend a long time picking up one book and then another, unaware of the time Dorothy was spending to complete her shopping. In the beginning, he was able to buy only a few books, but as his business flourished, his personal library began to increase to formidable proportions.

He had always enjoyed perusing garden books and in time would accumulate over a hundred of them. Gardening had entranced him ever since he was a boy in Hong Kong, and when he was living on Ash Street, it was his favourite form of relaxation. The mild climate of Vancouver meant there were always some flowers or vegetables struggling in the garden, even in the depths of winter. For a brief time, he even worked on a garden allotment on the outskirts of the city, since his enthusiasm for the work exceeded the space in his backyard. When they moved to their penthouse apartment on Comox Street, David did his best to bring his garden with him. Boxes and large pots of earth were arranged on the balconies and earth-filled containers were placed on the roof. Flowers, vegetables, small trees and bushes were planted and tended with loving care, with results that satisfied not only his needs but his daughters' growing families as well.

As they could afford it, David and Dorothy got involved in other activities such as tennis, skiing and golf. Over the years, David became a competent golfer, but not necessarily one whom a club would select to represent it in a competition. Reflecting on the sport, he once told a reporter, "Golf is a game that is very humbling. Just when you think you know the system, it all falls apart. But I don't let it get me down. I just go out and have a good time."

Another sport David had loved since his Hong Kong days was sailing. He could not afford to indulge in it in Vancouver until the early 1970s, when he bought a small sailboat. The purchase of the sailboat was not a matter of walking along a dock to see what was for sale. He attended the Jib Set sailing school to learn how to handle and navigate a small yacht, and later had Dorothy and one of his daughters take the course as well. While this was going on, he bought a Tanzer-style yacht which would comfortably take four people anywhere up and down the coast. He called it the *Selah*, a Hebrew word which ends verses of the Psalms. He later bought a larger, forty-two-foot craft and became a member of the Royal Vancouver Yacht Club.

Once he started to sail, he found he enjoyed it so much he would use his yacht whenever he could, enjoying the tranquillity and quietness it gave him. "I had my share of motor boating in Hong Kong," he reflects. "I have never enjoyed it because it means just sitting there, dressed in a blazer with a drink in your hand, bouncing up and down going somewhere, yelling at each other instead of talking because of the noise level. To me, it's nothing."

For David, there was no better way to relax than to go sailing, to slip out of the harbour with a favourable wind filling the sail, the cabin's galley well stocked with food and perhaps a friend or two with them to enjoy the trip. Frequently, it would last only a weekend when they might go to the yacht club's outstation on Alexandra Island. There they would moor the yacht, go walking on the island and perhaps do a little fishing or scuba diving. Some other favourite spots were Harmony Island and Desolation Sound. British Columbia's coast was a marvellous place for sailing enthusiasts, and David and Dorothy soon had favourite spots to visit like the others. If too many boats crowded around an anchorage or the dock, they could always slip away to a quieter place.

David and Dorothy both liked to travel during his vacation. In their early years in Canada, the family travelled by trailer over a great deal of British Columbia and well south into the United States. Aside from business trips to Hong Kong, David's first major trip took place shortly after he and Dorothy received Canadian citizenship, when with some friends, they went on a tour of South America. There were more travels after that, most of them made with groups connected with the Vancouver Aquarium.

David's association with the aquarium began in the 1970s and grew out of his interest in scuba diving. He had learned diving by himself in Hong Kong, but the opportunities there were limited by the small size of the colony. In British Columbia, with its huge coastline and numerous islands, the sport attracted hundreds of enthusiasts whose choices for locale seemed limitless. At first he dove at Lion's Bay, not far from Britannia Beach, setting out from a dock with a spear gun to catch some bottom fish and, at Dorothy's insistence, a rope around his waist, with her holding it as a lifeline. Conversation with other divers convinced him that he should not be diving by himself, and that he should get professional instruction in the sport. He accepted their advice, and he and Dorothy went to Willoughby's Divers Den to be properly trained and certified. (Dorothy took the course primarily to know about it rather than be involved in it.) At the diving school, someone suggested that he join the Vancouver Aquarium, which every year organized diving expeditions to various parts of the world. The Lams decided to join, and at the first opportunity, signed up for one of the expeditions.

On one such tour, he met the aquarium's director, Dr. Murray Newman, and his wife Kathy. David and Dorothy had been visiting the Great Barrier Reef off the coast of Australia and en route for home, met up with the Newmans and the tour group in Fiji. They formed an immediate liking for each other. Newman remembers that David was "extremely hospitable and gracious while at the same time being curious, energetic and enterprising. Wherever the group would go, David would find the best Chinese restaurant in town. So we were all invited out, the whole group of us, to Lam's party in the Chinese restaurant in Suva."

Their meeting in Fiji led to more socializing in Vancouver. Later, when Newman organized a tour to French Polynesia, the Lams went along to collect tropical fish for the aquarium. Once again Newman was impressed by his new friend. On the island of Rangiroa, they collected a large number of fish of various species, enough to make getting them back to Vancouver a problem. David responded to the challenge with a foray into the kitchen of their hotel, where though the cuisine was French, the cooks were Chinese. He managed to get from them a supply of empty, one-gallon plastic cooking oil containers as well as numerous large glass jars. The aquarium staff had brought with them little individual pumps and air tubes to keep the water aerated, and with these in place, the group headed for the airport. In Los Angeles, David helped get the fish through the custom authorities as well. "He was a natural leader," Newman recalls, "very smooth and personable and able to convince people that we were not doing anything illegal, just transporting small tropical fish in oil containers." The whole collection was taken back safely.

Newman had served with the United States Marine Corps during the Second World War and spent most of his war years in the South Pacific. He knew the area well and had been on some of the islands they visited. He arranged a tour of Micronesia in 1978, and again the Lams took part. The group stopped off in Truk, an archipelago used during the war by the Imperial Japanese Navy. During the war numerous Japanese ships had been sunk there, and in time, they became a haven for marine life. It was an excellent place for scuba diving and the group decided to spend a few days there, swimming among the old shipwrecks and studying the fish.

The normal practice for visiting scuba divers was to bring their own regulators and buoyancy compensators but to rent their compressed air tanks and weight belts locally. They dove in pairs for greater safety so that if one got into trouble, he or she could rely on their "buddy" to help. Newman and David agreed to be diving partners, and they and a few others rented their gear and went out in a small boat to a wreck called the *Sankisan Maru*. The ship had been sunk in February 1944.

Newman describes the wreck: "It was an armed freighter that was unloading military equipment when it was sunk, and it was absolutely fascinating to look at. It is a habitat for all kinds of marine life, surrounded by beautiful coral fishes and encrusted with corals and sponges and cobwebs of marine life. It was like a haunted house because you could go down and you could see the moment of terror. The shell casings were still there around the anti-aircraft guns. You could swim into the spaces inside the hull and see, for example, broken chinaware." The wreck lay upright in about a hundred feet of water, its mast barely showing above the surface. The bow of the ship had settled on a large rock while its stern rested on a sandy bottom, leaving room to swim completely under the hull.

Tying their boat to the mast, David and Newman slipped over the side. David recalls that they agreed to head for the bottom, and comments, "I did not have a gauge on how much air I had in my tank, so I looked at Newman's gauge. He still had more than half so I assumed mine was half full because all the equipment was rented from the local guide. So we started going down. We went through the hull and we saw tanks and guns and trucks. They were all rotted and encrusted, but still there. We saw schools and schools of fish inside the hold of the ship, which was covered with coral growth and barnacles, all different colours and extremely beautiful."

When they had reached the bottom of the ship on the exterior of the hull and swam under the keel, Newman suddenly saw David making him a signal. He was pounding his chest and then drawing his finger across his throat. He was out of air.

"When I ran out of air," he recalls, "it was a very shocking experience because you don't run out of air in a gradual sense. You just suck in air and 'clunk,' there is nothing. I signalled to Murray and he gave me his mouthpiece and thus air. I gave it back to him and he gave it back to me. This was buddy breathing. That was okay, but *you* try to do it 110 feet under the water with all the panic and scary feeling. So we started ascending." David knew he was not supposed to shoot straight up from 100 feet due to the damage that expanding air could do to his lungs. The two breathed back and forth but still came up a bit too fast, and David didn't get a chance to expel enough of his air. When they got to the surface, David was coughing blood. "I knew that was a bad thing in the South Pacific," he says. "When you have cuts or blood in the water that would attract sharks. We waved to the boat about 100 yards away to come and pick me up. It was scary. I felt faint and numb, holding blood in my mouth."

The two men were hauled on board and the boat immediately sped to shore. Dorothy saw him coming towards the hotel with a lot of blood on his chest and was alarmed. Both men were taken immediately to the hospital at Palau. The local doctor was afraid that David might have bubbles in his blood stream; if any lodged in his brain, they might cause a stroke. He insisted on keeping him under observation and medication for three days. When released, he and Dorothy continued on with the tour.

The experience at Truk was the last time David scuba dived to any depth, which made Dorothy very happy. On the rare occasion he used his gear to drop over the side of his yacht to fix his propeller, Dorothy made sure he had a rope around his waist and that she was holding on to the other end of it.

Some time after the event, Newman was given a well-deserved silver medal for bravery by the Royal Lifesaving Society. The man who presented the medal was David Lam, who embraced him and again expressed his thanks.

Another trip David took with Newman and the aquarium was to the far reaches of the Canadian Arctic in the summer of 1976. David had never been there and was curious to learn more about the North. The tour lasted nine or ten days and was organized with considerable care. Some time earlier, the aquarium had acquired a narwhal. With its long spiral tooth that looked like the mythical horn of a unicorn, the small white whale caused a lot of excitement in Vancouver. Unfortunately it died, and the aquarium authorities wanted to find out why. It was thought that a closer examination of the animal in its local habitat would yield more information.

This was to be an all-male tour of about a dozen people. Among them were Peter Pollen, mayor of Victoria; Bill Hughes, a well-known CKNW radio broadcaster; Dr. Bristol Foster, director of the B.C. provincial museum; and Ron Longstaffe, vice-president of the Canfor forestry products company. The number was determined by the capacity of their twin-engine Otter aircraft, which had to take not only the passengers but their sleeping bags, winter clothing and emergency supplies. Flying from Vancouver to Edmonton and then on to Resolute Bay, they picked up their chartered aircraft and for the next week hopped from one place to another in the Far North. Its oversized tires allowed the Otter to land in many places without an airstrip.

David found the area wonderful. The brilliant blue skies, great white icebergs and dark blue waters of the seas and straits were a revelation to him. He was interested in everything he saw, especially in the native people and their culture. At one place they landed, they were fortunate. Only the Inuit were allowed to kill narwhal for food, and one was caught when the group was there. The hunters hauled it up on the ice and began to gut it, giving the scientists with the tour the opportunity to obtain some of its internal organs for examination. David saw some of the natives cutting pieces of the whale's skin, chewing it and swallowing it. He had heard this was how they obtained their vitamin C. If they enjoyed it, he thought, perhaps he would too. He took out his pocketknife, cut off a little bit, washed away the blood in sea water and put it in his mouth. "It felt," he said later, "as if you had cut a little piece of foam rubber that had been impregnated with raw cod liver oil."

The group went to Bathurst Island, stopped on the Grinnell Peninsula of Devon Island and flew on further north to Axel Heiberg Island. They stopped briefly at the world's most northern lake, Lake Hazen, where David caught an Arctic char. He pan-fried it over a little oil stove and declared it to be the best fish he ever tasted. Their northernmost stop was the top of Ellesmere Island, only a few hundred miles from the North Pole.

On their way home, the aircraft stopped overnight at Resolute, a small settlement on Cornwallis Island, which frequently acts as a base for various projects in the Northwest Territories. By that time, Newman recalls, the men in the group were a very rough looking lot: "We had been out camping and maybe we didn't smell too good either."

After unloading their gear, about eight of the group looked for a pub where they could get a beer. The only place available was the Musk Ox Inn, a private establishment which boasted a television set with rather erratic reception. They obtained permission to go in. Bill Hughes, whose "Roving Mike" program on station CKNW was very popular in Vancouver, had his tape-recorder with him and wanted to interview the members of the group before they dispersed. The sound from the television set was too loud, so David went over and reduced the volume. "No sooner had I touched the volume," David remembers, "when a commissionaire came up and said, 'You. Out.'"

I said, "Why?"

"I don't have to give you a reason," said the commissionaire. "You touched the control of the TV set. No one touches it except me!"

"You mean to say you don't welcome me?"

"I don't welcome you. Out."

Then Peter Pollen, the mayor of Victoria, spoke up. "Wait a minute. We're together. How come you are kicking him out?" he demanded.

"Who said that?" roared the commissionaire, who then ordered Pollen out as well.

The commissionaire was a huge man, well over six feet tall and with the physique of a professional bouncer. On the other hand, there were over half a dozen men from the aquarium group. They had all become very friendly with each other and regarded an insult to one as an insult to all. Pollen felt David was being discriminated against because of his Chinese origin, and he refused to be intimidated. Seeing this opposition, the commissionaire called the Royal Canadian Mounted Police, and two constables arrived shortly afterward. David describes the denouement: "The RCMP officer said, 'Look, you are making it embarrassing for me. This is a private club. If they want you out, you have to go.' 'But,' I said, 'is that right given to this fellow?' He said, 'I don't know how they run the club.' So we each ordered one more round of beer and holding it in our hand, we all walked out."

Despite this incident, everyone agreed that it had been a marvellous tour. David was entranced with the trip. In the past fifteen years, he had seen more of Canada than most Canadians.

David's connection with the Vancouver Aquarium was by no means limited to his participation in their tours. He thoroughly enjoyed those but was aware of the public support needed by the aquarium to raise money. His commitment was such that he served for a time as one of its governors and later as its patron. Dr. Newman was pleased to have his support and his influence as well.

A typical example of the latter occurred when the aquarium's beluga whale gave birth in the late 1970s. Baby whales are difficult to keep alive and at the time there was little known about how to maintain the animals. Newman talked to Dr. Norman Louie, a physician friend of his, about the baby and the need for better facilities to look after it. Louie said that in the Chinese culture, it was customary to wait thirty days before celebrating the birth of a child. At that point, the parents have a "red egg party" when relatives and friends come bearing gifts, and the baby is given its name.

"I discussed this with David," Newman recalls, "and he thought that was a really good idea." A red egg party for the baby was organized in short order. Dorothy and David provided invaluable help in reaching out to the Chinese community, and the event was a complete success. Recalls Newman, "We had a marvellous party, and David was in the receiving line to welcome guests."

While the Lams did a great deal of socializing, it was at home that David could indulge in another hobby he greatly enjoyed. As a young boy in Hong Kong, he was always interested in the activity going on in the kitchen of his father's house. The cook must have been an unusually patient man, since busy as he was preparing meals for a large household, he never seemed to mind the young boy watching him prepare meals. Many years later, David had the opportunity to take some professional lessons himself. These included a two-week course in Perugia, Italy, where, under the instruction of a well-known chef, David, Dorothy and a group of enthusiastic amateur gourmet cooks learned some of the finer points of Italian cooking.

Closer to home, David heard about a resort on Saltspring Island called Hastings House. It had an excellent reputation for its cuisine, and once or twice a year, its chef gave cooking lessons over the weekend to small groups. David and Dorothy took several courses there, enjoying the serene pastoral setting as well as the lessons on gourmet food preparation. Reflecting on cooking's attraction for him, David says, "I found that it was very creative and very relaxing to do some cooking because it is challenging to the mind. At one time I told Dorothy, 'Let us just completely run the kitchen pantry and the refrigerator empty.' 'What do you mean?' she asked. 'Let's take whatever is there without buying anything and just consume it all to see what kind of dishes we can continue to create.' Of course, it is easy for the first couple or three days. Then it gets harder and harder, but it is very challenging and creative. And then I found that when I started sailing, I became the cook more than anyone else because I helped buy the provisions and I stored them and nobody knew where to find them."

Even if someone could find the stored provisions, there is every likelihood that David would have volunteered his services in the yacht's galley. "He enjoys that sort of thing," Doreen says of her father. "He likes to experiment and he can whip up a dinner or anything with whatever is at hand."

Over the years, some of the hobbies in which David was involved—flying and horseback riding, for example—claimed less and less of his attention. The joy of cooking was to remain with him, however, and many guests invited to his Comox Street apartment were to find that their host was also the chef.

TEN

Active Retirement

BY THE END of the 1970s, David was a successful and wealthy businessman with a wide network of clients stretching from Taiwan to Singapore. His friends and acquaintances included many of the wealthiest men in Hong Kong. While he admired them, he sometimes questioned their unremitting drive to obtain more and more money to the detriment of enjoying life.

David was quite happy to make money, lots of it, but he never thought it should be the main goal in life for anyone. He felt that the energy some of his acquaintances put into piling up more money was based on insecurity. In Hong Kong, for example, many had come to the colony to escape the Japanese invaders of the 1930s and, later, the revolutionary years of the Communist takeover. Their livelihood had been shattered. When they had the opportunity to recover their lives in Hong Kong and began to make money, it almost seemed that they equated money with security: the more they made, the less likely they were ever to endure their former suffering again. Similarly, he had met wealthy Canadians who had never forgotten what they had experienced during the Great Depression of the 1930s. Again, he felt, they sought to acquire wealth as a means of security and became locked into this activity to the exclusion of everything else.

"When a person cannot develop other interests in life that can round off all his time and energy," David observes, "they become a very lonely kind of person, and business becomes a loner's activity. They use the excuse 'Oh, my business is driving me crazy.' That is an excuse, because they cannot face themselves having very few intimate friends, very few hobbies, very few sports and very few activities. A lot of rich people are like that. They would come here and say 'I am so busy.' I would say, 'Wait a minute. Slow down. What are you trying to do?' They would hear what I said, but they couldn't do it. It takes a person with a philosophical mind to think through a lot of things, one who can look at the evening star and listen to Mozart's music in the still of the night and thinking through things—not business, but life. Where am I coming from? Where am I going? What should I do? What service can I do to make me happier?"

For David, life holds far more than the pursuit of money. The soul, too, must be nourished. "When I get a chance to sail," he says, "I am very close to the might of nature. When I anchor off a small island, the sky is clearer. There are no city lights. I can see more stars. Those are the times that I become very religious, very conscious of the might of the Creator."

To his mind, security cannot be measured by money in a bank vault: it can only be found in a peaceful and contented mind, especially when one has a strong Christian faith and strives always to live up to the teachings of Christ. David believes his life would have been quite different had he not been brought up as a Christian, and he derives great comfort from the teaching he received in the Baptist church. He also believes that during the course of his life, particularly during the wartime years when he escaped death several times, the Lord had a guiding hand on his shoulder.

As the decade drew to a close, David gave more and more thought to retiring when he reached the age of sixty in 1982. It would give him the opportunity to share with others some of the benefits he had received through God's grace. By the late 1970s, he began to make plans to withdraw from the real estate business.

One of the early moves he made concerned his residence on Comox Street. David and Dorothy now owned half the building and let the other owner, Frank Stanzl, manage it. Almost three years after they bought out their Sunnyvale clients, Frank Stanzl died. His wife wanted to sell his various interests, including the Comox Street building, and move back to Germany. "I am so Chinese," David recalls, "that there is just no way I could see myself negotiating, particularly with a widow of a former partner." He tried to persuade Mrs. Stanzl not to sell, telling her that Canadian International Properties would help her manage the building and that he would do everything he could to assist her.

David could be a very persuasive person but in this case, he lost out. A short time later Mrs. Stanzl sold all of her husband's holdings. David's first intimation of this came with a telephone call from Nelson Skalbania, a man who had been gaining a reputation in the Vancouver real estate business as a wheeler-dealer. Skalbania informed David that he had bought out Mrs. Stanzl's properties, including the half interest in the Comox Street apartment building, and that he was now David's partner. He wanted to convert the rental apartments into condominiums, sell them, and make a good profit from their sale, he said, and asked if David had any objections to the deal. David did. He thought the building was a gem, and he didn't think it should be cut into little pieces with the tenants being forced to buy or move. Skalbania then suggested David might wish to buy him out at a considerable profit to himself.

Faced with a possible long-term confrontation with the new half-owner, and most unwilling to move himself from the penthouse apartment and his roof gardens, David arranged for Canadian International Properties to buy the other half of the building from Skalbania. The latter got his profit, but the building was such a good rental property that the loans David had to arrange were soon paid off, and his roof gardens continued to flourish.

David's decision to wind up his business affairs took time to accomplish. There were almost three dozen companies in which he had partial ownership of 10 per cent or more. Canadian International Properties was owned solely by David and Dorothy and would be easy to wind up, but careful preparations had to be made for the other companies' sale or continuance under different management. David had no sons to whom he could pass on the business, and none of his three daughters were interested in a business career. Doreen, after graduating from university, had started to work in real estate in another firm and had done exceptionally well for two years. Eventually, however, she had taken further studies at Regent College. Daphne had also worked in real estate in Calgary, but married life and children cut short her career in that field. The eldest daughter, Debbie, had concentrated on charitable endeavours and had no desire to become a businesswoman.

David had considered accepting into his firm some sons of friends in Hong Kong who were also his partners in several of his companies. He knew many of them so well that they called him "uncle," and their fathers felt David would be an excellent person to teach their sons the real estate business. The problem with this proposition was that David wanted to retire when he was still mentally and physically able to pursue a variety of things that interested him. Accepting the sons of friends into his company would mean continuing on as president for longer than he wished and would push back his own retirement five or ten years. Under the circumstances, he decided not to accept trainees in the firm.

During this latter period of his active business career, David made two real estate deals which are worth noting. The Vancouver General Hospital on 12th Avenue owned a block of houses close by. Part of the block was needed for a carpark and the hospital wished to sell the remainder. David felt the property had good potential if the houses were replaced with rental apartments. He formed a company in the usual fashion with each overseas client contributing to the capital needed to construct the building. On this occasion, however, his timing was not good. Although the duplexes he built were first-class, they didn't sell well. David wanted to withdraw from the venture but did not want those who had invested with him to suffer a loss. He had an excellent reputation which he valued and all of his companies had been profitable. He had persuaded his clients to come into the deal with him and they trusted him implicitly.

Faced with this problem, David took a step which surprised his staff. Earlier he had bought a couple of properties on Broadway and had built condominiums on them. This was his own venture and at his own risk. His timing was right, and he sold them at a profit of a little over a million dollars. He decided to take that money and give it to his partners who had made nothing on the hospital property. This decision engendered considerable protest from some of his senior staff. It did not affect them financially, but they argued that David had no obligation to cover the losses of his clients. A deal was a deal, they argued. Sometimes you won, sometimes you lost.

David felt differently. This was to be his last real estate venture, and he was determined that not one of his clients was going to have any reason to complain, even if he had to dip deeply into his own pocket. David gave the order to his accountant to transfer the money. Today, he sums up the story with cheerful simplicity: "That's what I did, and I'm happy and I'm not any poorer."

A partial explanation for this very unusual and generous act on David's part may be found in a speech he gave in 1986 to students at the University of Victoria. In it, he said: "I was brought up in an education process which placed tremendous importance on Chinese philosophy as well as Christianity. Christianity is the religion by which I live my life, but I continue to draw insights from and be guided by Chinese philosophy. Harmony is the goal of Chinese philosophy. It stresses harmony with oneself, harmony with nature and harmony with humanity. Harmony starts with a sound mind which is at peace with one's self, with nature and with humanity." David's decision gave him more peace of mind and inner contentment than any other course he might have followed.

The loss suffered from the former hospital property development was unique among the companies which David organized and managed over the years.

In the process of winding up his affairs, David did very well for himself and Dorothy with the sale of the Insurance Exchange Building in San Francisco. They had bought it for $5.4 million, of which only a small portion was cash. Twenty-five per cent of the money came from the Floribunda Philanthropic Society, a charitable fund which David and Dorothy had created in the 1970s. David had felt sure this investment in the building would grow, and with it his ability to distribute the money for charitable purposes.

In 1983, five years after he had bought the building, David was ready to sell. The market value of the building had increased approximately five times. Richard Ellis and Company, a large real estate firm, was interested in buying the building on behalf of a consortium of pension funds in Great Britain. David sent Andrew Grant to San Francisco to negotiate the transaction. Grant found it tough going, however; the buyer's agent was excessively cautious and wanted to examine every comma in the contract. When he telephoned David to say that he appeared to be getting nowhere, David told him, "Life is too short. Forget it. Come back to Vancouver."

There was another man interested in seeing the sale completed, however. This was Blake Bromley, David's lawyer for the Floribunda Philanthropic Society. Bromley had looked forward to a considerable amount of money coming to the society, and when David told him the deal was about to collapse, he asked who the buyer was. On being told that it was Richard Ellis, he asked if David knew Don Bodell, who was in charge of the American branch of the company. David had no knowledge of his connection with the company but he certainly knew Bodell. He had been a property manager in Vancouver when they first met. David had been so impressed with him that he invited him to join as a partner in his first company. Bodell had progressed up the ladder with other firms and had been very successful. David told Bromley to telephone Bodell and ask him if he remembered David Lam. David wanted to find out why Andrew Grant was having such a hard time with Bodell's agent in San Francisco and he wanted to find out from the top man.

As David tells the story, "Don Bodell phoned me early in the morning and said to me, 'How can you ask Blake to ask me if I remember you? You were the one who offered me a partnership.' I said, 'Okay, Don, I'm the one selling the 433 California Street building. You are the buyer. If you are not buying, let's not talk. If I'm not selling, there's no point talking. But I am selling. You have a fellow in San Francisco who is so difficult that my man has just quit and come back.' He said, 'I have just hired him and he wants to be very cautious. He was a banker.' I said, 'That explains it.' Then he said, 'Ask your man to go back down. I'll phone my guy.' Naturally, after that, everything went smoothly."

When Andrew Grant returned to San Francisco to continue the negotiations for the sale, he found the atmosphere quite changed. There was a lot of work to be done, but in due course David and Dorothy flew down to sign the final documents. In the office where the papers were prepared, there were numerous lawyers and accountants. "It was very intimidating," David recalls. "Everybody was so serious. I said, 'I'm not going to sign because you guys are too serious. You intimidate me. I want you to smile.' So everybody smiled."

After the signing, the Lams left the lawyer's office and walked into the bright California sunshine. David was elated. He had sold the building at five times the price he had paid for it, and in the years he owned it, revenue from the building had paid back the money he had borrowed to buy it. He remembers saying to Dorothy, "Let's get a taxi and go home." She replied, "Why take a taxi? We usually take the bus." He said, "Okay, fine."

But he was so happy he chose the wrong bus and they ended up at Fisherman's Wharf. It was a long way, but they walked back to their condominium on Nob Hill where Andrew Grant and Ken Williams, his controller, were wondering what had happened to them.

David had sold other properties in the United States and he faced having to pay both American taxes and Canadian taxes, since he wanted to move his money to Canada. The combined taxes, he estimated, would come close to $10 million. David decided to send Ken Williams back to San Francisco to examine the tax situation and report back to him. In due course, Williams telephoned back with the astounding information that David did not have to pay any taxes. At the time of the sale, the San Francisco building was 75 per cent owned by David and Dorothy and 25 per cent by their philanthropic society. Under a joint Canadian-American agreement still in effect at that time, a Canadian company owning less than 80 per cent of a real estate firm in the United States was not required to pay the normal business tax on money returning to Canada, nor would it be subjected to a Canadian tax. The same held true of an American real estate firm in Canada. It was a tax loophole which was in the process of being plugged by both governments, but David's sale just got in under the wire.

Later, when people praised him for his astonishing sense of timing on the deal, David disclaimed any particular perceptiveness. When he used 25 per cent of his charitable society's funds to buy the building, he had no idea of the role it would play in tax consideration. When he sold the building, he had no idea of the changes in tax laws being negotiated by Canada and the United States. It was pure chance. After he had double-checked with the Canadian tax authorities to make sure it was not a dream, however, he sat down with Dorothy to talk about the windfall.

"This is something that is given by God, but it should not change our lifestyle," was David's way of putting it. Dorothy wondered what they should do with it, and David felt they should donate it for the benefit of others. "It is up to you," replied Dorothy. "You made the money." David decided that instead of taking 75 per cent for himself, he would assign that proportion to a second foundation for charitable giving. He then had Blake Bromley establish the David and Dorothy Lam Foundation. During the next five years, he was to devote a considerable amount of his time spending millions rather than making them.

David was most generous when he decided to retire from his business career. On November 24, 1982, Canadian International Properties became Canadian International Enterprises. All of the business connections, office furniture and other equipment were turned over to his senior executives. Andrew Grant, Ken Williams and Felix Ts'o thus inherited a thriving business rather than having to go and look for employment elsewhere. David retained the assets he owned, such as the apartment building in which he lived as well as several other properties in Canada and the United States. The company itself was earning good revenue from property management, and continued to look after properties belonging to David's numerous friends in Hong Kong and elsewhere. He also had sent Andrew Grant and Ken Williams and their wives on a trip to Hong Kong to meet some of his clients and get at least a nodding acquaintance with the hustle and bustle of the colony's business activity. Later renamed Pacific Canadian Investments, the firm continued to flourish. Arrangements were made for David to have the use of an office whenever he wished. His secretary, Sarah McSevney, was to find that even though her boss had retired, she was to be kept quite busy with the new activities he entered into.

Promoting racial harmony was one of David's long-standing interests, and a theme he frequently touched on in speeches to business organizations or the Rotary Club. He strongly believed that harmony could best be achieved through understanding and education. In one such speech to the Richmond Rotary Club in 1988, he expressed the core of his belief: "When people of different races, cultural backgrounds and values meet, the first and natural response is usually a feeling of intimidation. It is quite natural to have a fear of strangers from different racial and cultural backgrounds. However, if we let this feeling grow, it easily builds into rejection. Rejection turns the area of contact into a battleground, and what we really need to find is a common ground. However, finding a common ground is really not enough because we really want to enjoy friends, to learn from them and to have our lives enriched by them. So through common ground we must reach a higher ground with people—the higher ground of enjoyment, learning and enrichment."

A few years after he retired, David was asked to join another group which caught his imagination. The Asia-Pacific Initiative was an organization sponsored by both the federal and provincial governments. It was co-chaired by Pat Carney, the member of Parliament for Vancouver Centre who became minister of International Trade, and Grace McCarthy, a senior cabinet member in the provincial government. The mandate of the organization covered a variety of fields but its main purpose was to promote Canada and British Columbia's presence among the Pacific Rim countries. By this time, Canada's import-export trade with these countries had grown larger than its trade with Europe, and as far as could be seen, it would continue to grow. Committees were formed to deal with matters such as transportation, tourism, communication, trade and cultural exchanges. David was asked to provide ideas to improve social and cultural relationships.

One idea that he proposed, based on his own experience and his observation of newcomers to Vancouver, was the production of a Chinese-language educational video program. He recalls, "I wanted to make it interesting and entertaining so that the message, hopefully, can be retained. People, when they go to a meeting and hear a speech that is good and interesting and maybe humorous, tend to retain the message a lot longer than if someone stands up giving you the 'do's' and 'don'ts.' So I suggested that we must have a good producer, good quality video and also a couple of well-known Chinese actors and actresses."

David found such actors, a husband and wife team who had recently moved to Canada, and then helped assemble a group which included everyone from a scriptwriter to a producer. The theme of the video was how newcomers could best fit into Canadian society once they arrived. The video was filmed and produced in Vancouver, and turned out to be very popular. In Hong Kong, all those who had been granted Canadian visas were invited to view it by the Canadian Commissioner, and his reports on its reception were good.

David himself had a role in the video. One scene was taken from the balcony of his penthouse apartment which looks over Vancouver harbour. He is shown talking to the actors, representing a recently arrived couple, and he explains to them that now they are in Canada, they should burn the mental bridge tying them to Hong Kong. "It's as if you are standing in two boats," he tells them, "one leg in one, and one leg in the other. If the two boats go apart, you are in the drink." Once you are accepted, he continues, then it is up to you to start belonging to your new country and contribute to it. This was a theme he had used in speeches many times before and he was to repeat it many times later.

Another activity in which David became involved was dragon boat racing, a tradition over two thousand years old which Milton Wong describes as "one of the noisiest and oldest regattas in the world." In Hong Kong, the Dragon Boat Festival is held on the fifth day of the fifth lunar month. People take the day off from work to watch the activities in the ports and fishing villages. Accompanied by cymbals and drums, amateur crews from a variety of organizations paddling long, slim boats race each other over an 800-yard course in a series of elimination contests.

In Vancouver, the Chinese Cultural Centre initiated the races as one of the cultural events associated with Expo 86. David had seen it and thought it had considerable potential. One evening when Vancouver businessman Milton Wong was at David's penthouse for dinner, David suggested to him that the event be expanded to include teams from other countries. It would provide a more international flavour. "His focus," Wong remembers, "was to cause the people of Vancouver to look at themselves as part of the Pacific Rim and to cause the intermingling of the various different cultures of the Pacific Rim." Wong promised to help, and eventually became chairman of the Canadian International Dragon Boat Festival Society. Others were encouraged to volunteer their services. The Chinese Cultural Centre was firmly behind the idea, and those involved in the Asia-Pacific Initiative gave it their support.

There was an immense amount of work to be done. It was not a government-funded affair so for the first few years David subsidized its deficit until it could stand on its own. The races were held in False Creek. Using six lanes, each 640 metres in length, the boats and their twenty paddlers competed with each other. As word spread about the festival, more and more teams began to participate, both local and from other countries. Moreover, the festival broadened to include other sports as well as multicultural events. By 1989 there were forty teams competing in the dragon boat races, thirty restaurants served various ethnic foods, and a host of acrobats, singers, jugglers, dancers and others entertained the thousands of people who flocked to see the event. It was a hugely successful affair and Vancouver now sends teams to similar events as far away as Hong Kong and Singapore. The festival was just the sort of event David was happy to promote, both financially and otherwise. There was no racial or cultural boundary to participation, and from his point of view, mixing groups of different nationalities in competitive games and entertaining activities could only lead to greater understanding.

During the 1980s, David frequently spoke on the problem of racism. At the turn of the century, anti-Asian sentiment was rampant in British Columbia. There had been riots in Vancouver over the number of Chinese, Japanese and Indian immigrants coming into the province. Chinese immigrants, most of them from the coolie class, were willing to work for less money, and working people saw them as a threat to their own security in the labour market. An attempt was made to exclude further immigration, and though that was eventually disallowed, their numbers were limited and a head tax imposed to discourage all but the most determined. Restrictions on their voting rights and their ability to attain university degrees in certain professions were further burdens they bore. It was only after the Second World War that Canadians of Chinese, Japanese and other origins were given full rights of citizenship.

Most Chinese immigrants to Canada in the 1960s and 1970s came from different economic and social strata than those who had arrived in the first half of the century. Some of the newcomers tended to look down on those who were born in Canada, particularly if they were not fluent in Chinese.

David had never encountered any racial discrimination since coming to Canada, but it pained him to see comments in the local papers which might revive old racial tensions. Typical concerns can be seen in the following extract from a June 25, 1989 article in the Richmond *News* about Hong Kong immigrants:

> In the past year house prices have soared by fifty per cent—a house on the residential west side now costs as much as $500,000—forcing middle income groups into marginal areas. Thousands have been evicted from modest apartment blocks to make way for expensive new housing (36 per cent of those who rent in Vancouver are below the official poverty line).
>
> The newcomers often buy a traditional wooden framed, clapboard house with garden and trees, only to demolish the lot (trees as well) and erect a substantial concrete mansion. Having acquired Canadian citizenship, many return to Hong Kong to cash in on the last few years before the 1997 handover.

The issue also received national coverage. An article in Toronto's *Globe and Mail* of October 20, 1989, suggested that the number of Chinese immigrants in future years would be colossal if Canada's immigration policy remained the same. Describing the flow of capital into B.C. as having reached "flood proportion," the article's tone was reflective of a mood that seemed to be growing in the city:

> Asian immigrants love the large lots and good schools but not the old houses and beautiful gardens. As a result, terrible things are happening to the neighbourhoods of Kerrisdale, Point Grey, Dunbar, Oakridge, Shaughnessy and South Granville. When a house sells, a scorched earth policy goes into effect. The house is razed and with it every tree, shrub and blade of grass. In its place rises a structure so stupendous in size and alien in appearance that it might have dropped down overnight from Mars.

Predictions that the number of Chinese immigrants coming to Canada would increase proved to be correct. Thousands of Hong Kong students were coming to private schools, colleges and universities in Canada, and by 1990 it was estimated they formed one-quarter of Canada's total foreign student body. Vancouver was particularly attractive to Chinese immigrants and critics were beginning to refer to it as "Hongcouver."

David felt that he should do what he could to lower the level of apprehension among resident Canadians while, at the same time, trying to point out to the newcomers some of the cultural differences they should expect in their adopted land. He spoke constantly on this theme whenever the opportunity offered—to business groups, cultural societies, school children or service clubs. The majority of these talks were to Chinese audiences. He was the first to admit that, as a young man, he had to make a determined effort to teach himself to be more tolerant. "I was conditioned by my upbringing in Hong Kong to be so aware of differences," he told his audiences. "Even among Chinese you do have differences between northerners and southerners. Discrimination started over the next hill, on the other side of the river."

One piece of advice he gave time and again to Chinese immigrants was to "demystify" themselves. As a visible minority with a language quite different from English, they were difficult for Canadians to understand. As a result, he said, "we fall victim to rumours and innuendoes—some malicious. We become stereotyped in the Hollywood version of Fu Manchu and Charlie Chan."

"Demystifying" involved a number of steps. The first, and probably the most difficult was to learn English, for without it immigrants would tend to cluster together in ghettos rather than trying to mingle with mainstream Canadian society. Advising prospective migrants in Hong Kong, David constantly repeated the old Chinese saying that one cannot be in two boats at the same time. If a person was going to a new country, he or she should be prepared to enter wholeheartedly into its culture.

"Be sensitive to Canadian values," he told them, "especially the respect for a clean and beautiful environment, the reverence with which older buildings are held, the social heritage of friendliness, caring and serving, and the cultural heritage of the English and French languages. Learn to speak the English language, the friendly communication of a smile, the all-important words "please" and "thank you." Enquire about the well-being of others. Eye contact is important, and failing to maintain it often conveys disinterest or unfriendliness." Above all, he said, they should make a commitment to be Canadians first: "Being a Canadian means that we share more, serve more, give more and care more than many people. Rather than concentrate only on financial matters, I urge you to be a volunteer, to contribute to society."

There were characteristics some immigrants brought with them which were not very acceptable, David suggested. "Speaking too loudly is rude, and having the tendency to look someone up and down, not acknowledging them with a smile, is considered hostile in Canada," he advised. To some of the wealthier immigrants, he warned that a friendly gesture could be made in the wrong way. For example, they might invite neighbours to their home, lavish a nine-course dinner on them, show off their belongings, talk about the many cars they bought and complain about the maid. "Although this may be accepted in Hong Kong society," he said, "a Canadian may feel uncomfortable for not being able to reciprocate such hospitality." Canadians would prefer meeting new neighbours with coffee and doughnuts in the kitchen, or perhaps exchanging garden vegetables over the fence in the backyard.

The overall theme of David's various talks and speeches was to urge new immigrants to be good Canadians. He described coming to Canada from Hong Kong as crossing a bridge. Once crossed, the bridge should be burned, and newcomers, though maintaining ties with their homeland, should devote themselves to their new country. He advised contributing financially to good causes, and urged even more for them to serve in some voluntary organization whose objective was charitable or useful to society. Among other benefits, such service would bring the volunteers in contact with other Canadians, widen their horizons, promote understanding and result in more progress towards intercultural harmony.

As for charges about racism in Canada, David could be quite blunt. "Sometimes people from Hong Kong who have any kind of problems in Canada find racism a convenient banner to wave," he said. "In my twenty-one years as a Canadian resident, I can honestly say I never encountered it once. Sure there are misunderstandings. If you are used to being a pedestrian in Hong Kong and you walk the same way in Vancouver, sooner or later someone is going to tell you that you shouldn't ignore red lights. That's not racism. If you are working in Canada and lose your job, that's most probably not racism. Canada isn't a racist society. Instead it is a wonderfully varied, multi-ethnic, very caring and compassionate society. That is why I tell Hong Kong people who immigrate to Canada: Give money to charity and donate it to schools and other worthwhile things in Canadian society. Become caring and compassionate like Canadians around you."

David knew this advice could not be followed with the expectation of instant changes in attitude. Nevertheless, he hoped it would indicate a path the immigrant could pursue. Sometimes he used a saying of the Chinese sage, Lao-tzu—"The journey of a thousand miles begins with one step"—to suggest they might make the initial move. "Take small steps to develop friendships with Canadian and other racial groups," he suggested. "Cross the ethnic boundary. That is the quickest way to learn about Canada."

While he spoke many times to Chinese immigrants about the need to become integrated into Canadian society, David also took the opportunity to talk to Canadians about the newcomers. He stressed that people from Hong Kong brought with them entrepreneurial skills and a great capacity for hard work.

He frequently pointed out the financial and economic benefits that Canada, and particularly British Columbia, had received over the previous decades from Hong Kong immigrants. While by no means all were wealthy, many of them were affluent and had long experience and wide connections in the Asian business world. Quite a number were comparatively young people who, once they obtained residence requirements and Canadian citizenship, returned to Hong Kong to make more money at a much faster pace than they could in their new country. In a sense, these immigrants formed a Canadian bridgehead into the Asian market which, in mainland China alone, had a population of over a billion people. These entrepreneurs knew all the subtleties of doing business in Hong Kong, Taiwan, China or Singapore, as well as dealing with North American markets. They served as commercial links to a Pacific Rim economy which was booming and had a direct impact on British Columbia's export trade. While language and cultural barriers had long made Canada a minor player in this economy, David thought this should change.

He wanted to reach a wider public, and one means of doing this was by supporting the Laurier Institute. Founded in 1989, the organization's mandate is to carry out research on social conflicts and to disseminate its findings to the public so that it would have factual information for debate. The institute depends on private rather than government financing since it was felt that its research must be above reproach. There was a great deal of discussion on racial problems in the 1980s in the media and in public forums. If these discussions were based on fact rather than rumour, then imaginary grievances would yield to logical solutions. This, it was hoped, would have an influence on political decisions.

The institute attracted David. He knew one of its founders, Milton Wong, and became one of its first financial supporters. In 1990, the institute published a study which examined the causes behind sharp rises in B.C. land and housing prices. Many thought that it was due to the influx of Asian immigrants into the province, especially into the Greater Vancouver area. Assisted by the B.C. Real Estate Foundation, the Institute found that the increase in real estate prices was caused more by people coming from other parts of Canada than by immigrants from Asia. "When that hit the press," Wong notes, "it really and truly mitigated social conflict, improved attitudes and ameliorated a lot of pressure even to this day." This was just the sort of project David was happy to assist.

David did not favour the building of so-called "monster houses" in Vancouver and Toronto, nor was he in favour of Hong Kong investors speculating in residential houses. Buying an office tower, a mall or a hotel was one thing, but purchasing houses, especially those which were rental houses, could cause a great deal of strain and stress if people had to move. Frequently, a displaced renter would drive by his or her former house a few months or a year later and see it empty. This built up resentment. David spoke openly against this practice in Hong Kong as well as in Vancouver. To Canadians, he explained that Canadian houses seemed cheap to Hong Kong buyers. If the buyer offered an amount well above the market price, David felt there would not be one seller who would sell for less as a matter of principle. The only way to control this type of inflation, he believed, was for local politicians to exercise some control over the residential housing market. He thought the construction of "monster houses" could also be controlled by local authorities as well.

David found it difficult to get his message across regarding this particular issue. Again, it was a culture clash which would take time to resolve. But if the law permitted "monster houses" to be built, and if the buyers faced no restrictions, what could he done? David had his own ideas, most of which involved bylaws and zoning.

At the same time, he felt that understanding could be reached on a personal level between a wealthy Hong Kong immigrant and his new neighbours when one of these large houses was being built. David enjoyed relating the following story (reprinted here from the December 1992 issue of *Vancouver* magazine) as an example of the understanding and harmony he was trying to promote:

A good friend of mine bought a house in the heart of Shaughnessy, and when the builder told him he could tear it down and give him double the size of the house, he went for it. He kept going back to look at the construction and noticed his neighbours looking at him rather coldly. One of the neighbours told him pointedly that he was chairman of the Anti-Monster House Society. One day a lady came to him and complained: "You had a beautiful maple tree and you chopped it down." He said: "No, I didn't. I dug it up and put it in front of my garage because there was another hole [to replant it] when the house is enlarged. Overnight somebody came by and helped themselves. It's gone."

Another neighbour asked him: "What are you going to build between my house and yours?" He replied: "According to the plan, a fence." The neighbour said: "I hate fences." "What do you like?" "A hedge so that from my kitchen I can look through the leaves and see the view." "Okay! Done."

So he went around like that and did what most of the people wanted. The day after he moved in he sent a box of fortune cookies and moon cakes to each of the neighbours with a note saying that over the last months there had been so much dirt and dust that he felt very badly about it. Then he got an invitation from all the neighbours.... They decided on a progressive dinner, with hors d'oeuvres in house A, soup in house B, salad and the main course in house C and ended up with dessert in yet another house.

The friend he described was Tom Chan, the son of David's old Hong Kong friend Dr. Chan Shun, who was also chairman of one of his "Sunny" companies. David admitted that while there are a lot of wealthy immigrants, "there are not many Tom Chans who are willing to go out and meet neighbours halfway."

During the years following his retirement, David had the opportunity to speak to a great many people in the province, in Hong Kong and elsewhere. In 1989 he was designated as Communicator of the Year by the British Columbia chapter of the International Association of Business Communicators. The organization cited David's "outstanding leadership in the cross-cultural communication" and lauded his personal commitment to maintain and sustain British Columbia's multicultural heritage. It was a fitting and well-deserved tribute.

ELEVEN

Caring and Sharing

THERE IS MUCH truth in Alexander Pope's assertion that "as the twig is bent, the tree is inclined." Certainly, this appears to be the case with David Lam. As a young boy he was raised in a household where Christian principles were always emphasized and practised. The idea of serving and giving was deeply imbedded in his father's Christian belief, so much so that in the businesses which he owned or controlled, he insisted that the companies' articles of association include a clause stating that 10 per cent of the profits should go to charitable enterprises. This was a most unusual requirement, but as we have seen, Lam Chi Fung was an unusual man.

Along with the concept that charity was a Christian virtue, David was brought up with the idea that giving brought joy to the giver. As he says now, "What the heart gives away is never lost; it stays in the heart of others forever." At the same time, he feels that giving has a value in its own right. "Giving is not bargaining," he insists. "It's not a business deal. One should not gift with the intention of expecting a return. If you are expecting a return, it is almost like gambling in Las Vegas. Some people think, 'Okay, Christ, I don't have to give this dollar but I'm giving it to you. Would you give me back something? Give me a blessing.' You see, it's almost like gambling. You put one dollar on the roulette wheel, and expect back thirty-six dollars. And then when God doesn't give you the thirty-six dollars and your dollar is gone, you put in another coin and say, 'Let me remind you, God, this is my second dollar.' That is not giving, that is gambling. One should look at giving as an obligation of good citizenship, of being a good fellow human with a spirit of caring, sharing, serving, compassion and giving. With that kind of spirit you give automatically and very naturally."

The spirit of giving, however, is beset with problems and David was always well aware of them. As a young man, he made a modest salary despite his position as general manager of the family bank. At the same time, particularly after he was married, there were a lot of things he wanted, and his "wish list" grew longer. He wanted to travel, to build a house, to buy stock and to indulge in his numerous hobbies. These demands on his dollars competed with those for charitable donations, and like many he was tempted by the idea of retaining the principle of giving but putting it off to a future time when personal demands would not be so strong. The difficulty here, he knew, was that the demands never cease. Should one wait until the children grow up, until they finish their university education, until they get a good job or even until one accumulates sufficient money to ensure a comfortable retirement?

David was determined to overcome these temptations and make donations less painful. He already had income tax deducted automatically from his salary, so he instructed his accountant to deduct 10 per cent of his income for charity at the source as well. This money was put into a separate account and could not be used for any other purpose. With that account established, David found he could reply to a request for funds without going through any mental process of wondering about personal priorities.

"It almost seemed," he says now, "as if I was writing a cheque on some other person's money because it was in a separate account. There would be someone come—maybe they would be in desperate circumstances—and I would give them a few hundred dollars. Or perhaps a small Baptist chapel was looking for a new piano and I would buy one and give it to them. This kind of little giving gave me tremendous joy. When I left Hong Kong I made sure that every cent, even in the piggy bank, would be taken to Canada because I knew that we would be faced with the unknown. But it never entered my mind to see how much money I had in that donation account, even though we went through a period when every cent counted. A short time ago, my accountant told me there was still $10,000 to $20,000 in that donation account. What should be done with it? I said, 'Take $3,000 to pay for your own services, and pay the balance to the Hong Kong Baptist Hospital.'"

During the 1970s, and particularly during the 1980s, David gave away a large amount of money, much of it anonymously. Some of this gifting was in Vancouver, some in Victoria and other parts of Canada, and some in Hong Kong. The amounts he gave depended in part on the needs of the organization he wished to support, partly on his own interests and partly on his desire to be an active and creative giver rather than a passive donor. He preferred the former to the latter as we shall see, but his interests were widespread.

In August 1985, David received a letter from the Vancouver Police Historical Society. In the following year, the Vancouver police force would celebrate its hundredth anniversary. The force had retained all its records and noted that in the early 1920s it had one of the best police museums in Canada. The museum had been located in the basement of the building which housed the police but expansion of the force had made it necessary to reclaim the space. The society wanted to reinstitute the museum as a centennial project. The city of Vancouver had given the society a heritage building to house the new museum, but it was left largely to the society to renovate. Volunteers had put in a lot of work cleaning, painting and repairing it, but a critical stage had been reached and an estimated $50,000 would have to be raised to complete the task. Joseph H. Cohen, a friend of David's, was the Honorary Chief of Police, and he suggested the society write to David for financial support. Cohen suggested that perhaps each of them should donate $25,000 to finish the job.

David accepted the suggestion although perhaps not for the reason Cohen may have thought. The police museum was located close to Chinatown. David knew that most Chinese immigrants, both old and new, had an almost inborn aversion to police. To many, policemen represented authority, and in China that frequently went along with repression. Rather than automatically approach a policeman for help, there was a strong tendency to solve one's own problems and evade involvement with anyone in uniform. David felt that a public museum might be one way of bringing the immigrants into closer contact with the police. This would encourage greater rapport, lead to greater cooperation and establish a harmony which was sorely needed.

David made it clear that he wanted no personal recognition for his donation. Rather than a plaque with his name on it, he suggested that it need only say that the money came from the Chinese community. When the museum opened in April 1986, that was how the plaque was worded.

As an immigrant himself, David was interested in helping others who came to Canada with the hope of establishing themselves in a new land with a different culture. He was aware that there were hundreds of Chinese coming to British Columbia who were finding it difficult to cope with Canadian customs and laws. He sympathized with them and understood the difficulties they encountered on arrival.

In 1974 the United Chinese Community Enrichment Services Society (SUCCESS) was formed. A major non-profit social service agency for the Chinese community, it had several objectives. It assisted immigrants of ethnic Chinese origin to overcome language and cultural barriers. It helped immigrants to assume greater responsibility towards achieving self-reliance. It wanted to foster and promote social awareness and community involvement through civic education. Among the range of services it provided were family and youth counselling, referral services, programs for women and seniors, and English language and citizen training programs for immigrant adults. SUCCESS grew rapidly because it filled a need, and soon there were branches outside Vancouver's Chinatown, in Burnaby, Richmond and elsewhere.

It was just the kind of organization David wanted to encourage, and he donated to it almost from the beginning. Similarly, he was a great supporter of the Chinese Cultural Centre. During the 1980s, the centre was busily involved in completing the construction of the first of three phases of a complex to house the centre. An old friend and Lingnan alumni colleague, Dr. K. T. Yue, was chairman of the centre, and no one could have been more delighted than he in 1987 when

David donated $250,000 toward the construction of the multi-purpose hall in the complex. On this occasion, in order to provide encouragement to other potential donors, he raised no objection to the desire of the centre's board to name it the David See Chai Lam Auditorium.

As with any householder, he received the usual appeals in the mail ranging from the Salvation Army to the Heart and Stroke Foundation. They would all receive something. Appeals with which he had some association, naturally, received more. The Oakridge Baptist Church which he and his family attended could always count on his generosity year after year, and now and then he would help another Baptist congregation struggling to build a new church.

Hospitals, of course, were always looking for funds to enhance the good work they were doing and David frequently gave to them. St. Paul's Hospital, the Royal Columbian Hospital, the Vancouver General Hospital and the Mount St. Joseph Hospital all benefited from large donations over the years.

In 1990, for example, he gave Mount St. Joseph's $300,000 to help it complete its Diagnostic and Imaging Centre. Other wealthy Chinese-Canadians also contributed very generously to the hospital's campaign, some in the six-figure range. This was the sort of caring and sharing by his fellow immigrants David liked to see and one he frequently propounded in an increasing number of speeches in the late 1980s. Although he gave a great deal of money anonymously, he sometimes allowed the recipient to mention his name on a plaque or in some other manner. He felt it would encourage his compatriots to donate heavily as well. He was careful when he allowed this to happen, however, as shall be seen.

The variety of causes and institutions which benefited from David and Dorothy's donations in the 1980s was very wide. On the religious side, not counting his own church, there was Young Life of Canada, the Church of the Good Shepherd, the Billy Graham Crusade, the Chinese Christian Mission, the Chinese Presbyterian Church, the Salvation Army and the Saltspring Island Baptist Church. He supported cultural and music groups such as the Vancouver Symphony Orchestra, Canadian Music Competition and the Chinese Cultural

Centre. He supported service clubs such as the Rotary Club and the Lions Club, and art societies such as the Vancouver Art Gallery, the Banff Centre and the Royal Theatre. Organizations such as the United Way or the Variety Club, whose purpose was to raise money for general charitable work, could rely on his help. Institutions dedicated to educating the public such as the Vancouver Aquarium or the Cranbrook Museum found David to be a generous donor as well.

Although Greater Vancouver was the major focus of David's gifting, there were other areas which felt his generosity. Stan Hagen, provincial minister of education under Premier Bill Vander Zalm, once brought to his attention the need for an improved library at the Camrose Lutheran College in Alberta. A member of their faculty had been Chester Ronning, who had taught in China before the Second World War and later became the first Canadian ambassador to the People's Republic of China. The work Ronning had done in China impressed David, and he presented the college with a large cheque to help build a new library.

There were occasions when David would give money quite spontaneously without being approached. A classic example occurred in the spring of 1994 when he was asked by a Chinese group in Vancouver to speak at a fundraising dinner. There were about five hundred people in the restaurant, and when David talked to the group's executive and heard about their plans to improve cultural relations, he was impressed. On enquiring further, he found that after the dinner, there would be an auction to help fund the group's mission. David made an immediate decision. He told the chairman that he would match, dollar for dollar, the money raised by the auction. "May I announce that?" the chairman asked. "Yes," David said, "and ask people to bid high because every dollar they bid they get one extra." The bidding was better than anyone could have anticipated and by the time it was over, the group had raised $66,926. A few days later, David sent them a cheque matching the amount as he had promised.

In another unexpected move, David purchased a $5 million life insurance policy and arranged for the money to go to a charitable foundation rather than to his family. As he explained with deadpan humour in a speech to the Institute of Chartered Accountants of B.C.

in 1989, "To a lot of laymen, the deal was kind of complicated, but to the insurance company it was quite straightforward—the longer I live the better. But to the beneficiary of my $5 million life insurance, it wouldn't hurt if I should die as soon as possible. I am, of course, neutral. However, I side a little bit with the insurance company."

The idea of creating a foundation had been simmering in David's mind for some time. One reason was the Canadian income tax laws which permit a person to deduct a maximum of 20 per cent of annual income spent on charity. If David earned $100,000 in one year and wanted to donate $30,000 for charitable works, the government would only allow him to claim $20,000 for tax purposes. This did not stop him from giving more than he could deduct, but it irritated him that the government curbed what he wanted to give.

Another reason for creating a foundation was a change in his own philosophy of giving. In his mind, there were two categories: reactive and creative giving. "In reactive giving," he explains, "you react to requests. In creative giving, you go out and ask yourself, 'Why isn't something done? What would it take to have it done?' And you start planning on it and getting people together and working on it. It is a lot of work but is also very exciting because you are creating something from nothing. And you only play a part by putting in a certain amount of money as a challenge to all parties to fulfil and complete the project."

David's first involvement in creative giving began with his fundraising for the Hong Kong Baptist Hospital. Although initially he was not able to contribute heavily to it financially, he volunteered hundreds of hours of his time to get the project underway. Later, when his business in Canada began to flourish, he made large donations to it in the same way he did to Canadian hospitals. This type of creative giving gave him great satisfaction, and he felt if he was to do the same sort of thing in Canada he should organize his affairs to ensure the maximum amount of his donations went directly to the recipients.

It was for these reasons that David formed the Floribunda Philanthropic Society in 1982. Floribunda, which in Latin means "abundant flowers," was nontaxable, as its chief and sole role was to distribute money to worthy purposes. It also meant David and

Dorothy could give anonymously. Its board of directors was kept very small. Decisions on how much to give and to whom were made by David and Dorothy with one or two others—his accountant, Ken Williams, and later his tax lawyer, Blake Bromley—giving them advice and suggestions, primarily about the efficient management of the society. Neither Dorothy nor David were paid a penny for their work nor did they charge any of the expenses relating to their activities as board members. There were no office charges. A meeting of the board usually consisted of four or five people getting together in David's office to consider a major donation. Originally, the files could be kept in a briefcase and, later, in a single filing cabinet in David's office. The funding for the society was provided by the Lams, and with good management, the original capital provided a considerable amount of interest, dividends and capital gains. (An outstanding example of the latter was the sale of the Insurance Exchange Building in San Francisco described in an earlier chapter.)

The David and Dorothy Lam Foundation was formed in February 1985, and has always emphasized creative rather than passive donations. Like Floribunda, there is no staff or office overhead. Meetings of the board take place only a few times each year. It receives no outside gifts and its asset management is quite independent. Its grants usually are in the $1 million range and, where feasible, it avoids taking on the support of any one program all by itself. Its grants may be used as seed money to start a program, with the expectation that the program will be self-sustaining within four or five years.

Blake Bromley, a well-known Vancouver tax lawyer, helped David establish the foundation. Born in China, the son of a Christian missionary, Bromley has observed over the years that David's giving is divided. "David the Christian," he says, "is a reactive, emotive giver. David the philanthropist is a proactive, strategic giver."

When David was studying for his diploma at the University of British Columbia, one of his professors in the Faculty of Commerce was Dr. Michael Goldberg. Early in 1982, Goldberg was doing research on ethnic Chinese real estate investment behaviour and contacted his former student, who was able to give him a lot of information. The two became quite friendly. In the summer of 1984 David suggested they have lunch at Pierre Dubrulle's French Culinary School on Broadway, where David had once taken some cooking courses. During the lunch, Goldberg mentioned that the Faculty of Commerce was doing well but needed a research library devoted to business and economic matters. It often took a long time to receive information about a specific company or any organization, particularly in the Far East, and the faculty wanted the information to be available at UBC to serve students and the business community. David liked the idea and said, "All right. It's a small library, why don't I give you a million dollars to start, and we will do it?"

Rarely, in any professor's lifetime, does he receive a proposal like that. Goldberg almost fell off his chair. "I tried to remain deadpan and dignified," he remembers, and managed to reply that a million dollars would be "very helpful."

Goldberg's superior, Dean Peter Lusztig, also found it difficult to believe. Both men had long dreamed of establishing a management research library and a research centre. Some years earlier, they had visited the Harvard Business School and had been shown around the Baker Library. It was the world's most extensive university business library. Both realized the benefits a similar institution would bring to UBC and the province. On their return, they began to plan such a library for their own campus, reaching out for advice to improve on what they had seen and even arranging to sketch plans and build models of their project. They presented this idea to David at another luncheon.

The project was huge and would cost far more than David's grant. A 210,000-square-foot building was planned to house several research bureaus, a management conference centre, a graduate placement centre and the research library itself. In all, the price would come close to $10 million. Goldberg and Lusztig's strategy was to get the library endowed first and then to find a donor to get a new building constructed. They knew that it was usually much harder to get an operating endowment than it was to get someone to put their name on the building, so they decided to do the harder thing first.

David was very much in favour of the idea, particularly as the library would be very useful not only to the academic community, but to labour, government and business as well. He also liked the idea of starting on the library first and collecting money for the building later. Once assured of the university's cooperation respecting the proposed building site, he wrote out a cheque as promised. The donation was in the form of a "forgivable loan;" the money was theirs provided the project was completed. If not, the university would pay it back.

The David See Chai Lam Management Library opened in June 1985. In David's speech at the opening ceremonies, he said he wanted to use this occasion to say "thank you" to Canada. "Very few countries offer the opportunities for success which enable an immigrant without capital to accumulate enough money to put something back into the community," he stated. "My contribution to this library is but a small payment to the debt of gratitude which I owe."

The complete Management Research Centre was opened with its new modern library in April 1992. Funds had come in from a variety of sources, including Vancouver's Chinese community. From the time the foundation was being built, Lusztig and Goldberg had wanted the new structure to be named after David, but he thought it was not a good idea. He felt that if the fundraisers wanted to get a really large grant it might be easier to attract such a donor if the building was not named after him. When the campaign ended, however, it was found that David had made the largest donation. With a little arm-twisting, he allowed his name to be used. "I thought it very important," Goldberg said later, "that there be a symbol of Chinese philanthropy so we could dispel immediately the mythology that Chinese merely look out for themselves and their families, and they don't look after society."

The Management Research Centre was by no means David's only contribution to UBC. In the late 1980s, David and Dorothy gave $500,000 towards the creation of two new chairs in the Faculty of Education, one called the David Lam Chair in Multicultural Education and the other the Dorothy Lam Chair in Special Education. The former supports research to help train teachers to deal with the multicultural classroom and incorporate the richness of these cultures into the classroom experience; the latter coordinates the development of materials for special needs children.

Another major contribution David made was to UBC's special garden area. Established in 1975, the university's Asian Garden sometimes was described as one of Vancouver's best kept secrets. It was accessible only from the far side of the UBC Botanical Garden, through the Moon Gate at the end of a tunnel under Southwest Marine Drive. In order to not only improve the garden but provide better access to it, David gave well over $1 million to UBC.

When the improvements were completed, a much larger number of people were able to enjoy the garden. "It is an extremely beautiful place to visit in almost any season," David says with considerable satisfaction, "particularly in the spring. There is the tranquillity of walking in a virgin forest with all kinds of flowers." Among other species, the garden includes thousands of rhododendrums, camellias and hydrangeas. When the garden's education and visitors centre was opened in September 1990, the Asian Gardens were named after David. What gave him even more pleasure, however, was to have a newly-developed hybrid rhododendrum named after him and officially recorded with the Royal Horticultural Society.

David's gifting to the university had numerous indirect beneficial side effects. By allowing his name to be used on the Management Research Centre, he was suggesting that other wealthy Chinese-Canadians should follow his example. He became a strong supporter of the university's campaign fund and used his considerable influence to persuade people in Hong Kong as well as in Vancouver to contribute. One was a man in Hong Kong whom David had known for many years and greatly admired, Dr. Chan Shun. As we have seen, he had been chairman of one of David's earliest companies, Sunnyvale Developments.

Dr. Chan had done exceedingly well in business and had become a philanthropist on an international scale. For some years, his two sons, Tom and Caleb, had been conducting business in Vancouver. Much of their father's spirit of giving had been inherited by the two sons, and no one was more delighted than David when they pledged $10 million towards the construction of a much-needed performing arts centre. When completed, it was named after their father. This was the largest single donation ever made by a Chinese-Canadian family. Like David, they at first wished to remain anonymous, but were persuaded to let the public know. By the end of the 1980s, there could be no doubt that Chinese-Canadians were contributing a great deal of money to many institutions and charitable organizations in Vancouver. The old myth that the Chinese-Canadians rarely contributed to the community at large was fading away as David hoped it would.

One institution on the UBC campus which attracted David's attention and support as early as 1982 was Regent College, a trans-denominational institution welcoming men and women of all ages no matter what their church membership. It was founded in 1968 by people in Vancouver and Victoria who were members of the Plymouth Brethren Church. Although the college originally had only a few faculty members, mostly from Oxford and Cambridge, and held only summer classes for the first few years, the founders wanted to have the college located on the campus where it could benefit from the university's well-established educational facilities. Rather than establishing another theological seminary, they conceived Regent College as a place which brought Christian studies together with other disciplines of the academy and integrated them in a holistic world view for dealing with life.

The original faculty members, particularly Dr. James Houston, soon attracted an increasing number of students. Although in time the college became a fully accredited seminary offering a Master of Divinity program, its principal, Dr. W.C. Wright, explains, "We still would define our distinction as training men and women for life in the world, not for leadership in the church. We do that only secondarily. We see ourselves having the same role institutionally as a local church would have, to equip the person sitting in the pew to live out their faith in the world."

David had become aware of Regent College partly through his lawyer, Blake Bromley, who had taken several courses there and was to become a member of its board of governors. Other businessmen David knew had attended some of its courses, seminars and special lectures, and David sat in on a number himself. He was impressed by its wide-reaching Christian message, the vision of its founders and the fact it was attracting more students from Asia as well as other parts of North America.

When David first became involved, the college was located in two former fraternity houses on Wesbrook Mall. These were crowded, unfortunately, and the need to construct a proper building was obvious. Unfortunately, obtaining land on campus was not an easy task since final permission had to be given by the provincial government.

The college decided to launch a major fundraising campaign with a target of $5 million. In the spring of 1982, David made a pledge of $1 million towards the construction of the new building. He made one important proviso. His million could not be drawn upon until the college had raised the first $4.5 million. It was his way of guaranteeing, to the extent he could, that the project would be completed. According to Douglas Bennett, one of the fundraisers, "It was the right thing for him to do because it kept our feet to the fire . . . I think he was very wise."

Raising money in the early 1980s was not an easy task. In February of 1984, David wrote the college complaining he had seen no evidence of progress. He requested a quarterly report and suggested that he was putting a timetable on his own donation unless more was done. David understood, however, that one of the major problems was getting government permission to acquire the proposed building site. In the same letter, he promised he would approach Grace McCarthy and Bob McLellan, two provincial cabinet ministers, to find out why the government had delayed making a decision for several years.

David kept his promise. He wrote the ministers. Receiving no answer, he had his secretary telephone them to try and arrange a meeting. She could get no firm date. The break came unexpectedly one day when David was in Victoria's Union Club, where he was invited to lunch by the chancellor of the University of Victoria, Dr. William Gibson. Going through the dining room, he heard someone call his name. He turned around and there was Grace McCarthy. David recalls, "I went back to her and said, 'You know, for a number of days my secretary tried to get a ten-minute appointment for me with you and she got nowhere.' 'Oh,' she said, 'I had absolutely no idea. For you it's not ten minutes, it's ten hours any time.' I said, 'No, it is not that simple. I have pledged one million to Regent College but the government has been dragging its feet on making the land decision. If you help quickly to push the decision through, I will give the million. Otherwise, I'll send it to Hong Kong.'"

Within a few weeks, the obstacles to the college's expansion were removed and it acquired the land it needed. With that in place, the fundraising campaign began to produce results.

Well before construction had started, David had talked to the college authorities about starting a Chinese Studies Program. He wanted Chinese students who came to Canada to get to know the country better and Canadians to know more about China and Chinese culture. A greater cross-cultural exchange of information would lead to greater understanding and that, in turn, would promote greater harmony.

Around that time, he had heard a recorded speech by In-sing Leung, a postgraduate student working on his doctor's degree. Leung's comments about East-West culture, the difference and similarities among Eastern and Western religions, and other topics so impressed David that he tracked him down to the University of Hawaii and telephoned him about coming to Vancouver. Leung had heard about Regent College and was agreeable to the suggestion of a visiting scholarship. David's next step was to approach the college principal, Dr. Carl Armerding. David would put up the money for Leung and his family's transportation to Vancouver as well as his salary for a year as a visiting scholar. Armerding and the college senate agreed, and everything worked out well. This was the first step in the creation of the Chinese Studies Program which is now flourishing.

Looking back on it, David says, "To me, it had the same excitement as making a business deal. You bring people together, you bring opportunity together, you bring everything together, and then you start to bake a cake."

Before the new building was formally opened in 1988, David gave the college an additional $250,000 to help fund the Chinese Studies Program. It was attracting students not only from Canada and the United States but from Singapore, Malaysia, Hong Kong and Taiwan. Within six years of the opening of the new structure the college had five hundred full- and part-time students, over 25 per cent of whom were of Asian origin. While David attended the opening ceremony, a ceremony more important to him was the one held in September of the same year to mark the opening of the Lam Chi Fung Auditorium. David was touched that the college named the new auditorium in honour of his father, who had worked so hard over many years to help the Baptist cause in Hong Kong and elsewhere. Most of David's brothers and sisters also attended in this tribute to that truly Christian gentleman, who had died in April 1971.

David and Dorothy's major funding grants were by no means confined to the UBC campus. In 1978, for example, David learned of the Chinese Cultural Centre's plan to establish a 3.5-acre Chinese classical garden in the heart of Vancouver's Chinatown. The city of Vancouver had established a Chinese Garden Advisory Committee, and in 1980, representatives from the Suzhou Garden Administration arrived from China on a visit. They felt the site was suitable to create a park and garden similar to those for which Suzhou was famous. To do so properly, however, would require craftsmen from China and authentic building material, plants and shrubbery. The estimated cost of the project was over $5 million.

When David first began to make enquiries about the garden, he encountered a lot of planners but no single authority in charge. He let it be known that he would be willing to pledge $1 million to the project, but with conditions. The money could not be used initially "to dig holes in the ground," as he put it, but it would be available when major funds had been collected to ensure its completion. To attract other donors, he even deposited a $1 million letter of credit with the bank as proof of his sincerity. This established the credibility of the project's capital campaign. Furthermore, several of the most prominent citizens of Vancouver became involved and began a five-year tireless campaign of fundraising. A few months later, the Dr. Sun Yat-Sen Classical Garden Society was formed with the specific aim of overseeing the completion of the garden.

Because of a downturn in the economy, raising funds was not easy despite David's pledge. Ron Shon, who became the society's president, had to work particularly hard to meet the deadlines imposed on construction both in China and at home. Early in 1985, the first of the fifty-two artisans from Suzhou arrived. Materials needed for constructing the bridges, pavilion and other structures in the garden arrived in seventy seagoing steel containers. During the next year, Chinese artisans and gardeners worked steadily until the garden was opened officially in April 1986. David and Dorothy were there for the opening of the only classical Chinese garden in Canada.

During the winter of 1984–85, the premier of British Columbia, William R. Bennett, called together a group of businessmen and academics to discuss prospects for developing economic relations with China. It was at this meeting that David met Howard E. Petch, the president of the University of Victoria. The two men got along well together, and in March, Petch invited him to Victoria to visit his campus. At that time, David was in no position to travel even the 70-mile distance to Victoria. He was in the hospital and was to remain there for two months. The doctors seemed unable to find the cause of his illness, and X-rays and other tests revealed nothing. Ultimately, David insisted that an operation should be performed so the surgeons could actually see what was the matter. It was well he insisted, for his gallbladder was filled with fine crystal particles which the X-ray could not detect. Inflammation had spread to his pancreas and was close to his liver. He remembered his father had had a similar illness in Hong Kong and only surgery had revealed the cause. After the operation, David recovered quite rapidly.

When he finally got to the University of Victoria in 1986, one of the academic staff he met was Dr. Jan Walls. He had taught Chinese language and literature at UBC from 1970 to 1978. Petch had wanted to start a centre for Pacific Rim studies, and he brought Walls to the University of Victoria to try and get one organized. David asked Petch if he could help the university and invited Petch to write him with specific proposals. Petch had made a number of suggestions—scholarships, fellowships, buildings and so on—but none seemed to arouse the response he had hoped for. In October 1985, however, he caught David's attention with a proposal, drafted in consultation with Dr.

Walls, that the David and Dorothy Lam Foundation assist in providing operating expenses for the first four years of the Centre for Pacific Rim Studies.

When David had the opportunity to discuss the proposal in more detail, he felt it was something he should support. There were, as Petch had written to him, "growing demands on this critical field across Canada." The centre, later called the Centre for Asia-Pacific Initiatives, would fill a need and the timing was right.

A short time later, over a luncheon in Victoria, David told Petch that he had decided to give the university $1 million. The money was to be used as an endowment fund. Interest and dividends from the fund were to be used to support the centre for its first four years, after which David expected it to be able to generate funding from other sources, as indeed was to be the case. At the end of that period, the president would present him with a new project for four-year funding and continue doing so every four years. These terms were met, and have so far resulted in two new bodies at the university: the Institute for Dispute Resolution and the Centre on Aging. Petch said at the time that the arrangement was unique and exciting, and commented, "It is a creative adaptation of the endowment concept and should help to ensure long-term development of this university. In effect, it is a perpetual development fund." Since the time will come when David is no longer available to scrutinize and approve new proposals, provision has been made for the incumbent lieutenant-governor to take his place.

To show its appreciation, the university named one of its largest auditoriums after David. A few months later, in the spring of 1986, a pair of rare Chinese dove trees were planted in his honour.

The $1 million endowment grant was followed by smaller donations in later years. One in particular, however, deserves mention. When Dr. Petch was nearing retirement, David thought he should be presented with a really nice gift in appreciation of his years of hard work at the university. He was thinking of a gold watch or fountain pen, but he put out feelers about an appropriate gift. One of the ideas which emerged for David's consideration was a fountain to be located in front of the library. Picturing a fountain of water splashing into a small goldfish pool, David calculated it might cost about $30,000. It was about ten times what he had in mind originally, but he indicated he liked the idea and the university began to develop plans for it. Sometime later, David was invited to come to Victoria and examine the architect's proposal. Viewing the model, he realized it was not a goldfish fountain but a large pool surrounded by a tree-shaded sitting area. For David, it was a considerable mental leap from a pen or watch to a beautiful pool with water cascading over huge rocks. Still, he was attracted by the idea and the provincial government agreed to match the money he was willing to donate. When the pool was opened officially on June 13, 1990, David felt he had done the right thing. As he put it, "The pool is something for enhancement and enrichment, for tranquillity, for art and for beauty, for creating an environment everyone on the campus can enjoy." Certainly it has become a favourite spot for the students to congregate, but instead of feeding goldfish, they delight in feeding the dozens of mallard ducks who swim about there for most of the year.

There was a third university in British Columbia which benefited from David's creative gifting on a large scale in the late 1980s—Simon Fraser University. Two men in particular managed to interest him in activities at SFU. One was Dr. Jan Walls, who had left the University of Victoria in 1985 to become vice-president of the newly established Asia-Pacific Foundation of Canada. In 1987, he was invited by Simon Fraser University to help create a Centre for Intercultural Communication in downtown Vancouver. Walls and David, by this time, knew each other well and were on friendly terms.

The other major influence was Dr. William Saywell, president of the university. He had studied Chinese history at the University of Toronto, learned to speak the language and, like Walls, had spent a year in Peking working as a cultural attaché for the Canadian embassy. In the late 1980s, the university began a campaign to raise funds which would be matched by the provincial government. It was decided to target certain persons to donate funds for projects which would be of special interest to them.

As Saywell recalls, "In the case of the Lams, we knew of their interest in Asia-Pacific issues, in cross-cultural communication, multiracial harmony and that sort of thing. We were attempting to set up a new downtown campus at Harbour Centre that would be committed to the study of intercultural communication focussed on Asia. It was not just language, but how do you deal with the cultures of Chinese, Japanese, Koreans, Malaysians, et cetera. How do you do business with them? How do you understand them?" It was planned that the centre's instructors would be able to speak a variety of languages, and its focus would be, in a very practical way, to instruct business, government, professional and other people in the art of learning about the cultures of nations they would be visiting on the other side of the Pacific. Equally important, the centre would be used by visitors from Asia wishing to learn more about Canada.

When David met Saywell, it was the first time he had ever met a Canadian university president with whom he could converse in Chinese. He was interested in the centre for cultural communications—after all, the subject was something he had been advocating for years—and he was pleased to hear that Walls would be in charge of the centre.

At the same time, there was another proposal by Saywell which interested him as well. This was the creation of a graduate research centre at the W. A. C. Bennett Library on the university's main campus.

After thoroughly examining both proposals, and keenly aware of the provincial government's matching grant, David wrote the president saying that he was going to give the university $1 million. One-quarter would go to the new Centre for International Communication, one-half to the Graduate Research Centre and the remaining quarter to the president's discretionary fund. In the letter, he made it clear that he and Dorothy wished to make the donation "in a way that does not attract a great deal of attention to our contribution." The university respected their wishes. Dr. Walls, however, was very keen to have at least the Centre for International Communication named after David. It took a lot of persuasion and three different attempts before he agreed, but when the centre was opened in June 1990, it bore David's name.

In very short order, the centre was operating and beginning to generate its own funds. The Department of External Affairs gave it a hefty grant and utilized the centre's expert staff to help prepare Canadian diplomats and business representatives to meet their opposite numbers across the Pacific. Saywell remembers the centre's first contract: "Alcan came to us and said, 'We're bringing twenty-six factory chiefs from China to Canada for about three months to network with them, to try and do business with them, to show them Canada. We are going to show them our plants. We would like you at the centre, for the first three weeks, to teach them about Canada, how we bank, how our insurance industry works, how our transportation industry operates, so that we can take them into the country and they will have all that background.' We set up a three-week intensive program to teach the Chinese leaders about Canada and we gave all the lectures in Chinese."

By 1995, the centre was providing courses to about four hundred people a year in Mandarin, Cantonese, Japanese, Korean and Bahasa Indonesia, the language spoken in Indonesia. Some take immersion courses, while others come for several hours a week, over a number of months or years. At the same time, they receive instruction on cultural behaviour, which Dr. Walls calls "a cross-cultural vaccination against foot-in-mouth disease."

Although he gradually moved from passive to active giving, David never gave up the former. Appeals from the United Way, the Red Cross or the Children's Hospital received his support but the larger donations required more scrutiny. "My money is used as a yeast," he liked to say, "as in the baking of bread." He had no interest in projects which would exist just because he supported them. Each project had to be able to stand on its own. In sum, David wanted to get the best value for his donated dollar. He sought long-term benefits over as many years as possible, and the longer the potential life of a project he funded, the happier he would be.

Today, he sums up his concept of giving with his trademark mixture of practicality and philosophy. "Anyone can write a cheque," he says. "Anyone can give money away, but that is not the key to charity. To run a charitable organization carries a lot of responsibilities. It is 'to what project, to whom, how, how much, when, under what control, what follow-up, and how much should one give?' That must be thought through and exercised wisely. Failing that, it is an abdication of responsibility."

"Giving during one's lifetime," he adds, "has the added joy of seeing how your money is being used. When it is being used very wisely, then you give some more. When it is not, then you stop giving to that organization. Some people have a simple idea. A good friend of mine said, 'I'm going to give everything to my church.' I said, 'You are going to kill that church.' When there is money in excess in that church, the board of deacons for sure will say, 'Let's build a daycare centre. Let's build a home for the aged. Let's expand. Let's branch out. Let's help foreign missionaries. Let's help religious education. Let's do something in the medical field.' But you cannot really do it all and do it well. The board will likely quarrel and might split the church."

David continued to give generously in the years that followed. Each of the three universities to which he had made major grants awarded him—and in one case Dorothy also—the honorary degree of Doctor of Law in appreciation of his gift. He received well-deserved wider recognition from the federal government in 1988, when he was made a Member of the Order of Canada. (More recently, he was appointed to the higher grade of Officer of the Order.) In the twenty-one years he had been in Canada, David had achieved a greater level of success than he might ever have imagined when he first arrived. Unknown to him at the time, he was to reach higher levels in the following years.

TWELVE

Queen's Representative

DURING THE FIRST five years following his retirement, David spent a considerable amount of time on his philanthropic activities, travelling, and had more time for sailing and learning the art of gourmet cooking. He remained active in the Rotary Club and, with more leisure available to him, his golf began to improve. Aside from looking after his personal properties, David accepted a directorship on the board of Barbicon Properties, which kept him mildly occupied in the real estate scene all across Canada in an advisory capacity. He also continued to devote time to the Asia-Pacific Initiative and the Dragon Boat Festival.

In 1982 David was invited to join the board of Canada Place Corporation. The Crown corporation was created in the early 1980s to oversee the construction of a major complex on the Vancouver waterfront which would include docks for cruise ships visiting the city, a large convention centre, and a world-class hotel. The huge venture involved the municipal, provincial and federal governments, as well as private capital. Its chairman was R. G. Rogers, a well-known businessman who had recently retired as president and CEO of the forestry company Crown Zellerbach. Rogers would appoint some of the board members; the federal government, the remainder.

David was neither a Liberal nor a Progressive Conservative. When he was asked by the federal Liberal party to accept a directorship on the corporation, he agreed to do so as a service to the community. The board met once a month; the directors were paid a few hundred dollars when they were attending the meeting, and that was it. The income from such an appointment was negligible to David. He regarded his appointment as a logical one, considering his knowledge of Vancouver's real estate market, and as an acknowledgment of the role of the Chinese-Canadian community in the life of the city.

After about two years on the job, R. G. Rogers resigned when he was appointed lieutenant-governor of British Columbia. A short time later, in the fall of 1984, the new chairman and all the appointed board members were asked to resign when the Progressive Conservative government was elected and placed its own appointees on the board.

There were few times in his life when David became angry. This was one of them. Someone in Ottawa phoned his office. His secretary took the message: David was to send in a letter of resignation from the board immediately. David remembers his reaction when she told him: "I blew my top." There was not even a letter thanking him for his work, merely a nameless political staffer in Ottawa intent on getting rid of Liberal government appointees. David had not accepted his appointment as a political favour. He accepted it to serve. He was a hardworking board member with experience the corporation needed. To be swept out merely because a new government had come to power struck him as insulting and, moreover, it reflected badly on the Chinese-Canadian population as a whole.

In the years that followed the Progressive Conservative party's rise to power, David had numerous opportunities to express his mind on his dismissal. Occasionally, he would meet senior cabinet ministers at social gatherings and would let them know that he did not appreciate being treated like a political lackey, to be swept away without so much as a thank you. Each of them expressed surprise and said something must be done about it. "The result," David says, "was that I kept hearing from people in Ottawa saying they were very regretful. They wanted to apologize to me, and would I consider serving on the board of Air Canada or the Bank of Canada or the Canada Council?" There was even mention indirectly of an appointment to the Canadian Senate.

David had no particular desire to fly back and forth across Canada to sit on a board of directors. He had already turned down offers to be a director on the boards of other companies. Sometime later, however, Senator Gerry St. Germain asked him if he would be willing to serve as a British Columbia member on the Canada Council. The council's mandate is to encourage the study and enjoyment of the arts, humanities and social sciences. It provides grants for scholarly research, artists, orchestras, book publishers, and a variety of artistic and cultural organizations and associations across Canada. This appealed to David. He accepted the appointment and soon was inundated with a mass of papers to read and petitions to hear. One of the latter was from the Vancouver Symphony Orchestra, which had gone broke. A well-known Vancouverite, Ray Peters, had organized a group determined to raise money for its continuance, and in David he found a very sympathetic listener. Late in 1988, the symphony received enough money to resume its musical offering to the public.

One of the most unexpected calls David received about an appointment for a government position came in 1988. The caller was the premier of British Columbia, Wilhelmus ("Bill") N. T. M. Vander Zalm. He had become leader of the Social Credit party in July 1986 and led his party to victory in the provincial elections in October of the same year. David had met him casually at several functions. He remembered one in particular. He and a group serving on the Asia-Pacific Initiative had been invited to dinner at Government House in Victoria, the residence of the lieutenant-governor. He wanted to catch the last airplane back to Vancouver that same evening. David and some friends had rented a car at the airport, and after the dinner they hopped into their car. Time was short and no one was familiar with the route through the city to the highway. Eventually they found their way, and with little time to spare, David drove faster than the speed limit. A police car pulled him over to the side of the road. Using all his considerable charm, David explained that it was urgent he catch the last plane.

Luck was with him. The officer said to follow him, so David and his friends roared down the highway behind the police car with its siren howling. Despite this effort, it was too late. The last flight had gone.

At dinner, however, David had overheard Vander Zalm and Grace McCarthy talking about taking the government jet for a late flight from the airport. He got in touch with the airport tower and requested that the official contact the premier's aircraft just as it was moving towards the takeoff runway. Vander Zalm agreed to take David and his friends on the government aircraft, and en route to Vancouver, they had the opportunity to talk. It was only a twenty-minute flight, but it was the longest chat David ever had with him.

Early in 1988, David received a telephone call from Bill Vander Zalm, who had been asked by the federal government to suggest three names for nomination of the next lieutenant-governor. While stressing that Ottawa was not bound to accept any one of the names, Vander Zalm said he would like to nominate David as one of the three. David asked if he could give his answer immediately, and said, "The answer is no, thank you very much." When Vander Zalm observed that it was a great honour he was turning down, David said, "Honour, yes, but I feel very intimidated by the whole idea. I don't want to change my lifestyle and I'm very busy doing a lot of things—my foundations, my volunteer work." Vander Zalm said, "Why don't you think about it for a few days. Talk to Mrs. Lam. Think about it." David agreed.

Sitting in his office at the time he received the phone call was an old friend from the banking business, George Siborne. When David told him the reason for the call, Siborne's initial response was, "David, you don't want it because you will sit for five years in a glass cage." David discussed the matter with Dorothy. If David was found acceptable, she would be living in the "glass cage" with him. Dorothy was not enthusiastic. She felt she would be intimidated by the publicity, the style of life and the fact that her English was not as good as David's. It would be a different world altogether, she knew, and she did not think she would be able to help him.

During the next two days, David found no reason to change his original answer to Vander Zalm. His English was better than Dorothy's, but it was still his second language. He knew little about the role of a lieutenant-governor—in fact, he was more familiar with the role of a colonial governor such as Hong Kong's. He was also a bit sensitive that a bout of Bell's Palsy had caused a partial paralysis on one side of his face; although hardly noticeable to a stranger, it was very noticeable to him. Two days later, the premier called again while David was at home having tea with Dorothy and their daughter Doreen. Again, he was asked if he would let his name stand, and David once more declined. When he hung up the telephone, the two women clapped their hands.

This was not the end of the matter. The next day, the Lams went to the Oakridge Baptist Church, where David talked about his decision with his pastor, the Reverend Campbell Henderson. Henderson told him that they should pray together for guidance. "In our life," the pastor said, "whatever comes, God will fix a path for you to follow." He advised David that this could be a very important milestone in his life. Historically, it was important in that if he was chosen, he would be the first Chinese-Canadian ever to fill the post. "You should not take it lightly," he added. "But I already said no," David replied. "Then you should pray some more," the pastor advised.

Back home, Dorothy and David talked about the nomination again. He told her, "I don't feel uncomfortable if it is God's will that I should take up an additional challenge and change five years of our lives by taking on this position." They discussed the matter with a variety of friends, all of whom agreed it was an honour he should not turn down should he be offered it. Dorothy now felt she should change her attitude. "I thought to myself," she remembers, "that later, when David looks back, he might regret that he refused such an honour because of me. So I told him, 'I will fully support you just as I did when we first came to this country. We worked hard together. We went through a lot together. I will do that again if you want to take on this big job.' "

David reconsidered his position. It was unlike him to think negatively, and after a few more days of reflection, he decided to telephone the premier. If the offer to nominate him was still open, he told him, he would accept. Vander Zalm was delighted and told David he would phone Ottawa that same day.

The fact that David's name would be put up for nomination did not mean that he would be asked to fill the position. The person who made the decision was the Canadian prime minister, who at that time was Brian Mulroney. David had met him once at a fundraising dinner for the Progressive Conservative Party in Vancouver. Mulroney would receive perhaps a dozen names as potential candidates. Names might be put forward by a number of people, from politicians to private citizens, but the final selection was up to the prime minister after consultation with his political advisers.

The post of lieutenant-governor is regarded as a "political plum." Considering the background of those usually asked to fill the post, the salary is by no means its most attractive lure, being comparable with that of the president of a small college or a successful lawyer in a modest law firm. It did, however, carry with it a great deal of prestige and put one automatically at the summit of provincial society and precedence.

There was no job description for the position. British Columbia, the third-largest province in Canada in both size and population, covers an area of almost 950,000 square kilometres, larger than most of the countries in Europe. If the lieutenant-governor was to be seen and heard by the three million people living in the province, he would have to do a lot of travelling. If he did not wish to make the effort, there was nothing compelling him to do so. As Her Majesty the Queen's representative in the province, there were certain constitutional duties for him to perform, but these normally took up only about 5 to 10 per cent of his time. There were no limits on his other duties.

During the late spring and early summer of 1988, David waited for word about the appointment. As the weeks went by with no answer, he put the thought back in his mind to the point where he no longer expected it. Dorothy was secretly happy that they would be able to continue their quiet, homey lifestyle while David, though retired, continued to be busy with his various projects. They were almost startled, therefore, when late in July, Gerry St. Germain called to say that David had been chosen to be British Columbia's next lieutenant-governor.

When the news was made public, it surprised many people. Peter Newman, a well-known Canadian writer, commented in print that previously, candidates had been of British stock, tended towards Anglicanism "and were probably raised on porridge. This self-perpetuating daisy chain was abruptly snapped with the appointment of British Columbia's twenty-fifth lieutenant-governor, David See Chai Lam." Almost immediately, David was inundated with newspaper reporters, television cameras and others.

David enjoyed the tumult, but after a full day of interviews, he left the city. He had promised to take Dorothy sailing and saw no reason to change his plans. "I wanted to get away from the telephone," he told reporters later. "Also, I wanted to live off the land, so I packed two days' provisions for a ten-day cruise. We caught salmon. We ate steamed clams with garlic butter and barbecued oysters. I kept the radio turned off, and every night I sat in the cockpit and looked at the stars. It brought me back to the magnitude of creation and my own insignificance. I looked at the stars and I said to God, 'You could have killed me half a dozen times but you didn't. I think you had a path for me and I am on it now.' "

After sailing a few days up the coast to Jervis Inlet, David used his radio telephone to call his office. His secretary told him the prime minister was trying to reach him. He tried several times to reach the telephone numbers Mulroney had left but was unable to contact him. An arrangement was made for him to call at a specific time the next day so he sailed farther up the coast where he knew there was a public telephone near a good anchorage. Holding a handful of quarters, he lined up behind others wanting to phone and in due course reached the prime minister.

After congratulating him, Mulroney asked when he wished to take over the appointment. David thought for a moment. On September 7, many of his brothers and sisters would be coming to Vancouver to attend the official opening of the auditorium at Regent College named after his father. He suggested that the changeover ceremony could take place two days later. It would give the family members time to visit Victoria and be on hand. Moreover, September 9 was the anniversary of his engagement to Dorothy. On top of that, it was the ninth day of the ninth month, and the double nines had special significance in the Chinese language since the sound is synonymous with the word everlasting. The date was acceptable and preliminary planning could start.

On the telephone to his secretary, David learned that news of his appointment had created a great deal of interest around the Pacific Rim and elsewhere. He had been called by Reuters and United Press International, and by friends and newspapers in Hong Kong, New York, Chicago, Dallas, Los Angeles, Australia, Singapore, Kuala Lumpur and Taipei. Newspapers serving Chinese communities in North America were particularly interested in interviewing a person who, twenty-one years earlier, had come to Canada as an immigrant and now represented the Queen in British Columbia.

In the weeks between talking to Mulroney and the swearing-in ceremony at Government House, there was a great deal to be done. David and Dorothy visited Government House to take a closer look at their new home, and both had a long talk with the Honourable Robert G. Rogers and his wife Jane about their experiences. David also met Michael Roberts, private secretary to the lieutenant-governor, who had served in that position since 1979. There was no one more knowledgeable than he was about all aspects of the office. While David and Rogers were discussing the business of the office, Dorothy was escorted by Jane Rogers to see the mansion, particularly the private suite which would be their own quarters. While Dorothy had experience running the large Lam residence in Hong Kong when David's mother was ill, she had not had a servant in her own house since coming to Canada. She was a bit awed by her new responsibilities, but Mrs. Rogers advised her to "just take this as your home. There are so many things to do, but don't try so hard to do everything." To make her point she later handed her the master keys of the house, which were held together by a chain inscribed with the words, "One Day at a Time."

One of the things David had to discuss was the swearing-in ceremony. Naturally, the incumbent lieutenant-governor wanted a few of his friends there. Most of the guests, however, were to be invited by David, and only a limited number could be accommodated. Given his large number of friends and relatives, it was a very difficult situation. "Some people may not forgive me to this day for having left them out," David says ruefully, "but I was under a very tight constraint as to the number I could invite."

On September 9, the ballroom of Government House was crowded. About a dozen television personnel roamed around the fringes of the audience recording the event for the evening news broadcasts. The 150 guests included 20 members of David's family, with most of his brothers except Daniel. The premier and his cabinet were there, as were a variety of people from the federal government and senior representatives from the universities, church, armed forces and so forth. It was his old neighbour from Ash Street, Chief Justice Allan McEachern, who swore David into office. Finally, after brief speeches, the ceremony was over and the guests departed. David had made arrangements for a bus to take his family members to enjoy dinner at Butchart Gardens. That night, since their private quarters in Government House were being repainted, David and Dorothy slept in the Royal Suite.

During the next weeks and months, David was to learn a great deal about the operation of his new office. His position carried with it certain privileges. One was precedence. When he first came to Canada, knowing that women usually preceded men when entering a room, he would sometimes have to push Dorothy gently ahead of him. Dorothy became quite accustomed to this. Now that David was lieutenant-governor, he had to reach out and tug her back so that he could enter first as protocol demanded. He now had his own official flag which flew over Government House when he was in residence, was hoisted on the mast of any ferry on which he travelled and flew from a small standard on his car. He had a chauffeur, John Mager, who also acted as steward, valet and piper. For formal dinners, Mager would don traditional Highland garb and pipe the guests into the dining room. He had been hired originally by a former lieutenant-governor, the Honourable H. P. Bell-Irving, who had a long association with the Seaforth Highlanders of Canada. David had no Scottish blood in him, but he liked the tradition and carried it on.

Although he had a chauffeur, for the first few years the provincial government did not provide him with a car. David, therefore, bought the limousine owned by his predecessor. The car had a special gold-plated licence plate displaying the coat of arms of British Columbia. He also had the privilege of being the first to be allowed on and off any B.C. ferry, and did not have to pay for travel on the ferry when on official business.

There were several other perquisites which went with the position such as honorary membership in the Vancouver Club, the Union Club of British Columbia in Victoria, and certain golf and country clubs. He could anticipate being made a Knight of Grace of the Most Venerable Order of the Hospital of St. John of Jerusalem, and serving as vice-prior of the order in the province during his term of office.

From a more practical point of view, David found that both the provincial and the federal government contributed to the upkeep of the office. The provincial government provided a budget to maintain Government House and the salaries of the dozen people who worked in it, ranging from his private secretary to the housekeepers and maintenance personnel. In earlier years there had been more, but now it was less expensive to contract out tasks such as mowing the large expanse of lawns, rather than retaining full-time gardeners. For large functions, extra part-time staff were hired.

For its part, the federal government paid David's salary and allowed him approximately $25,000 per year for travelling and $30,000 for "in-capital" expenses incurred while he was in the capital city of the province. During the years he was in office, both amounts were reduced. As David soon found out, neither grant was sufficient to pay the costs of travel or entertainment he was expected to undertake. This was a problem familiar to previous incumbents which David was to resolve in his own way.

As lieutenant-governor, David received invitations to speak at a large variety of functions ranging from the mess dinner of a local army regiment to the opening of a flower show by a horticultural society. As he had nobody to write his speeches or do research for him, he started out by writing his own. Then, a week after he was sworn in, he gave a talk at a fundraiser for the Vancouver Symphony Orchestra. It was a dark and cloudy day. David read from his speech, saying how much he valued and appreciated the orchestra. "I wanted to wish the symphony orchestra to go from crescendo to crescendo," he remembers.

"When I said 'crescendo,' the loudest crack of thunder in the history of Vancouver broke over the convention centre. It was so loud. I had never had such a sound hit my eardrums. Many people ducked in their seats. At that moment I looked up to the sky and said, 'God, thank you. With God as my soundman, I really don't need a speech writer.' I concluded my speech right there and brought the house down. That helped to mould the style of speech I developed."

From that time onward, David rarely used a prepared text. While he might write a few notes ahead of time, more often he would scribble a few notes on the back of an envelope or menu while having dinner before he rose to speak.

If his speeches were frequently made "off the cuff," his engagements were very carefully timed and prepared. Since there were often several in one day and their locations could be miles apart, a one-, two- or three-page "operations order" was usually issued, covering such things as the time and date of the engagement, dress for Their Honours, the name of the event, the place and address and even a small map of the area. If the lieutenant-governor was expected to speak, the order said for how long and on what topic. Then there would be a detailed sequence of the meeting which would include who was to greet him, whether there was time set aside for him to mingle with the guests, a list of the head table guests, a brief history of the society he was talking to and the anticipated time of his departure. Everything had to be choreographed like a ballet so that the event would proceed with style and dignity.

Most of the time everything went well, but now and then it did not. One such moment came when David was crossing to Vancouver by ferry. His car was first on the ship and thus positioned at the exit gate to be the first off. When the ferry docked and the ramp was lowered, the chauffeur tried to start the car, but an electrical fault had drained the battery. Several hundred cars could not move until the battery was jump-started and its engine roared to life. A rather embarrassed David hoped not too many ferry passengers recognized him as the car sped up the ramp to the dock.

Of all the functions he attended, the opening of the Legislative Assembly was the most important. This was one of his constitutional duties and involved a considerable amount of traditional ceremony. On this occasion, he wore a heavy black jacket laced with gold braid, black trousers, a cocked hat trimmed with feathers and a sword. He would arrive in front of the Legislative Building as the last of a fifteen-gun salute was fired by the local artillery battery. A hundred-man guard of honour, accompanied by a band, was lined up for his inspection. After he had inspected the troops, he was met on the steps of the legislature by the premier and other dignitaries. Then, in solemn procession, he was escorted into the Legislative Chamber to read the Speech from the Throne, an ancient parliamentary tradition performed in the British House of Commons by Her Majesty the Queen. Following the ceremony, he was escorted back to his car, and with a final salute from the military forces, he went back to Government House and got out of his uniform as quickly as possible.

The pomp and circumstance of such occasions attracted the attention of the press and the television crews, and perhaps left an impression on the public mind that this was all a lieutenant-governor did. David himself thought that way until he really became involved. He decided to give the position a higher profile during his term. It would be an excellent platform to promote his ideas on education, racial harmony and other topics dear to his heart. A few weeks before assuming office, he told the Richmond Rotary Club, "I am determined to work hard to bring harmony, good will and prosperity to this province. I pledge to use my knowledge and connections, both here and abroad, to build bridges between British Columbia, the Asia-Pacific countries and the world. I believe we can learn from each other and can be beneficial to each other."

Accomplishing this task was to take up a great deal of his time, particularly as he began to accept more and more invitations to speak, from one end of the province to the other.

David talked to former judges, constitutional experts, professors and others knowledgeable about constitutional matters so that he would be fully aware of his role and responsibilities. "The more things I learned," he says, "the more I realized that the lieutenant-governorship was not quite what I thought it was."

Even though many previous lieutenant-governors had been closely associated with one political party or another, the incumbent was supposed to be non-political. The lieutenant-governor was not supposed to comment publicly on any action taken by the party in power, nor on any other politician. The provincial government, in the course of its business, would pass a number of bills, laws and orders-in-council, and provided these were within their proper guidelines, they would be made legal with the signature of the lieutenant-governor. In the extremely unlikely possibility that the provincial government decided to print its own money, establish a head tax on immigrants or change the provincial boundaries at the expense of an adjoining province, the lieutenant-governor could negate the action by withholding his approval. If the premier failed to maintain the confidence of his own political party, the lieutenant-governor would ask for his resignation. For a lieutenant-governor to interfere in this manner was extremely rare, and it was not the sort of situation anyone in that office wanted to encounter.

Prior to coming to Government House he had been given a lot of advice about not crossing certain lines. One suggestion was that a lieutenant-governor should be "seen but not heard." He did not see his role in that light. Shortly after he assumed office, he called his small staff together and told them, "We are going to go all out. We are going out to reach and touch the lives of people and encourage them to touch me." He wanted to bring messages of good will, compassion and understanding, to be a vice-regal cheerleader for the province and to make his office and himself better known. He intended "to put Government House on wheels," but with a limited travel budget to reach out to a province almost three times the size of Germany, it was going to call for a lot of planning.

David first thought he might be able to travel the province by bus or train. After making enquiries about the costs involved, he quickly dropped the idea. He found out, too, that some of the smaller towns were apprehensive about the cost they might incur in entertaining a lieutenant-governor, his wife and his aide-de-camp, when he paid them a visit. David had the opportunity to solve this early in his term when the mayors of the Union of British Columbia Municipalities held a conference in Victoria. Most were accompanied by their spouses. He decided to invite the spouses to tea at Government House. After tea, he suggested to them the best, least expensive way to invite him for a visit. They need not worry about his travel expenses. He would come using a government jet aircraft or by a commercial flight.

"It will cost you nothing," he said. "I will arrive around ten in the morning. If you arrange to have some school or combination of high schools meet together in a gymnasium, I will talk to them and answer questions, and then I will leave. I'll go to one of your local radio or television stations and be interviewed and take questions. After that, I will go to one of your service club luncheons and if they want me, I'll speak to the members—Rotary, Lions, Kiwanis, anyone. After that I would want to see the sights of the community, usually in a car supplied by the RCMP. After that, take me to the municipal hall to meet the mayor and council. Later, I could come and visit one of the seniors' homes, have tea and meet them. If you want me to stay for an evening dinner put on by the Canadian Club or a volunteer group, I will do that and then fly home."

The women thought it was a wonderful idea. But David wasn't finished. He added, "I want you to go back and carry this message to your spouses. Now you are my agents. When your spouse is not working, you needle him. Better still, you take up this project, and if the mayor agrees, then you head up the organizing, and I'll be there."

David started to get letters asking him to speak from all over the province, and soon what began as a trickle developed into a flood. David's first speech after assuming office was to the United Way of the lower mainland. One year later, he spoke again to the same group. He told his audience that in the last 12 months, he had made 126 ferry crossings of the Strait of Georgia and about 10 by air. He had visited over 20 smaller communities in the province and presided over 24 ceremonies in schools and colleges. In June alone, he spoke to over 8,000 students. He had attended roughly 4 events and activities a day, 7 days a week, and over 153 official functions.

As a look at Government House records shows, each day brought with it different demands. October 29, 1992, was a typically busy day. At 8:30 in the morning, David's aide-de-camp, one of many volunteers who served him, arrived at Government House. Ten minutes later, they left for a downtown hotel, Laurel Point Inn, where David was to take part in a conference for disabled aboriginal people. The ceremony began at 9:00 A.M., David spoke at 9:10 A.M. and left after his speech. He had to return to Government House to receive the Honourary Consul of Morocco, Mr. Pursey Von Lipinski. Shortly before noon, David and Dorothy were off to the Victoria Conference Centre to attend a luncheon at the Canadian Vocational Association's national conference. Following that, Dorothy visited the Greater Victoria Multicultural Association on View Street in Victoria. After about an hour there, she had to dash back to meet David since both of them were catching the 4:30 P.M. helicopter flight to Vancouver. Two hours later, David addressed the Simon Fraser University president's dinner at a downtown hotel. It was a long day.

Although David and Dorothy packed in several meetings on that occasion, frequently a considerable amount of time could be spent attending only one. In November 1994, for example, they went to Courtenay. They had been to the Courtenay-Comox area several times and enjoyed their visits. A new elementary school—Valley View Elementary—had recently been built, and David received over one hundred letters from students asking him to open the school officially. It was an organized appeal. David turned the mass of letters over to Dorothy to read, and she urged him to go since it meant a great deal to the children.

On the appointed day, they went out to the Victoria airport. There was no government jet aircraft available so they took the early plane to Vancouver. There was a wait for several hours before a flight left for Campbell River and, after another wait, on to Courtenay. By the time they reached Courtenay, light rain was falling. From the airport they went by car to the school arriving in the early afternoon. The students greeted him with songs, the ribbon was cut, David spoke to all the classes in the gymnasium and then dropped into each class to say hello. He planted a rosebush as a memento of his visit, then went to the home of Stan Hagen, the former minister of education. After tea with the Hagens, it was back to the airport to catch the same circuitous flight back to Victoria where they arrived after nine o'clock in the evening. Neither had the opportunity to have lunch or dinner, so they told John Mager to drive them directly to Chinatown. While he waited, they had a quick Chinese dinner and drove back to Government House. By the time they got to bed, they had been on the go for almost sixteen hours.

Sometimes, the hectic pace of official functions went on for several days in a row, particularly when it involved travel to the more isolated parts of the province. Access to the interior by road and by rail was comparatively easy, but along the sea coast of British Columbia, there were many communities which were difficult to reach. For a long time no lieutenant-governor had visited these isolated coastal towns and Indian villages.

It was an annual practice for one of the Royal Canadian Navy destroyers based in Esquimalt to sail north along the coast, putting into coastal settlements to "show the flag." When Rear-Admiral R. E. George approached David to enquire if he would like to go on such a cruise, he jumped at the opportunity. Since the more modern destroyers carried helicopters, the cruise on HMCS *Huron* would enable David to reach beyond the bays and inlets where the ship would dock.

David and Dorothy took their first trip on the destroyer in June 1989, accompanied by Michael Roberts and John Mager. On the first day out, after a two-hour sail from Esquimalt, David and Dorothy found themselves in a helicopter flying to the village of Ucluelet. They landed in the high school playground. After visiting and speaking to the students, they had lunch with one of the local service clubs. Then the helicopter took them off to Tofino where they visited the mayor, toured the town and visited the community hall. Walking back to the helicopter, David saw an old church and stopped to shake hands with the pastor and greet people along the street.

After flying back to the ship, the vice-regal party very quickly changed and freshened up. Half an hour later they arrived in Port Alberni, where over three hundred guests were invited to the ship for a reception. After that, there was a joint meeting of service clubs like the Kiwanis, Lions, Gyros and Rotary Clubs for the Lams to attend. Then they went driving around to see the sights of Port Alberni before finally returning to the ship. That was day one, and they kept going for five more days with a similar schedule.

It was fortunate that David was able to speak without having to write his speeches. He had a good memory, and if he needed some specific facts and figures, his secretary, Carole Simpson, could usually find the information he wanted. Using just a few notes allowed him to keep eye contact with his audiences, and he discovered they preferred this type of interaction to a more formal presentation. The requests for him to speak increased each year, coming not only from within the province, but from other parts of Canada, the United States and Hong Kong. Sometimes he was requested to "make a few remarks," and at other times he would have a topic suggested to him.

He liked to spice his talks with humour, frequently directed against himself and based on some of the situations he encountered. He liked to tell the story of a woman who came to him after an official ceremony to say that her daughter liked him and wanted to know how many uniforms he had. David replied he had only the one he wore when he read the Speech from the Throne. The woman said her daughter loved his red uniform. "Wait a minute," David said, "That is my aide-de-camp, an RCMP officer." The woman replied, "Then no wonder my daughter said, 'All night long, the lieutenant-governor didn't get to say a word. There was a Chinese fellow who did all the talking.'"

Incidents during formal occasions could also cause a smile. At a dinner in Government House, the piper led the guests into the dining room where the table had been laid with flowers, sparkling silver, embossed chinaware and individual menus in front of each place setting. Just before they came in, one of the servers entered and quietly began to take each menu away. Having collected all of them, she returned to the kitchen. David made no comment at the time, and it was not until after the guests had gone that he learned that a printing error had listed the main course as "Roast of Lam."

David had no previous military experience, so he was somewhat nervous when the time came to review the troops as he was sometimes called upon to do. The cocked hat he wore on opening the Legislative Assembly did not balance well, and he had never saluted. He made a creditable attempt the first time, but it was pointed out to him later that the fingers and thumb of his right hand should be held together rather than apart. To do otherwise would convey a wrong impression. Similarly, when reviewing the troops, it was normal for the inspecting officer to walk along the front rank, then the second and finally the third. He did that, and then went to inspect the band. Going by reason rather than experience, he noticed the bandsmen held their instruments in front of them. Rather than dodge around drums and trombones, David decided to walk through the files rather than the ranks of the band. It was probably the first time the band had been inspected from the side rather than the front, and later David had a great laugh over it when he was told about his error.

David received a large number of guests at Government House. All foreign consuls and consuls-general usually made a courtesy call at least once during their posting to British Columbia. They were normally invited to tea or perhaps to lunch. Foreign ambassadors to Canada visiting the province usually paid a courtesy call as well and might be invited to dinner. Newly appointed ministers in the provincial legislature were sworn in at Government House and senior officers in the armed forces traditionally made courtesy calls there. David enjoyed this contact, however brief. During his years in office he would visit and review almost every regular and reserve unit of the Canadian Forces in the province, and it made his visits more comfortable if he had already met the commanding officer.

In earlier years, there were times when Government House hosted thousands of guests. One was the traditional garden party when the public came into the grounds, shook hands with the lieutenant-governor, moved on to partake of refreshments and walked around the garden meeting friends and listening to the band music. Another was the State Ball held at the same time as the opening of a new session of the Legislative Assembly. This was a splendid event, and invitations to it were much sought after. It was a formal affair which offered an impressive banquet and a good orchestra playing in the ballroom. Budget restraints had brought these two functions to an end before David was appointed to the office, but one traditional event which brought large numbers of people to Government House continued—the New Year's

Day Levée. This had been practised by the early colonial governors and had its origins in a much earlier period in Europe. Anyone was welcome to drop into Government House, meet the lieutenant-governor and his wife and share some tea, coffee, punch and sandwiches. At the Lam's first levée in 1989, a total of 1,816 guests arrived. David's hand was sore from handshakes.

With such numbers, the line-up of guests waiting to enter sometimes stretched to the street, several hundred yards away. With many aides-de-camp in attendance, everything normally went smoothly. On one occasion, however, a local protest group called the Raging Grannies attempted to disrupt the affair. Although small in number, they were very adept at attracting media attention. After going through the reception line, they gathered in the ballroom to start their protest. They had scarcely begun when one or two aides informed them that such action was inappropriate: Government House should not be used as a platform for any protests under any circumstance. The television crews in attendance that day were easily persuaded not to show any film of the group on the evening broadcast, which without a doubt, the Raging Grannies had counted on. With their attempt frustrated, the group left with such grace as they could muster.

There were numerous times when the lieutenant-governor was expected to entertain visiting groups for teas, dinners, luncheons, cocktails or some similar sort of function. Even though Government House could purchase liquor and wine free of duty, expenses could mount. There was not only the food and drink to consider, but the extra staffing as well. For a dinner of over a hundred, the chef might require five or six extra helpers in the kitchen. Additional help would be needed to serve guests both before and after the dinner, and to clean up afterwards. One or two people would be needed to serve in the cloakroom, additional commissionaires to direct parking, and several people to move furniture and set up the tables and chairs in the ballroom and then take them down into storage on the following day. Whether the guests came in ones and twos, or whether there were a hundred or more, the budget allowance could shrink alarmingly, and the incumbent had to take that into account.

Shortly after David assumed office, the former comptroller of Government House retired. He was replaced by Brian Rowbottom, who worked with Michael Roberts to try and live within the budget allowed. Henceforth, all staff members, no matter what their rank or position, would pay for their lunch, or even for their coffee during a coffee break. The arrangement was "cost neutral," with the price based on the actual cost of buying and preparing the food. Other changes were made to schedules and duties. For example, the chauffeur was now paid not for an eight-hour working day, but rather for the time he was actually performing his duties.

David found he did not need two full-time housekeepers, so their hours of work and duties were also revised. As he explained later in a speech, "So we now have half a maid. Why? Because when we eat alone, if I serve my wife, she will clear the table; if she serves me, then I will clear the table. So our arrangement is perfect. In fact, I would rather serve than clear the table, so I run to the dumbwaiter and grab the dishes before her. It works just great. My wife keeps reminding me, 'Remember, in five years' time, you're going to go back and do the dishes.'"

David and Dorothy also economized on expenses when they went to Vancouver. In the beginning, they stayed in hotels when they were there on official business, but soon Dorothy suggested that they simply go home to their Comox Street apartment. David remembers, "The first visit we had after we went home was a visit of eleven members of Parliament from New Zealand. I said to my wife, 'Okay, now you serve all the drinks.' And she said, 'Okay, now you wash the dishes.'"

Actually, Dorothy's idea was a good one. It saved hotel bills and thus helped the budget. However, there were numerous times when David had to meet people in Vancouver and entertain them with more than a drink and for longer than an hour. An arrangement was made with one of the better downtown hotels to rent a suite for a morning or afternoon only. That allowed him to entertain thirty or so visitors using the hotel's staff and catering services. This system worked very well for the rest of his tenure, although Dorothy sometimes found herself busier in Vancouver than in Government House.

Increasing budgetary pressures made it a constant challenge to live within the amount allocated while maintaining the traditional hospitality and ambience of his office. Government House is located on some thirty-six acres of ground, of which a considerable portion is cultivated. The mansion contains about one hundred rooms. There are seven large suites, including the Royal Suite and the lieutenant-governor's private suite. In addition, there are twelve bedrooms and offices, reception rooms, a large kitchen and a variety of entertainment areas—the drawing room, ballroom and dining room. Building on the base of a core government staff, David and his senior managers augmented the six volunteer house tour docents and forty volunteer flower arrangers with ten volunteer office assistants and over three hundred garden volunteers.

While Government House was used to entertain official guests, it could also be used for personal guests as well so long as the costs of the two groups were kept separate. If David had friends from Hong Kong, Vancouver, Texas or elsewhere visiting him, he might send his chauffeur to meet them. In that case, he would pay the chauffeur's wages for the hour or so it took for the return trip to the airport. If the visitors were staying at Government House, David would pay the cost of preparing and cleaning their room, placing flowers or chocolates in their room to greet them, and any meals or other expenses. The same held true of his personal long-distance telephone calls. If he planned to go to his home in Vancouver and took a steak or a bottle of wine from the House kitchen for his dinner, he was charged for that as well. There were no "freebies" at Government House.

Every two years, the lieutenant-governors of the provinces and the governor-general met for several days either in Ottawa or in one of the provincial capitals to exchange views and experiences and be brought up-to-date with any changes in government policy relating to their own office. It did not take long for David to realize that the lieutenant-governor's residence in British Columbia was one of the best in Canada. A few provinces had no vice-regal residence and their lieutenant-governors worked out of offices in provincial legislative buildings while living in a house which had no facilities for anything but a small dinner party. If there was large-scale entertaining to be done, they had to use private facilities such as a hotel, where the expense was much greater. In Victoria, everything could be carried out under one roof, from a small tea party to a reception for four hundred people. The British Columbia government took advantage of this as well. During the year, the premier and cabinet ministers often requested permission to hold some function at Government House—an award banquet, for example—with the cost to be covered by the minister's budget. Doing so saved the government a great deal of money, while at the same time providing an ambience for the guests which could not be matched by even the best hotels in the city.

David found the provincial government to be very helpful when he had to request assistance for running his office, such as a new computer or painting one of the rooms. But even more, he was pleased at its acceptance of the role that Government House could play in recognizing citizens for volunteer work, achievements in music and education, bravery in the police, fire fighters and military, or long-term service in the government. With its beautiful house and gardens, Government House performed a very significant service on behalf of the people of British Columbia, he felt. "I don't want to turn it into an elitist place," he said with considerable feeling in 1993. "We want to show our recognition of and appreciation for people who serve, who care, who share, who give. These kinds of people, no matter whether they are in arts or education, in culture or in service industries, they are constantly recognized here."

As the months and years went by, David's activities as lieutenant-governor rarely slackened. He worked hard to bring messages of good will to the people of British Columbia and to act as one of the province's best "public relations" representatives when travelling abroad. He soon made a reputation for himself in the public service as he had in the business community.

THIRTEEN

Cultivating the Future

IT DID NOT take long for David and Dorothy to become accustomed to hosting a continual stream of people at Government House. The president of Iceland paid a visit a few weeks after David was appointed, and in May 1989 he held a dinner for His Excellency Wan Li, chairman of the National People's Congress of the People's Republic of China. Two days later, David had the pleasure of hosting Prince Philip, the Duke of Edinburgh.

Prince Philip's visit was the first time David had to welcome a member of the Royal Family. He had been informed well in advance that His Royal Highness would be accompanied by a party of three, including Major Sir Guy Acland, his equerry. The Duke was en route to Los Angeles and had planned an overnight stay in Victoria as a rest stop for his air crew as well as his own party. It was very convenient for him to stay at Government House, which he remembered from an earlier visit.

David and Dorothy looked forward to meeting him but were unsure about protocol. Should they go to the airport to meet him? David would have preferred that, but since he was the Queen's representative in the province, it was not required. Should he meet him when he arrives and steps out of his car or wait until he enters the door? Should he address him as Your Royal Highness every time he speaks to him? Should Dorothy curtsy? There were a dozen questions to ask.

As it turned out, the brief visit was a huge success. David met him outside the door and they quickly established a warm rapport. Lunch was held in David's private suite and the conversation was very relaxed. One topic that arose was inter-cultural communication. Prince Philip told the story of how he once visited "the Orient" and was taken to a communal farm. While there, he requested to visit a washroom. The translator gave instructions and someone brought him a washbasin and towel. That was not what the Duke had in mind, so he used a more direct term. Again, the translator gave instructions and a few minutes later informed the Prince that unfortunately, it was not the season for "sweet peas." The Duke experienced great relief when the interpreter finally understood what he wanted.

One of the topics David brought up during lunch was his plan to improve the gardens at Government House. Seeing the Duke was interested, he drew a rough sketch of how various types of gardens might be created in different areas of the grounds. Impressed by David's passion for the subject, Prince Phillip told him that if he completed his plans to improve and expand the Government House grounds, he would call him "Capability" Lam. He was referring to the famous eighteenth-century landscape architect, Capability Brown.

After lunch, Prince Philip decided to roam the grounds to get a first-hand view of the potential sites. Leaving the house by a side door, he climbed over a low iron railing and started down the slope. A gardener saw him and waved him away, saying the area was not open to visitors. A little explanation resulted in an embarrassed gardener having a chat with the Duke who then continued to look around. Nobody had seen him leave, and the heavy side door had shut behind him. After he completed his garden tour, he found that he was locked out. He made his way around to the front door and was spotted by a security man just as he was about to push the doorbell. On his next visit several years later, David jokingly asked him if he would like a duplicate set of house keys.

The discussion he had with Prince Philip about his plans to improve the gardens was a topic dear to David's heart. Over the next several years he spent a considerable amount of his time and money on improving the Government House gardens and his efforts deserve more than passing mention.

Victoria has long been known as the "City of Gardens." It has a mild climate and in February and March, when other parts of Canada are experiencing frozen rivers and plenty of snow, in Victoria the residents are beginning to mow their lawns and enjoy the crocuses and early daffodils. The winter of 1988–89, however, was an exception. February was exceptionally cold, with freezing temperatures and high winds. The freezing wind came whistling up the side of Government House and played havoc with the rose garden planted on high ground by David's predecessors, the Rogers. By the end of the month, about 80 per cent of the rosebushes had been killed by the cold due to their exposed position. David was well aware of the care Jane Rogers had given to the rose garden and considered what he should do. Should he try to replace them or salvage what he could? Would another rare wintry blast repeat the damage? He also felt that more people should be able to enjoy the gardens' peace and tranquillity and that additional areas of the grounds could be utilized for public viewing and pleasure.

During the spring, David began to consider various plans to rescue the surviving rosebushes and start another rose garden in a more protected location. By chance, he happened to read in the local newspaper about three well-known Victoria gardeners—Elizabeth Kerfoot, George Radford and Phoebe Noble—each of them specialists in their fields. David had never met them, but he telephoned and invited them individually to tea. He wanted their advice on where best to plant the gardens he had in mind and welcomed any suggestions they might have. Finding all to be positive and enthusiastic, he described the lack of funds and asked if there might be people in the city, now living in apartments and condominiums, who would enjoy a chance to get their hands dirty. He described the type of volunteer program he had in mind. All three thought there would be a good response and agreed to help.

Since he now had three leaders but no followers, David's next step was to telephone Colin D. McCullough, the publisher of the *Times-*

Colonist and a member of a small advisory group called the Government House Foundation. He asked the publisher for some free publicity on what he hoped to do in the garden. When the news came out about the need for volunteers, there was an immediate response from both men and women. Most were retired people, and many were apartment dwellers who missed the opportunity to work in a garden. Once they found how much they enjoyed it, they brought in more friends and soon David had to ask his operations manager, Brian Rowbottom, to organize the volunteers more formally. Brian protested he knew nothing about gardening, but David assured him that all he had to know was the difference between a vegetable and a flower. In due course, the Friends of the Government House Gardens Society was formed.

During the next few years, the society grew from two dozen to almost two hundred volunteers. Each member paid a small annual fee for membership, and the society also made arrangements to accept financial donations for the upkeep of the gardens. The most generous donor was David himself. For the six years that he was lieutenant-governor, he donated his salary to the improvement of the gardens. This was extremely helpful, but David was keenly aware money had to be found to keep the gardens maintained for the enjoyment of the public after he stepped down.

Meanwhile, David was beginning to think of a major project which he knew was beyond the scope of the volunteers. He wanted to create a rose garden in a more protected area near the exit gate from the grounds. Although he searched through his dozens of garden books for ideas, he found none that appealed to him. Then, while on a sailing trip to Desolation Sound months later, he stopped at a small village to buy supplies and picked up a magazine called *Garden Designs*. On the centre page was a photograph of a lovely restored Victorian rose garden at Warwick Castle in England. The garden had been designed just outside the walls of the mediaeval castle in the late nineteenth century. It was just the design he was looking for, and on his return, he contacted the owners of the castle to see if he could get a copy of the original plans. After a little negotiation, they agreed.

In July 1991, David and Dorothy travelled to Great Britain to pay a courtesy call on Her Majesty Queen Elizabeth at Buckingham Palace. It was normal practice for a lieutenant-governor to be received by Her Majesty at least once during the period he or she held office. While David and Dorothy had met her briefly once before on board Her Majesty's Yacht *Britannia*, this time they had half an hour's talk with her. Much of the conversation revolved around gardens and gardening, and later they had an opportunity to visit the private gardens at the palace. It was a most interesting experience for both of them and far more comfortable than either David or Dorothy had imagined.

They stayed a few extra days to visit Warwick Castle, where they received a warm reception from the castle's landscape advisor, Paul Edwards, and the general manager of the estate. There were many questions to ask on both sides. The castle's garden covered about an acre with a rockery, a small waterfall and a large variety of roses. David wanted to concentrate on the Victorian roses, a hardy variety whose flowers were mostly the single type in various shades of pink and some white. Well informed about the problems and difficulties he might encounter, David returned to Victoria full of enthusiasm for his new project.

The Government House gardens in the summer of 1991 were a blaze of colour. There was a noticeable increase in the number of visitors and tourists coming in to see the gardens, and it was becoming a popular site for photographing newly wed couples after wedding ceremonies. The various gardens were taking shape—the English Country Garden, the Cut-Flower Garden, the Woodland and Native Plant Garden, and the Rock and Alpine Garden, to mention only a few of them. There was some money coming in too, and several individuals and institutions had donated $600 each for garden benches, each of which carried a plaque with the name of the donor.

The Victoria Rose Garden, however, would need a considerable amount of money to see it completed. David decided to donate $150,000 towards the project and wanted the provincial government to match that amount. When he put the proposal to Premier Vander Zalm at a luncheon meeting, the premier, himself a professional gardener, was intrigued but non-committal. In due course, however, the government allocated its share. Knowing that David had donated several million dollars to the creation of gardens in Vancouver, a local newspaper reporter asked why he had limited himself to $150,000. His reply very nicely expressed his philosophy of giving: "The easiest way to kill a project," he said, "is to simply write a cheque. It will kill a church. It will kill a symphony. It kills incentive. Everyone must play a part. This is a grand opportunity for everyone to be involved. So often people look at something and say, 'This is the government's.' I want people to look at these grounds and say, 'This is my garden.' Once we put the word 'our' and 'mine' into people's mindset, we are really there."

The news of David's contribution stimulated even more volunteers to offer their services in the gardens, including experts who could be used as group leaders. Money to create a sustaining fund for the gardens came in as well, ranging from a $5 bill from a neighbourhood pensioner to an anonymous gift of $10,000 for summer students to clear invasive plants from the Woodland Garden. Donations also came in from various Hong Kong friends of David's, some of whom he had invited to Government House for dinner or an overnight stay. Even one of his former partners in the Hong Kong flower shop sent a generous cheque. By early 1992, the fund had topped the $100,000 mark.

David did what he could to advertise his garden project or other events, sometimes with surprising results. At a fete sponsored by the Victoria Art Gallery, he had arranged to have a table with pamphlets describing what was being done to improve the gardens. A volunteer was in attendance when an elderly lady stopped to chat. Through family connections, she told the volunteer, she had a long acquaintance with Government House. The story got back to David, who got her telephone number and asked the lady and her daughter to tea. As he fondly tells the story, "They came and left with me old photographs of bygone days. I showed them around Government House, had tea and told them of my grand plan of revitalization, not so much with money, but with love and spirit and sharing and caring of the volunteers. She was very touched. She said, 'Your Honour, I wish I had my chequebook with me. I want to show my support.' I said, 'I'm not asking for money.' They left, and she came back and left an envelope for me with the commissionaire at the door. It contained a cheque for $15,000."

Among other projects, David had mentioned a pavilion near the rose garden which was by this time under construction. He thought it would cost about $50,000, but it turned out to be closer to $100,000. The lady donated a further $35,000 which she thought would see the construction completed. When this proved insufficient, David again dug into his own pocket and provided another $50,000. When finished, it was named the Bruce Pavilion.

Eventually, so many volunteers called in to offer their services and expertise that David installed a telephone "hot line" just to deal with the garden. The movement, as he put it, became "unstoppable." In the back of his mind, however, was always the question of maintaining the new gardens once he had gone. Since David knew from experience that the provincial government might reduce the annual grant to Government House any time it wished, he felt there should be a separate, private fund established of at least a million dollars. With such an independent source of money and the enthusiasm of the volunteers, the gardens would thrive despite any government cutbacks.

A dinner was arranged to raise funds but the tickets, at $200 a plate, were selling slowly. Then a friend proposed something on a much larger scale. Why not have a David Lam Tribute Dinner? Some tables would sell for $25,000, some for $10,000, and in the outer circle, some for $5,000. Several friends, including Bob Lee, promised to go after large corporations to sponsor the more expensive tables, and in a remarkably short time all were sold. The Hotel Vancouver, where the event was held on May 4, 1993, announced that over eight hundred people had bought tickets and its dining room was filled to capacity. The gala dinner was a terrific tribute to David and Dorothy. Not only did it illustrate the high esteem in which they were held, but it raised approximately $350,000—the largest single donation to the garden fund.

During the first two years of his tenure as a lieutenant-governor, David exercised his constitutional powers in a routine way—swearing in new ministers, signing innumerable orders-in-council, opening and proroguing the Legislative Assembly, and so forth. There were numerous other duties to perform as well. As the official Visitor to the three universities in the province, he tried to attend all the convocation ceremonies they held, and as the patron of some two hundred societies in the province, he accepted as many invitations as he could to attend their functions. In Government House, there was the usual duty of hosting visiting dignitaries for lunch or dinner, and sometimes there was a request from a minister or even the premier to host a group or person of particular importance.

Late in August 1990, David's secretary received a call from the premier's office asking if it was possible for David to host a luncheon on September 6. The premier wanted the luncheon for a visiting group of Taiwan investors, one of whom was described as one of the wealthiest men in Taiwan. He particularly wanted the lieutenant-governor to be there. No names were mentioned. There was nothing unusual in the request and, with David's approval, arrangements were made for the luncheon. Late on September 4, there were media reports that the premier and his wife were considering the sale of their Fantasy Gardens property to a Taiwanese investor, Tan Yu, who controlled Asiaworld International. It was not until the following day, when the list of guests for the luncheon was received by Government House, that David knew who was coming. Tan Yu and his daughter, Emilia "Bien Bien" Roxas, were among the guests, as were Faye Leung and her husband. Leung was a well-known real estate entrepreneur in Vancouver. David had first met her when he arrived as an immigrant in 1967. Hearing he was a banker from Hong Kong, she had hoped to sell him a house. David had rarely met her since then.

David was interested in Tan Yu. His daughter was portrayed by the media as the decision maker, but David was skeptical that so young a woman could be in the driver's seat of a multi-billion-dollar empire. She was probably, he guessed, the front person on behalf of the father or the family.

Tan Yu was seated on David's right. Their conversation ranged over a variety of topics from philanthropy to British Columbia as a place for investment. At the conclusion of the lunch David stood up, welcomed the delegation and praised British Columbia's potential as

Canada's gateway to the growing Pacific Rim economy. Emilia Roxas, David noted, was about to stand up when her father signalled her he would reply. He gave a gracious thank you, praised British Columbia and said he looked forward to returning. The luncheon ended on a pleasant note, and David had confirmed his own suspicion that, although he kept a very low profile, Tan Yu was the man in control. After lunch, there was a swarm of reporters at the door asking questions, all concentrating on Emilia Roxas.

A few days later, it was revealed that Premier Vander Zalm was going to sell Fantasy Gardens for about $16 million. It is not the intention here to go into detail about the raising chorus of cries about Vander Zalm misusing his political position to benefit his private business transactions, nor the claim by Faye Leung that she had been squeezed out of her commission as a real estate agent. Briefly, the premier was accused of breaking his own guidelines on the separation of public office and private enterprise, and some members of his own Social Credit Party caucus announced their decision to resign. Certain aspects of the case were being investigated by the RCMP's commercial crime squad, and Faye Leung's pronouncements further muddied the waters about the sale of Vander Zalm's property. After public interest in the premier's financial affairs, whipped up by the media, led to other charges about his conduct, Vander Zalm asked the provincial conflict of interest commissioner, Ted Hughes, to review the case and make a report. Hughes began his task on February 14, 1991, and the report was released six weeks later.

Until the report was made public, there was a great deal of speculation about its finding not only among the public but in Government House as well. What the accusations might lead to was anybody's guess, but since it involved the premier, and thus the governance of the province, David and his staff had to be prepared to act.

From a constitutional point of view, it was a unique problem. What would Hughes's report say? What would the Social Credit caucus do? Would their MLAs stand behind their leader or would there be a division of their support? If there was a division, would the party demand a leadership convention? What would Vander Zalm himself do? His party was nearing the time when it must call an election. Would the premier "go to the people," as he sometimes mentioned? And if he did, would he campaign as a premier or an MLA?

There were over a dozen scenarios to consider and Michael Roberts had to try and envisage all possibilities so that he could present David suitable courses of action. Both he and David consulted numerous constitutional advisers during this period, but it was difficult to find a precedent. The premier was charged with a conflict of interest according to guidelines which he himself had introduced at the beginning of his term, but which had not as yet been approved by the provincial legislature. (Later, there were criminal charges laid against the premier, but he was found innocent of these.)

The report was given to David two hours before it was released to the public, and Vander Zalm received a copy at the same time. It stated that the premier had breached his own guidelines, and that he had used his position to have Tan Yu invited to Government House without revealing the negotiations underway for Tan Yu to purchase Fantasy Gardens. For all that, he had not overstepped provincial legislation, nor had he committed a criminal act. The Social Credit Party caucus met almost immediately to recommend a successor. Michael Roberts had suggested to the chairman of the caucus that should they select a new leader and present his or her name for consideration as a successor to Vander Zalm, it would be helpful if the document had the signatures of all those supporting the recommendation. In that way, David would be able to judge the candidate's degree of support in the assembly. His main concern was to ensure the smooth process of the government.

In the early afternoon of April 2, David received two calls. One was from the Premier's Office asking for an appointment for Vander Zalm, who wished to tender his resignation. The other was from the chairman of the Social Credit caucus presenting the name of the caucus's recommendation for premier, Rita Johnson. Those two telephone calls meant a potential crisis was over. David would not have to wield his constitutional power to sort things out himself.

The meeting with Premier Vander Zalm was brief. A letter of resignation had been prepared which he signed. He displayed no bitterness nor anger and David expressed his regrets at the circumstances which led to the unhappy event. When he left, for a few hours there was no premier of the province until Rita Johnson arrived. Seeing the caucus support she had, David had no reason not to accept her. After taking the oaths of allegiance and confidentiality, she was appointed premier of British Columbia. She would later return to Government House to present her cabinet, and David would swear them in.

Mrs. Johnson was in office only a short time. There was an election before the end of the year. The Social Credit Party lost power, and the New Democratic Party formed the new government. On November 5, David presided over the swearing-in ceremony of Premier Michael Harcourt and the ministers of his new cabinet. Traditionally, this would have been done at Government House, but the new premier wanted to make it a more public affair. The ceremony was held in a large auditorium of the University of Victoria which was packed with the party faithful and other invited guests.

The previous evening, David had been reading a book on Confucius and he decided to use a passage from it in his address after the ceremony. "As I thumbed through the book," he told the crowd, "I found one passage which said, 'The student of Confucius asked the master, 'Tell us about government.' Confucius said, 'There are three things very crucial to government—to have enough food on the table for the people, to have military might to protect them and to have the trust and confidence of the people.' A student asked, 'Master, if one of the three has to be sacrificed, which one should be let go?' Confucius said, 'Do away with the military.' "

At that point the audience applauded enthusiastically. David continued: "Then the student asked, 'Master, of the remaining two, if one must be sacrificed, which one should go?' And the master said, 'Of course, food.' The student said, 'Without food we will all die. How can you give up food and maintain confidence?' Confucius said, 'You asked me about government. Government stands on confidence and trust of the people. Without those the government falls. Insofar as food is concerned, it is a matter of dying sooner or later because everybody dies. If you don't have food, you die sooner. If you do have food, you die later. What's the point?' "

The audience loved the story, largely, David reasons, because it was subject to all shades of interpretation. To some, "I could be giving the New Democratic Party government a reminder that they must have the people's trust. To some, I was criticizing Vander Zalm because he lost the people's trust. I said no more."

David's relationship with the new socialist government continued to be as cordial as it had been with the previous one. There were few changes. At the opening of the new legislature in March 1992, the wording of the Speech from the Throne changed from the traditional "my government" to "this government." Since the speech was approved by the premier, there was no comment by Government House.

A year later, at the opening of another session of the legislature, David himself broke with tradition by attending in a formal civilian clothes rather than in uniform. Lieutenant-governors in British Columbia had worn the uniform known as "Windsor dress" on such occasions for over a century. Made of heavy melton cloth with a great deal of gold braid, it had been designed at a time when a lieutenant-governor would arrive in a horsedrawn carriage. Wearing it in an automobile was a different matter. The feathered cocked hat tended to slide over the eyes as one bent to leave the car, and the sword was awkward as one stepped from the car to the pavement. Worse, the jacket weighed almost thirty pounds and was stiff and heavy. Wearing it while reading the Speech from the Throne in a crowded chamber made the wearer uncomfortably warm. Neither the jacket nor the trousers had pockets, which was somewhat awkward. The cloth was so stiff that when David bent over, he was afraid there would be gaps opening between the clips which came down the front instead of buttons. To avoid exposing his skin, he wore it with a light teeshirt which was the same colour as the gold braid on the jacket. On the back was written "Dog Days—Vancouver Yacht Club."

By the time David inherited it, the uniform was almost half a century old and in need of repair or replacement. A tailor reported that it was almost impossible to mend, and replacing it would cost over $25,000 for the jacket alone. It was time for a change. When David arrived at the entrance of the legislative buildings, he wore striped trousers, a pearl-grey waistcoat, a short black jacket and Homburg hat.

Most of the other lieutenant-governors in Canada had adopted this dress years earlier.

When David arrived in front of the Legislative Buildings, Premier Mike Harcourt was waiting for him on the steps as usual. In front of the legislative building stood an unusually large crowd of people, many of them carrying signs and banners protesting the new government's lack of action on the environment.

All went well until, after receiving the traditional gun salute and inspecting the guard, David started up the steps to greet the premier. At that point, the demonstrators began to vent their anger, yelling, "We want Mike," and chanting their protest slogans in an increasing volume. When David and the premier entered the main door of the building, the troops moved away, as was customary, for a brief break from their duties. Scarcely had they left when the protestors, whipped up by agitators, advanced up the steps and entered the building, streaming towards the chamber where David had just started to address the members. The din was terrific as the mob made its way towards the chamber, pushing aside anyone who attempted to stop them. The doors of the chamber were closed and six commissionaires tried to prevent the protesters, now straining against the doors, from entering. One of the glass windows of the doors was broken. David, at the far end of the chamber, stopped speaking. At that moment, Brian Rowbottom, who was standing in for Michael Roberts as private secretary, stepped forward towards the premier, indicating by his action that a brief recess should be called until order was restored.

At this point, David was escorted through a side door to the Speaker's chamber. The noise and din continued as the young people milled about in the foyer. David remembers thinking, "It can only happen in a democratic country. If this should happen in a totalitarian country, they would all be arrested or shot or put in concentration camps." He had been in countries which would have sent policemen and soldiers into the mob, wielding batons and rifle butts to subdue the protesters. Saddened as he was by the unruly scene, he admired the restraint of the police when they appeared to take control. What would have happened if the protesters had been able to break into the chamber? David felt they would have wrecked the furniture and destroyed any symbol of authority. Yet even if they had, he still felt tolerating such an action was better than having policemen open fire to control them. There must be law and order for democracy to survive, but in David's mind, armed force was a last resort. He was happy that control was restored without any heads being broken.

Within an hour the sitting resumed, and David finished reading the Speech from the Throne. He left by an exit away from the crowd of protesters, which was still present with their banners on the front lawn of the legislature. It was the most unusual political event he was to encounter during his tenure of office, and one which he was not eager to repeat.

Among the dozen or more letters David reviewed every day, it was not unusual to receive a letter from the provincial or federal government stating that a certain dignitary or high official would be visiting Victoria and requesting that David invite the person to dinner or even accommodate him or her overnight. The more senior the guest, the more warning David would have.

During his first year in office, for instance, David hosted a formal dinner for Wan Li, the chairman of the National People's Congress of China. He was on the first leg of a visit to Canada and the United States. The federal government had provided an interpreter and Wan Li had one also. Partly because of the formality of the occasion and so others could understand, David spoke to Wan Li in English which was interpreted into Chinese by his interpreter, and vice versa. All went well, but the conversation was stilted and confined to small talk. This was not David's style. He apologized to his non-Chinese-speaking guests and told them he was going to speak in Chinese "to break the ice." Then turning to Wan Li, he spoke to him in Mandarin. His guest immediately warmed up, and soon they were cracking jokes and thoroughly enjoying themselves. The Chinese ambassador and Chinese consul-general and other Chinese-speaking guests warmed up in this relaxed atmosphere and the dinner turned out to be a resounding success. Soon after, David began to receive invitations from the Chinese government to pay an official visit. Unfortunately, about a month later, there was a brutal crackdown on Chinese students demonstrating in Tiananmen Square, and the invitations were turned down.

Later that year, Her Royal Highness Princess Alexandra stayed in Government House during her visit to present a new Queen's Colour to the Canadian Scottish Regiment (Princess Mary's). At dinner one evening, David mentioned that when her brother, the Duke of Kent, had visited Hong Kong many years ago, the governor of the colony held a ball in his honour. It was while dancing at the ball that David and Dorothy had realized they had more in common than family friendship. It seemed appropriate, somehow, that they were now entertaining the sister of the man who had unknowingly brought them together.

During his tenure at Government House, David had several visits from the governor general. On these occasions, the governor general's flag was hoisted over Government House while he was in residence. Protocol demanded that he had precedence over David, and those in charge of arranging ceremonies in Victoria sometimes found the tendency of Ottawa officials to change seating plans at the last moment a little hard to take.

On a few occasions, David and Dorothy hosted foreign royalty. The first was in June 1990, when Princess Margriet of the Netherlands and her husband arrived. As usual, there was a flurry of correspondence and telegrams to find out what sort of entertainment would be most suitable to the guests. The Princess opted for a trip to the Queen Charlotte Islands where she and the Lams were fortunate to see grey whales passing their sailboat. Before the day was over, the Princess and Dorothy were walking barefoot on the beach and behaving as if they were old school friends who had not met for years.

David also met a number of visiting dignitaries in Vancouver. Among the earliest was the president of South Korea, Roh Tae Woo. On the way to his hotel, the two had an opportunity to talk. The name Tae Woo means "big fool" in Chinese, and during the course of their conversation David asked the president about it. The president said it was simply the name given him as a baby. David thought about that for a moment and then said, "That's a good name." Asked why, he replied, "There is a Confucian saying, 'When a person is of extreme high wisdom, he often acts as if he is a foolish person.' The truly very wise person often does not let his wisdom or smartness show. You often look at that person and consider him a fool. Being Big Fool, according to Confucius, means you are a person of extreme wisdom." The president liked this observation and possibly wondered why David was not in the diplomatic corps.

Aside from the former president of the Soviet Union, Mikhail Gorbachev, the most important politician David met while he was in office was probably His Excellency Zhu Rongji, vice-premier of the People's Republic of China. This meeting was held in Vancouver on May 16, 1993 at the Waterfront Centre Hotel. When a very senior official of a country with a population of over one billion people comes on a visit, very careful plans are laid to ensure he has a cordial welcome. Zhu had expressed a wish to meet David, but the meeting was important for the federal government. As a Department of External Affairs memo put it, "The visit is a significant event in our bilateral relations and we attach importance to our relations with the People's Republic of China." Ottawa's objective was to establish good relationships with Vice-Premier Zhu, who was not only the key economic planner of his country but a person who, in time, might step into the shoes of the aging premier. His was the first high-level visit to Canada by a Chinese government leader since the Tiananmen Square tragedy, and both countries hoped to return to normal relations.

Arrangements were made to keep the meeting reasonably small. Zhu was accompanied by the Chinese ambassador to Canada and two senior government representatives. David brought senior officials from the Department of External Affairs, both of whom spoke Mandarin, and two representatives from the provincial government. Both parties had interpreters. The meeting lasted for about forty minutes. Zhu mentioned he had come to improve relations with Canada. He pointed out that Hong Kong, Japan, Germany and others were investing in China, but Canadian investors seemed reluctant.

David reminded him Canada used to be China's best friend, but the people had been repelled by Tiananmen Square. To talk about restoring the old friendship, David suggested, was to talk about untying a knot. He implied that Canadians would appreciate an apology at the very least regarding the brutal treatment of the Chinese students. He went on to talk about his own dream of bringing greater understanding between the Chinese in China and the Chinese living beyond its borders. Their conversation was wide ranging, informal and sincere. David offered to do anything he could to promote greater understanding and harmony between China and its Pacific Rim neighbours. He stressed the increasing interdependence among nations and the need to build bridges between different cultures with different ideologies. He touched on the future of Hong Kong and on his own desire to promote higher education for Chinese scholars wanting to improve conditions in China.

The meeting was a complete success. At a formal dinner that evening, Vice-Premier Zhu paid David many compliments and said he learned much from him. He acknowledged that, as David had put it, there was "a knot to be untied," and pledged that he would work towards that goal.

A few months later, when David was flying back from a visit to Hong Kong, he encountered Zhang Yijun, the Chinese ambassador to Canada. His Excellency told David how much the vice-premier appreciated their conversation in Vancouver and said he wanted to meet him again. He also enquired about David's plans after he stepped down from being lieutenant-governor. He suggested the Chinese government would be interested in David heading an international consortium to help China improve its railways, power-generating facilities or telecommunications system. David's reply was non-committal, but appropriately gracious.

David had been in Government House for over a year before he travelled to Hong Kong in November 1989. He had been invited by the Hong Kong Baptist College to speak at its commencement exercise. At long last, the college had achieved degree-granting status. Shortly after, a letter from the governor of Hong Kong arrived, saying he would be pleased to see him also. David informed both Ottawa and Victoria of his wish to go, and both strongly urged him to do so. When it was known he was coming, more invitations began to arrive. By the time the trip was over, David had attended 82 engagements in 16 days.

Almost every single meal he had during that period involved a meeting with either old friends or with a large group of people whom he was expected to address. In his speeches and press conferences David repeated his message to Hong Kong businessmen moving to or just doing business in Canada: "No one can be on two boats at once; they must decide on one or the other boat." He did not want the whole Chinese community to be known as a selfish ethnic group, he told them. "If every ethnic group just looked after its own interests," he said in one speech, "then we would have a lot of selfish people who are totally un-Canadian. I do not condone people who come in, make a big buck and then walk right out, nor do I encourage them. But we are dealing with people with very dead-set habits who are used to living a fortressed life. There are no easy answers to dealing with multinational tycoons who move in and out and become crybabies when not everything goes their way."

David's visit to Hong Kong was probably his busiest to date. He managed to squeeze in some time to visit some of his brothers and sisters, but since almost half of them by this time had immigrated to the United States, he probably saw more of his family on visits to the United States than he did in Hong Kong. His schedule was so packed and so many old friends wanted to invite him to this or that function that both he and Dorothy had very little time to themselves.

David's philanthropic activities had always included Hong Kong. As lieutenant-governor, he thought it inadvisable to make large grants in British Columbia and Canada during his term of office, though he continued to donate generously to a wide variety of good causes. There was nothing, however, to prevent him from donating large sums of money to institutions in Hong Kong. In June 1990, for example, the Hong Kong *Standard* reported that David had pledged HK$1 million to the Lingnan University Development Fund, another million to the Hong Kong Baptist College and yet another to a project called Breakthrough. The latter was a project initiated by Dr. Philemon Choi. A graduate in medicine from the University of Manitoba, he went to Hong Kong where he became interested in social work, particularly in helping poor street children. He had a strong Christian faith and was working towards making religious television programs to be shown on Hong Kong's cable television. David's donation was to encourage him in this effort which required a considerable capital outlay.

These donations were primarily passive grants, and David was more interested in creative giving. One project that particularly interested him was the idea of establishing a centre for international education as part of the Hong Kong Baptist College. It would be a centre where scholars from Hong Kong, the People's Republic of China, Taiwan and elsewhere could meet, upgrade their skills, hold conferences and seminars, exchange ideas and, in general, improve themselves professionally. David discussed the project with the governor of Hong Kong, and the colonial government agreed to grant land and provide some financial help. A committee was formed to raise funds, and one of its members was David. After another trip to Hong Kong in 1991 during which he did some fundraising, he sent off about two dozen letters to some of his wealthy friends, asking each one to donate HK$1 million to the project within thirty days. The fact that about three-quarters of them responded positively says much about the esteem in which he was held. The remaining one-quarter contributed some money, though not the full amount requested.

During the next few years, David visited Hong Kong several times, and whenever possible he worked to raise money for the Baptist College and its new centre. On another occasion, he visited a friend who had promised to give HK$1 million. David's description of the meeting is a study in unorthodox fundraising techniques: "He gave me a cheque and there was a ceremony where I took it. Then I told him, 'Shau-Kee, tear up this cheque. I don't want it.' He said, 'Why?' I said, 'Put in another zero.' He said, 'No, no, no, absolutely no. My budget is all gone.' And I said, 'Ask your secretary to come in.' He said, 'No, no, no.' I said, 'Press the button, ask her to come in.' So he pressed the button and she came in and I said, 'Change this cheque.' He said, 'No, no, no' again and left the room and went outside with the secretary. He didn't come back for two minutes. When he returned, he had a new cheque, this one for HK$2 million."

By 1993, he had managed to raise HK$20 million. In November of that year, the college honoured David by naming the new centre the

David C. Lam Institute for East-West Studies. Its objectives were the same as those envisioned in what David had proposed—a centre for promoting better understanding between East and West. The college further honoured him even while he was still fundraising by conferring on him the honorary degree of Doctor of Humanities. This was David's sixth honorary doctorate degree. His first was from UBC (1987) followed by Baylor University (1990), Simon Fraser University (both David and Dorothy—1991), Royal Roads Military College (1991), Eastern College (1991), and Hong Kong Baptist College (1992). He received another from the University of Victoria in 1995 and in 1996 one more from the University of Northern British Columbia.

During his various trips to Hong Kong, David always attended a multitude of functions at which he was frequently the keynote speaker. Both the federal and provincial governments took advantage of his visits as well, knowing he could draw a large crowd to hear him speak. The British Columbia government, for example, was interested in attracting Hong Kong investments to the province, and frequently asked him to participate in meetings in Hong Kong when he was there to promote the potential of British Columbia. Few immigrants had travelled throughout the province as much as he had. His own personal experience as an immigrant, his knowledge of Hong Kong, his ability to speak three Chinese dialects as well as English, his business relationships with numerous Chinese entrepreneurs—all this and more made him a very attractive and sought-after speaker.

David had been approached several times to visit the People's Republic of China, but it was not until November 1992 that he was able to accept the offer. The invitation came from the Chinese consul-general in Vancouver. There was to be a launching of a rocket carrying an Australian satellite into orbit, and David and Dorothy were invited to witness it. It was to be a private visit, but as a lieutenant-governor, David had to get clearance from both Ottawa and Victoria. When they arrived in Hong Kong en route to Beijing, David informed the Canadian Commissioner of his arrival and within a day or so, two diplomats from the Canadian embassy in Beijing arrived to give him a detailed briefing on Chinese-Canadian relations in various areas.

While he was in Hong Kong, David learned that the rocket launching was postponed owing to technical difficulties. Disappointed, he proposed returning to Canada, but the Chinese official in Hong Kong begged him not to do so. He was still wanted in Beijing, where a meeting had been arranged with Chairman Jiang Zemin, the general secretary of the Communist party in China.

David's opportunity to talk to the general secretary was unusual. His welcome and treatment was on the level an ambassador might receive, and the representatives from the Canadian embassy were more than pleased with the meeting. David could speak his mind quite freely without worrying about political consequences. He was there as a private citizen and, among other things, chatted with Jiang about his hope to bring more harmony between the Chinese living in the People's Republic and the many millions living in other parts of the world. Jiang seemed to be well aware of what David had been doing and they parted on friendly terms. "I got a lot out of talking with him," David said later. "It helped me to understand the situation in China very, very much. It changed my outlook for the future of Hong Kong and the outlook for China."

Before he left, David had the opportunity to see something of the tremendous industrial growth in China and have talks with various officials in Shanghai. He was impressed with what he saw and the progress which had taken place over the past few years. He would be invited to China again.

By the summer of 1993, David and Dorothy began to count the weeks before they would leave Government House and return to their normal life in Vancouver. Both had become very fond of Victoria, so much so that David had bought a condominium there. They enjoyed taking walks in the Oak Bay area where Government House is located. The tenure of the office was for a minimum of five years so David assumed he would be able to leave in September 1993. Dorothy, in particular, was looking forward to the day. She had made many new friends and learned a great deal as the chatelaine of

Government House, but she missed seeing her children and grandchildren in Vancouver. Their numerous trips there were usually filled with functions to attend so that she did not have the time she would have wished for family and old friends. Pleasant as Victoria might be, Dorothy looked forward to returning home and the end of public life.

When the term of office of a lieutenant-governor is coming to an end, rumours begin to circulate about the successor. David began to hear the names of some potential candidates as early as the spring of 1993. He had been approached indirectly to see if he was willing to step down early, again with the hint that a senatorship or perhaps an appointment as an ambassador would be his for the asking. At the same time, he began to hear that John Fraser, the speaker of the House of Commons, was a potential replacement. There was no indication from Fraser about his future plans, though from other sources, it appeared he was a likely candidate. David's reply to the question of whether he might be willing to step down before his term was up was a flat no. To his mind, it would be a poor reflection on him and would give the appearance he was being eased out of his office. The question was never raised again.

In June 1993, Prime Minister Brian Mulroney stepped down and the new leader of the Progressive Conservative Party, Kim Campbell, succeeded him. An election was in the offing and reappointing a new lieutenant-governor was low on the new prime minister's priority list. She wanted to avoid making any appointments until after the federal elections. Mulroney had been severely accused of patronage appointments and she knew her party faced a difficult enough time without her being accused of the same thing. David would have to wait.

The election brought in the Liberals with a good majority and a new prime minister, Jean Chrétien. The new prime minister was extremely busy forming his cabinet, preparing new legislation and undertaking many other essential duties, so once again David could do little except nudge the Prime Minister's Office periodically to remind them he was waiting. The first word he had was on Christmas Eve, when the prime minister telephoned him. David and Dorothy were out doing some last-minute shopping. Chrétien left his telephone number, so on Christmas Day, just before going to church,

David telephoned him at his home. The result of their conversation was that David agreed to remain in office until after the Commonwealth Games in early September 1994. David asked the prime minister to send him a letter to that effect, which he did.

During 1994, David continued his usual hectic pace. His appointment book was crowded with functions ranging from a visit to a local flower show to a cross-Canada tour speaking to various chapters of the Hong Kong-Canada Business Association. As the summer approached, the staff at Government House became busier than ever in preparation for a visit of the Queen and Prince Philip. Their son, Prince Edward, was president of the Commonwealth Games Federation. He was to arrive a few days earlier than his parents and would be staying at Government House as well. A large part of Her Majesty's activities would be involved with the Commonwealth Games, but David received permission to have an hour or so of her busy schedule set aside to have her officially dedicate the renovated gardens at Government House.

Late in May, David proposed a change to the date when he would step down. If the prime minister gave out his successor's name before the games, David would appear as a "lame duck" lieutenant-governor while the Queen and numerous Commonwealth heads of state were in Victoria. David felt that should be avoided. If the prime minister named a successor after the games, the takeover would be in October, the beginning of a very busy period of Government House activities. He suggested, therefore, that he remain in office until after the New Year's Day Levée. January was traditionally a quiet month and his proposal would give the prime minister more time to select a successor. The prime minister agreed to David's suggestion but did not propose a final date or name a successor.

The Commonwealth Games were a tremendous success in every respect. The weather was lovely, the pageantry impressive and the games were enjoyed by thousands of enthusiastic spectators. Her Majesty received a warm welcome wherever she went and seemed pleased and relaxed at her reception.

At Government House, David and Dorothy found her to be a charming guest. There was only one time when they could have lunch with her by themselves, but that occasion stretched on for an hour and a half. The conversation covered topics ranging from gardening to Her Majesty's various experiences during her long reign. It was just the type of informal and interesting conversation David enjoyed, and it was apparent that his guest was feeling very much at home.

Her opening of the renovated gardens was a well-attended affair. The weather was good, the speeches were short, and nothing pleased David more than walking with her through the garden and describing the tremendous work of the volunteer gardeners. The warm friendly feeling between guest and host was obvious from the moment the Queen entered Government House.

Quite unexpectedly, it was Her Majesty who decided on David's retirement date. When Prime Minister Chrétien came to Government House for a state dinner, David welcomed him and in the same breath asked if he had selected a successor. Chrétien smiled and said David was doing such a good job he didn't want to let him go. At that point, Her Majesty arrived and the conversation ended. It was not until two days later, while attending a musical concert at the University of Victoria, that David, Dorothy and the Queen had an unscheduled moment together. During a break, the Queen casually asked when David's term was finished. He explained that he had been waiting since the previous September, and related what the prime minister had said two days earlier. When the Queen observed that this was unfair, David felt comfortable enough with her to say, "It's no use to tell me that. The person who should really hear this is Jean Chrétien." She agreed, and as luck would have it, Jean Chrétien was talking to some people only a few paces away.

David remembers, "I walked over and brought him to the Queen. The Queen asked him, 'When is his term up?' Chrétien said, 'He is so good we won't let him go.' 'Naughty, that's not fair,' she said. At that point, Chrétien said, 'I told His Honour it is his call. Whatever date he said, that will be the date.'

David turned to Her Majesty and asked, "May I make a suggestion. Would you pick the date?" The monarch smiled and started counting her fingers. "March," she said decisively. "I want the prime minister to have six months to find a successor, and I want you to have further opportunity to enjoy your beautiful gardens." There were smiles all around, and Dorothy had the broadest smile of all.

It is customary for the Queen to have a "farewell" on the day she is leaving a residence in which she has been a guest. At the end of their 1994 stay at Government House, a small room was put at the disposal of Her Majesty and Prince Philip for this purpose. Selected members from the federal and provincial governments as well as several from Government House were called in one by one to be thanked by the Queen, often receiving a gift such as a signed photograph to show her gratitude for the particular service rendered.

David was the last to enter. He brought a gift for the Queen—a book of photographs of British Columbia taken from the air. Prince Philip held in his hands a two-volume set of books on the Royal Family for David. Before giving it to him, however, the Queen stepped forward with a small box in her hands. "What is this, Your Majesty?" David asked. "I am making you a Commander of the Royal Victorian Order," she replied. David was overwhelmed. The CVO ranks above the OBE (Order of the British Empire), which David's father had been awarded by the governor of Hong Kong many years ago, and the Queen has total discretion over its presentation. Later, he learned that he was the only lieutenant-governor to receive the award from Her Majesty. Another very surprised Government House employee was Michael Roberts, who was appointed a Lieutenant of the Royal Victorian Order.

A few hours after the farewell, the royal couple departed and the sovereign's standard, which had flown over Government House, was lowered. David said later that had she been any other woman, he would have given Her Majesty an affectionate hug before she went out the door.

During his remaining months in office, David remained busy but eased up a bit on his normally hectic pace. He had let the media know that he would be stepping down in March and this had stirred up interest again in his successor. Various names were bandied about, but it wasn't until the last moment that he knew who it would be. The number of people attending the New Year's Day Levée in 1995 was larger than ever—2,700 people. In March, when he delivered the

Speech from the Throne for the seventh time, he was warmly received both by the crowd of onlookers observing the ceremony and by the members of the Legislative Assembly. To commemorate his term of office, an Empress of China tree had been planted on the lawn in front of the legislative buildings. When he left the chamber after giving his speech, a choir from the University of Victoria was on hand to sing two songs in his honour. The second one, "Amazing Grace," was one of his favourites and brought tears to his eyes.

In the final weeks, he was swamped with invitations to farewell parties. All over the province, the media issued congratulatory editorials on the way he had performed his duties. He had worked hard, he knew. When he finally turned over his responsibilities to his successor, Garde B. Gardom, on April 21, he had given an estimated 1,900 speeches, entertained 79,000 people and signed 70,000 documents. The walls of his office were covered with plaques, photographs and memorabilia from his innumerable visits not only in British Columbia but all over North America and the Far East. These he could take home with him. The gardens he created in the grounds of Government House would remain as his gift to the public, cared for by his army of volunteer gardeners.

Rather than charge the government the expense of moving his own personal possessions, David had them crated and put in his Eurovan, and hired a driver to take the crates and boxes to his condominium in Victoria. As they packed, David and Dorothy reminisced about doing the same thing in Hong Kong twenty-eight years ago, wondering how they would make out in Canada.

On their last night in Government House, the Lams worked late as usual. After finishing their work, they walked in the dark to the upstairs dining room. A light rain was falling outside. As David and Dorothy looked out the window, they were overwhelmed by the memories of six and a half years of hard work, of the many things that had happened and the people they had met.

"We said a prayer and thanked the Lord," David remembers. "Why us? Why did He open the doors for us and open the road for us to walk on and give us the strength to face the sometimes insurmountable challenge? We seemed to have an almost naive, stupid, blind courage.

Where did it come from? How come we barged forward and suddenly so many people came and supported us so we didn't fall flat on our faces?" It was a miracle, they agreed, a gift from God.

And then? "Then we said we had better get to bed. We have to get up at six o'clock. It's going to be a busy day."

INDEX

Alexandra, Princess, 117
Americans, social customs, 49, 54
Armerding, Dr. Carl, 183
Asia-Pacific Foundation of Canada, 187
Asia Pacific Initiative, 159, 193

Bangkok, 67–68
Bank of Nova Scotia, 95
Banking, 62–64, 95
Banking Advisory Committee, 69
Baptist World Alliance, 73
Barbicon Properties, 191
Beijing, 232–33. See also Peking
Bell-Irving, Hon. H. P., 199
Bell's Palsy, 195
Bennett, Douglas, 182
Bennett, William R., 185
Blackmail, 81
Board of Trade building, 115–16
Bodell, Don, 156
Bromley, Blake, 156, 158, 177, 181
Brooklyn, 54
Business philosophy, 96, 101, 105, 106–7, 113, 118, 120, 122, 123, 126–27, 130, 133–34, 135, 136, 139, 151–52, 155
Butchart Gardens, 90, 199
Calgary, 104, 126
Campbell, Prime Minister Kim, 234

Camrose Lutheran College, 175
Canada Council, 193
Canada Place Corporation, 191–92
Canadian Arctic, 146–48
Canadian International Enterprises, 158
Canadian International Properties, 119, 129, 135, 153, 158
Canadian Scottish Regiment (Princess Mary's), 227
Canton, 12, 47
Carney, Senator Patricia, 159
Centre for Asia-Pacific Initiatives, 186
Centre for Pacific Rim Studies (University of Victoria), 185
Centre on Aging (University of Victoria), 186
Chan, Allan, 85
Chan, Caleb, 180
Chang-chiang, 128
Chan, Chak-Fu, 88
Chan, Dr. C. K., 21–22, 40–41
Chan Chik-Tung, 8
Chan, Dr. Shun, 88, 105, 180
Chan, Thomas, 168, 180
Charbonnages du Tonkin, 23, 26
Charity, thoughts on, 170–75, 189, 230
Cheng, Herbert, 81, 127
Cheng, Y. C., 58, 59, 64, 66, 69, 83, 127
Chiang Kai-shek, 31, 47, 55

INDEX

Chiap Hua Flashlights Ltd., 67
Chiap Hua Manufactory, 60, 61
Chinese Cultural Centre, 160, 161, 173, 184
Chinese family, traditions, 48, 59, 65, 72–73, 82, 89, 92
Chinese Garden Advisory Committee, 184
Chinese Studies Program (Regent College), 183
Choi, Philemon, 230
Chong, Richard, 138
Chrétien, Prime Minister Jean, 234, 236
Cohen, Joseph H., 172
Commonwealth Games (1994), 235
Communist Party, 48, 55
Comox Street apartment, 129–130, 141, 152–53
Confucianism, 18, 223
Coombs, Paul, 95
Courtenay-Comox area, 205
Cove Motor Hotel, 94

Dallas, 134
David and Dorothy Lam Foundation, 158, 176, 177
David Lam Asian Gardens, 180
David C. Lam Institute for East-West Studies, 232
David Lam Centre for Intercultural Communication, 187–88
David Lam Chair in Multicultural Education, 179
David Lam Farm, 16–18
David Lam Management Research Centre, 129
David Lam rhododendron, 180
David See Chai Lam Auditorium, 174
David See Chai Lam Management Research Library, 179
Dennies Frères, 30
Dorothy Lam Chair in Special Education, 179
Doctoral studies, 52
Dragon Boat Festival, 160, 161
Edward, Prince, 235
Elizabeth II, Her Majesty the Queen, 217, 235–37
External Affairs, Department of, 228

Fantasy Gardens, 220, 221
Feng shui, 81
Floribunda Philanthropic Society, 155, 156, 176–77
Fok, Chu-On, 35
Fort Bayard: David's first visits, 26; living there, 26–28; returns from Lingnan University, 35; leaves for Hong Kong, 36, 48
Foster, Dr. Bristol, 146
Fraser, Hon. John, 234
Friends of Government House Gardens Society, 216
Fung, King-Hey, 98, 100, 102, 105, 108

Gardening, 16–18, 82, 141, 180, 184, 214, 216
Gardom, Hon. Garde B., 238
George Williams College Camp, 51–52, 53, 55
Goldberg, Dr. Michael, 177–78, 179
Gorbachev, Mikhail, 228
Government House: Lams' first visit, 193; becomes lieutenant-governor, 198; budget, 200; activities, 203–5; guests, 208; volunteer help, 211; budget restrictions, 211; entertainment, 211–12; official visitors, 213; gardens, 215–18; pavilion, 219; end of term, 238–39
Governor general, 227
Grant, Andrew, 115, 116, 119, 120, 121–22, 129, 132, 135, 156–57, 158
Grantham, Sir Alexander, 86
Green Fields Flower Shop, 88
Gum Hong Baptist Church, 6

Hagen, Stan, 175, 205
Hainan Island, 30
Haiphong, 9, 27, 30
Hall, Bishop, 74, 75, 80, 81
Harcourt, Premier Michael, 223
Hawaii, 56
Henderson, Rev. Campbell, 195

Index

Hobbies: basketball, 29; boating, 83; bowling, 88; flying, 83; golfing, 52, 134; gourmet cooking, 149–50; hiking, 82; music, 16, 33, 49; sailing, 142; skiing, 141; swimming, 52, 82; tennis, 141; trailer camping, 111–12. *See also* gardening, scuba diving
Homes, 96, 122–23, 127, 129, 134, 152, 233
Honada (company), 127, 134
Hong Kong: Japanese attacks, 1, 19; origins as a British colony, 2–3; impact of Second World War, 3; Canadian troops in, 4; end of Japanese occupation, 46; postwar growth, 47, 57; impact of Korean War, 58, 76; growth of industries, 60
Hong Kong Baptist College, 47, 61, 79, 87, 103, 176, 229, 230–31
Hong Kong Baptist Hospital, 84–87, 172
Hong Kong Jockey Club, 17
Hong Kong Merchants Association of Vancouver, 98, 140
Hong Kong University, 13, 14
Honorary degrees, 190, 232
Honours and awards, 190, 200, 237
Hughes, Bill, 146–48
Hughes, Ted, 221
Immigration, 90–92, 160, 163–64, 173, 230
Indochina, 3, 9, 22, 26. *See also* Vietnam
Institute for Dispute Resolution (University of Victoria), 186
Institute of Chartered Accountants of B.C., 175
Insurance Exchange building, 130–33, 155–57
Interior decorating, 129, 134

Japan: expansionist policies, 3–4; attacks Hong Kong, 19; treatment of Hong Kong population, 22; thrust into S-E Asia, 23–24; naval defeats, 29, 34; retreat from Southeast Asia, 42–43; surrender of, 46

Jiang Zemin, Chairman, 233
Johnson, Premier Rita, 222, 223

Ka Wah Bank, 61–64, 90, 92, 95, 104
Kai Tak Airport, 19, 83
Kent, Duke of, 71, 227
Kerfoot, Elizabeth, 215
Kong, Eddie, 100
Kota Kinabalu, 117
Korean War, 55, 58, 76
Kowloon, 1, 3, 4, 19–20
Kuala Lumpur, 117
Kwei-liu, 35
Kwok, Stanley, 87, 115
Kwok, Tak-sheng, 108

Lam, Alexander, 16, 74, 93
Lam, Alice, 127
Lam Chi Fung: business, 1–2, 4; family background, 5; early education, 6–7; goes to Hong Kong, 7; marries, 8; strong religious conviction, 8, 15; starts own business, 8–9; religious and charitable interests, 9; children, 9–10; moves to Kowloon, 10; interest in sports, 15; protects house from Japanese, 20–22; moves family to Macao, 23–24; re-establishes business, 26; principal of Baptist High School, 28; life in Macao, 43; return to Hong Kong, 46–47; ventures with Cheng brothers, 59; family business, 65, 69; friend of Tan family, 70; and Hong Kong Baptist College, 79; illness, 85; awarded OBE, 86; golden wedding anniversary, 103; death of, 184
Lam Chi Fung Auditorium, 184
Lam, Daniel, 1, 12, 16, 22, 43, 46, 59, 61, 65, 68, 92, 104
Lam, Daphne, 74, 84, 110, 112, 154
Lam, David: attends Lingnan University, 2; bombed by Japanese aircraft, 5; birth, 9; influence of father, 10; early education, 10–13; enters Lingnan University, 14; Baptist upbringing, 14–15; musical interests, 16; family band, 16; studies

INDEX

Confucian philosophy, 18; studies Mandarin, 18; studies Japanese, 23; takes family to Macao, 23–25; assists father in coal business, 26; helps orphanage in Fort Bayard, 27; at Lingnan University, 30–34, 47; return to Macao, 36–41; bombed at dock, 36; chased by pirates, 37; shipwrecked, 38–39; return to Hong Kong and Macao, 40; speculates in Hong Kong dollars, 44–46; graduate studies in the USA, 48–56; return to Hong Kong, 57; becomes chief manager of Ka Wah bank, 62; thoughts on working for the family, 69; marriage to Dorothy Tan, 69–72; builds own house, 80–82; investments, 83, 88–89; considers emigration, 89–92; goes to Canada, 94; enters real estate business, 99; interests Hong Kong investors, 104, 107–8; forms own company, 119; deals in the United States, 128; hospitalized, 185; community service, 191–93; becomes lieutenant-governor, 197; returns to private life, 236. *See also* hobbies, lieutenant-governor, retirement

Lam, Deborah, 73, 110, 112, 154
Lam, Doreen, 74, 110, 112, 153, 195
Lam, Paul, 90, 94
Lam, Shu-Kee, 33
Lam Siu-Fun, 5; becomes a Baptist pastor, 6
Lam, Timothy, 25
Lau, C. K., 115, 117
Lau, Datuk G. P., 114, 116, 117
Lau, Geoffrey, 114–15, 116, 117
Laurier Institute, 166–67
Lee, Robert, 105, 106, 114, 115, 116, 119, 129, 133
Lee, Shau-Kee, 108, 231
Leong, Sydney, 88
Leung, Bing, 100
Leung, Faye, 220, 221
Leung, In-sing, 183
Levée, New Year's Day, 209, 237

Li Ka-Shing, 76
Li, Robert, 88
Lidvard, 48
Lieutenant-governor: proposed nomination, 194–96; swearing-in ceremony, 198–99; protocol, 199–200; expenses, 200; invitations to speak, 201; at Legislative Assembly, 201–2; constitutional powers, 203; visiting communities, 203–4; typical daily activity, 205; travel by naval destroyer, 206–7; speeches, 207; guests, 208; servants, 209–10; volunteers, 211, 216; official visits, 213, 226; gardens, 215–19; visits the Queen, 217; patronage, 220; resignation of premier, 222; official uniform, 224; riot at Legislative Building, 225–26; visits Hong Kong, 229–32; Queen's visit, 235; leaving office, 236–39
Ling Tung Baptist Mission, 6
Lingnan High School, 12
Lingnan Maru, 41
Lingnan University: in Hong Kong, 2, 14, 23; in mainland China, 30–32; campus life, 33; alumni, 34, 76; threatened by advancing Japanese, 34; returns to Canton, 47, 230
Longstaffe, Ron, 146
Los Angeles, 48
Lusztig, Dean Peter, 178–79

McCarthy, Grace, 159, 182–83
McCullough, Colin D., 215
McEachern, Chief Justice Allan, 96, 199
McKenzie Management, 113–14, 119, 120
McSevney, Sarah, 159
Macao, 4, 23; a haven for Lam family, 24–25, 35; David's return, 41
Mager, John, 206
Margriet, Princess (of the Netherlands), 227
Meiger, Ernie, 131
Mao Tse-tung, 47, 55

Index

Master of Business Administration, 51
Middle East trade delegation, 80
Missionaries, 5, 6, 12, 73, 79, 85
Monster houses, 167–68
Mulroney, Prime Minister Brian, 196, 197, 234
Mount St. Joseph Hospital, 174
Munsang College, 13, 14

Nanpang Island, 38
Neighbours, 96–97
New Democatic Party, 128, 223, 224
Newcombe, Edward, 99, 103
Newcombe Realty, 99–100, 103, 105, 125
Newman, Dr. Murray, 143–46, 149
Newman, Peter, 196
New Territories (Hong Kong), 5, 19, 21, 74, 82
New York, 53, 98
New York University, 53, 55
Noble, Phoebe, 215

Oakridge Baptist Church, 97, 195

Pacific Canadian Investments, 158
Pacific Centre, 119, 140
Peking Union Medical College, 6
Peoples' Republic of China, 55, 139, 228, 232–33
Perugia, 149
Petch, Dr. Howard E., 185–87; commemorative fountain, 187
Peters, Ray, 193
Petty, Tony, 86
Philadelphia, 48, 49, 50
Philanthropy: 177–90; Lam's thoughts on, 189–90; in Hong Kong, 230. *See also* charity
Philip, Duke of Edinburgh, 213–14, 235
Political contributions, 141
Poole, Jack, 126
Pollen, Peter, 146, 148
Pui-Ching Middle School (Macao), 46, (Hong Kong) 85
Pui-Ching School, 12
Racism, 89, 159, 161–65

Radford, George, 215
Rangiroa, 144
Rankin, Dr. Samuel, 85–87
Raylam Battery Co., 67
Ray-O-Vac, 67
Real estate: Hong Kong, 88; Vancouver, 99, 101, 106, 113; management, 121; location and timing, 125–26; in the United States, 127; development, 136–37; last deals, 154–55
Real Estate Institute of British Columbia, 101
Real Estate Institute of Canada, 101
Refugees, 57
Regent College, 181–84
Retirement, 153–55
Richards, R. L., 113, 114, 121
Ritchie, Cedric E., 95
Roberts, Michael, 206, 222, 225, 237
Rogers, Hon. Robert G., 191, 192, 198, 215
Roh Tae Woo, 227
Rotary Club, 77, 130, 159, 175, 191
Rowbottom, Brian, 210, 216, 225
Roxas, Emilia, 220, 221
Royal Bank of Canada, 132
Royal Columbian Hospital, 174
Royal Vancouver Yacht Club, 142, 22

SS President Cleveland, 56, 57
St. Germain, Senator Gerry, 193, 196
St. Paul's Hospital, 174
Saigon, 78
San Francisco, 49, 50, 127
Saywell, Dr. William, 187–89
School, Annie B. Jamieson Elementary, 109
School, Sir Winston Churchill High, 109
Scuba diving, 61, 143–46
Seattle, 90, 134
Selah, 142
Shanghai, 14
Shipbreaking business, 64, 69
Shatin, 74
Shon, Ron, 184
Siborne, George, 194

Simon Fraser University, 187–89
Simpson, Carole, 207
Singapore, 117
Sin Gin Maru, 36, 38, 39
Skalbania, Nelson, 153
Smith, Dr. James, 97
Social Credit Party, 128
Southern Baptist Convention, 79
Sudden Valley, 127
Sun Yat Sen Classical Garden Society, 184
"Sunny" companies, 102–103, 106, 129
Swatow, 5, 6, 7, 9, 59, 61, 66, 69, 76, 115
Sze Wai Company, 9

Tan, Dorothy: early life, 69; moved to Hong Kong, 70; attends Diocesan Girls School, 70; meets David, 70–71; marriage, 72; living in Lam household, 73–74; children, 73, 97, 103, 109–10; adjusting to Canadian life, 111, 123–24; on going to Government House, 195; return to private life, 238
Tan Yu, 220, 222
Temple University, 48, 50–51
Tiananmen Square, 226, 228
Tokyo, 116
Toronto, 95
Truk, 144
Ts'o, Felix, 158
Tucson, 134
Tung Man College, 6

Union Club of B.C., 182, 200
United Chinese Community Enrichment Services Society (SUCCESS), 173
University of British Columbia, 100, 177; Faculty of Commerce, 178–79; Faculty of Education, 179; Asian Gardens, 180; Regent College, 181–84
University of the Philippines, 1, 43
University of Victoria, 185–87

Vacations, 111–12, 134, 142
Vancouver Aquarium, 143, 146, 148–49
Vancouver Club, 200
Vancouver General Hospital, 174
Vancouver Police Historical Society, 172–73
Vander Zalm, Premier William 175, 193–94, 217, 221–22, 224
Victoria (Hong Kong), 21
Victoria (British Columbia), 90, 215
Victorian Rose Garden, 217
Vietnam, 27
Vietnam War, 67, 78, 79

Wales, Robert, 90–91, 92
Wall and Redekop, 105, 106, 113, 119
Walls, Dr. Jan, 185–86, 187
Wan Li, 226
Warwick Castle, 216, 217
Williams, Eva, 109
Williams, Ken, 157, 158, 177
Wing Wah, 30
Wong, Milton, 160, 161, 166
Wright, Dr. W. C., 181

YMCA, 11, 51
Yue, Dr. K. T., 33, 173

Zhang Yijun, 229
Zhu Rongji, 228

www.ingramcontent.com/pod-product-compliance
Lightning Source LLC
Chambersburg PA
CBHW030132240426
43672CB00005B/109